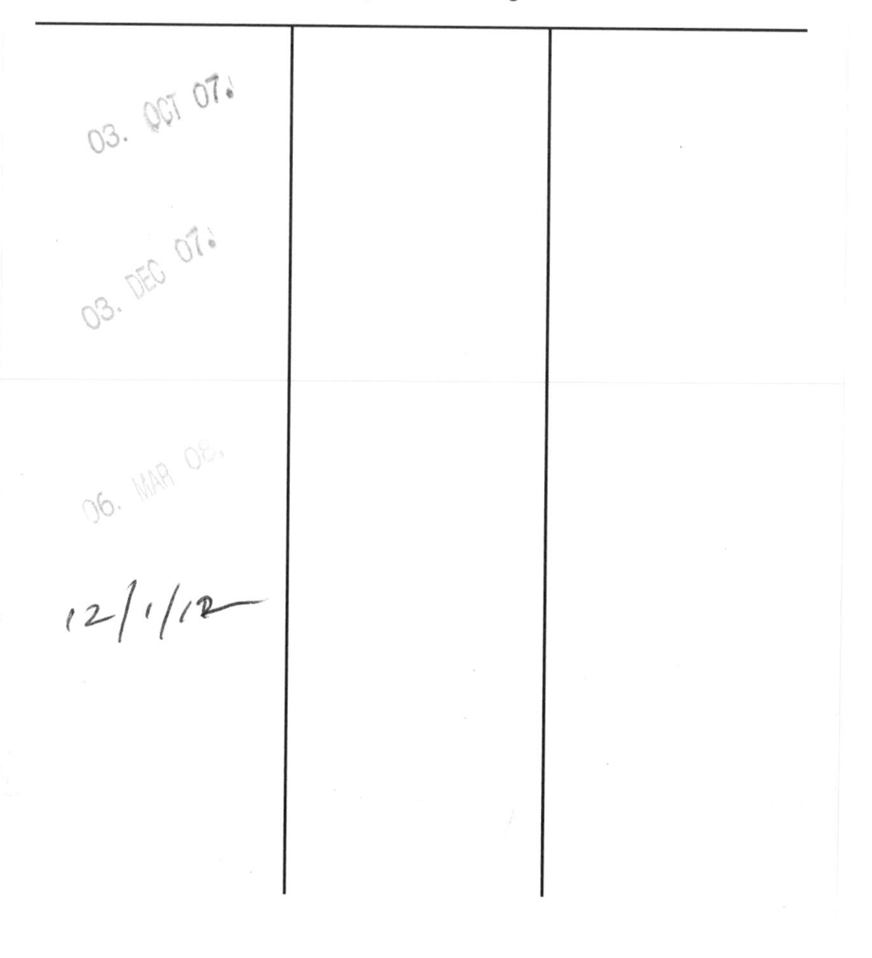
03. OCT 07.
03. DEC 07.
06. MAR 08.
12/1/12

Wicked Whispers

Wicked Whispers

Confessions of a Gossip Queen

JESSICA CALLAN

MICHAEL JOSEPH
an imprint of
PENGUIN BOOKS

MICHAEL JOSEPH

Published by the Penguin Group
Penguin Books Ltd, 80 Strand, London WC2R 0RL, England
Penguin Group (USA) Inc., 375 Hudson Street, New York, New York 10014, USA
Penguin Group (Canada), 90 Eglinton Avenue East, Suite 700, Toronto, Ontario, Canada M4P 2Y3
(a division of Pearson Penguin Canada Inc.)
Penguin Ireland, 25 St Stephen's Green, Dublin 2, Ireland (a division of Penguin Books Ltd)
Penguin Group (Australia), 250 Camberwell Road, Camberwell, Victoria 3124, Australia
(a division of Pearson Australia Group Pty Ltd)
Penguin Books India Pvt Ltd, 11 Community Centre, Panchsheel Park, New Delhi – 110 017, India
Penguin Group (NZ), 67 Apollo Drive, Rosedale, North Shore 0632, New Zealand
(a division of Pearson New Zealand Ltd)
Penguin Books (South Africa) (Pty) Ltd, 24 Sturdee Avenue, Rosebank, Johannesburg 2196, South Africa

Penguin Books Ltd, Registered Offices: 80 Strand, London WC2R 0RL, England

www.penguin.com

Published in 2007
1

Set in 12/14.75 pt Monotype Bembo
Typeset by Rowland Phototypesetting Ltd, Bury St Edmunds, Suffolk
Printed in Great Britain by Clays Ltd, St Ives plc

A CIP catalogue record for this book is available from the British Library

HARDBACK ISBN: 978-0-718-15295-6
TRADE PAPERBACK ISBN: 978-0-718-15340-3

www.greenpenguin.co.uk

Penguin Books is committed to a sustainable future
for our business, our readers and our planet.
The book in your hands is made from paper
certified by the Forest Stewardship Council.

For Mummy, Daddy and Jamie. It's not my fault.

Contents

1 Almost Mission Impossible 1
2 Dogs at Dawn 15
3 Fisticuffs 31
4 Shameless 61
5 Spice World 87
6 Planet Jordan 107
7 Racy Behaviour 145
8 More Bust-ups and Break-ups 171
9 Sugar Daddies and Secret Agents 191
10 Threats and Thrills 229
11 Turning Point 257
12 A Deadline of One's Own 283
13 Behaving Badly and Bowing Out 313
Acknowledgements 339

Me, Polly, Angelina Jolie and Eva

1. Almost Mission Impossible

Jostling for space in front of the mirror in the crowded ladies' loo and re-applying my lip gloss for the tenth time that evening, I catch sight of the stress lines on my forehead and the panic in my eyes.

'Where the hell is Tom Cruise? He should be here by now. What if he tells us to fuck off? What if I trip over in front of him and land on my arse? At least that'll get his attention, I guess. Bollocks, these high heels are killing me,' I mutter nervously to myself, frantically trying to shove my make-up back into my bag.

The lip gloss falls to the floor and rolls away. I realize my hands are shaking slightly. What is wrong with me? I need to calm down, I am going to draw attention to myself if I carry on freaking out like this in the bathroom.

It is a warm July evening in 2000 and I am at the Odeon Leicester Square at the premiere of *Mission: Impossible II* with my new work colleagues, Eva and Polly. It is our first assignment for the *Daily Mirror* as the newly christened 3am gossip columnists. Our orders are to talk to Tom Cruise and somehow, through any means possible, get our photograph taken with the A-list actor.

Failure is not an option. Being dragged off by the police or one of the star's bodyguards is fine, apparently, as long as I have managed to get that shot. Forget about worthy war-reporting, uncovering government scandals, campaigning for the rights of the underprivileged. Whether I manage to pose for a picture with Tom Cruise and my two colleagues is just as important, a matter of life and death in fact. Which is why I am stressing out, because if I don't pull this off, or if my two partners in crime succeed and I don't because I am sprawled on the floor thanks to my high heels, then I'll be given my marching orders.

We had left the office in Canary Wharf at 5.30pm to head to the cinema, the words of our showbusiness editor, Richard Wallace, still ringing in our ears. 'Get alongside Cruise, flirt, chat away, shove your arms round him, smile for the cameras, and bang, bang, bang – we've got him!' he'd barked. It sounded so easy and fun.

We'd been told that we had to glam up as best we could, and not look like the clichéd scruffy tabloid journalists that we were. I was yet to take on board Rule Number One of becoming a successful gossip columnist: when in doubt, get 'em out. Or to put it politely, use your feminine wiles whether it's by wearing a short skirt or a low-cut top.

Rule Number Two – blag, borrow or steal glitzy gear to wear to awards ceremonies and parties – clearly hadn't made an impact yet either. I looked pathetically unglamorous in my black Oasis top and knee-length, black flowery Top Shop skirt. At least I'd managed the high heels, with a pair of black slingbacks from River Island.

Polly, Eva and I snuck away to the ladies' loo on the newsroom floor, and I tried to work out how I could do my make-up without looking ridiculous. I was always a fan of the less-is-more look, but I knew I had to make some sort of effort so I hastily slapped on what I could, desperately trying not to look like I'd been taking make-up tips from Worzel Gummidge's girlfriend, Aunt Sally.

'Right, let's get out of here,' instructed Polly.

Eva and I looked at each other and tried not to laugh. Sergeant Major Graham was trying to boss us about and it was only day two. I had a feeling this was a taste of what was to come.

When Eva, Polly and I squeezed off the Tube at Leicester Square half an hour later and found ourselves caught up in the scrum of hundreds of screeching fans and baffled-looking tourists, we realized that our task was going to be a lot harder than we had expected.

'This is a bloody mission in itself just getting past the gawkers, let alone actually getting into the cinema or tracking down Cruise,' remarked Polly, elbowing several placard-waving kids out the way.

We stomped past the baying crowds and into the Odeon, waving our three tickets to the *MI: II* screening to the doormen. We had three tickets to the after-party as well in our handbags. The film company and the PR company hired to deal with the print press had been happy to oblige as a star like Tom Cruise loves publicity at his movie premieres. Albeit with the press at a safe distance.

We'd planned our assault on Tom with military precision. By a stroke of luck it had been his birthday a few days before, so we'd bought him a birthday card to wave in his direction and hopefully catch his attention while we were kept behind the rope with the rest of the media. This was our first chance to prove that three girls *could* work together rather than bitch behind each other's backs and plot to pull one another's pigtails after work.

We waited impatiently in the foyer of the cinema. We were in a roped-off area at the top of the first staircase, the rest of the press – the TV crews, print journalists and radio interviewers – all crammed in with us. It wasn't called the press cage for nothing. Everyone was getting a little bit restless. Deadlines were looming. The diminutive star was in the middle of one of his four-hour marathon walkabouts among the crowds that were to become his trademark in order to prove he wasn't really a Scientologist weirdo. My feet were already beginning to ache.

The security guards arrived and started clearing the lobby of rubber-neckers who had managed to acquire tickets to the premiere – corporate types who had shelled out to treat their clients to a starry night out – so that Tom could flash that famous wide, white, cheesy grin for the press and say yet again how much he loved England and his English fans.

Could Cruise be heading our way soon? I was desperately trying to contain my growing panic, although it was adrenaline-pumping nervous energy which would keep me going until the end of the night. Or at least until we managed to complete our mission.

Cruise, however, was still busy giving high fives to practically every person squashed behind barriers, snatching mobiles out of the hands of teenagers, demanding they call their parents and hollering 'Hey wassup?' down the phone.

'Bugger this. I'm not standing here all night. We'll never get near him standing near this lot,' snapped Polly, pointing towards the rest of the press pack. 'We need to be by ourselves, away from the other journalists, so that we don't look like reporters.'

'Well, how are we going to do that?' asked Eva, rolling her eyes at Polly, and not for the last time.

'The film is going to start soon and the security guards are going to make everyone go to their seats. We either stand with the rest of the media behind the barrier or we're going to be made to sit down inside the auditorium.' She had a point.

Eva had an idea. 'Why don't we wait in the women's toilets so when Tom walks past to get into the cinema, we can jump out and leap on him? Youngy will be following him with the other snappers, so he'd be able to take our picture no problem,' she explained. 'Youngy' was the nickname we used for Richard Young, our photographer.

We all agreed that it was a great plan. Chances were, if we managed to catch him totally by surprise, his bodyguards and his terrifying then-publicist, Pat Kingsley, wouldn't be able to stop us.

We slipped under the velvet rope and hurried towards the bathroom to wait for our big moment. A few burly bodyguards eyed us suspiciously. It must have looked strange – the other journalists were all waiting in the media area to scribble down a few snatched words from Cruise and we were legging it.

We marched into the loo and waited. And waited.

'This is shit boring. Where is he?' moaned Eva. 'I've done my make-up, like, ten times already. It's going to be deadline soon.'

I was fed up of waiting too. But my nervousness outweighed my boredom. I thanked God the other two girls were here with me; that way all three of us could back each other up. If I had been on my own, I would definitely have bottled it. But I had safety in numbers with Eva and Polly by my side.

Slowly the hordes of women in the bathroom who were attending the premiere, all dressed up in glamorous frocks and making me feel like an underdressed impostor, finished touching up their make-up and gossiping by the hand dryers and began to file out the door. Polly furiously tapped away at her mobile phone, texting a friend and sighing like a bored teenager while Eva painted on more black liquid eyeliner and I balanced on the edge of the sinks, trying not to get the back of my skirt wet.

The door swung open and a pale, spindly brunette with the most enormous pair of lips glided in. It was Angelina Jolie.

Polly, Eva and I looked at each other open-mouthed. I didn't have a chance to be star-struck. I was hypnotized by her ridiculous-sized pout. Bloody hell, we've got to talk to her, I thought to myself.

The Hollywood star was in England filming the first Lara Croft film and had arrived at the cinema wearing a white ankle-length skirt and top. Considering how dressed up she was when she was just a guest at somebody else's premiere, I always found it strange she didn't bother to put on a frock for her own *Tomb Raider* screening the following year. At that event she turned up in black trousers and a T-shirt.

'Hi Angelina, we're big fans. Do you mind posing for a picture with us?' I stammered.

'Sure. That's fine,' was her response.

That was all she said. When I met her again a year later at the premiere of *Tomb Raider* and then *Tomb Raider 2* in 2003, she had added only a few more words to her repertoire. While she didn't mind posing for photographs, you could forget about getting a chat out of her. But that was the point. What seemed to be a friendly lack of conversational skills actually turned out to be something much more powerful. You'd get a 'Hi. Sure, I don't mind doing a picture. Yes, I love England. The fans here are great' and a photograph, and then as you were ushered away you'd realize she had managed to reveal not one single fact about herself.

It was a tactic employed by lots of stars, including Ant and Dec, Kylie Minogue and Nicole Kidman, who would cripple you with politeness and in the process manage to distract you from the fact that they had given absolutely nothing away.

Even those male gossip columnists who prided themselves on their ability to chat up female stars never had any luck with Angelina. It was reassuring to see them getting flustered and be-mused. I saw one male hack say to her at a party, 'You're one of the sexiest stars I've ever met,' and a slightly glacial expression crept across her face.

In the end, her quote in our column was rewritten, unbeknownst to us. Apparently she asked us, 'Hey, are you guys important? I've never seen so much security. What's going on?'

That was my first lesson in how the conversations celebrities had with us often bore absolutely no relation to the words which were printed in the column. On the odd occasion – like this time with Angelina – I didn't even know the quotes had been rewritten until I read the paper the following day. I was also taught that most celebrities are not very eloquent and that many would be happy that we'd made them 'sound more intelligent' by rejigging their words. Well, there was rejigging and then there was making up entire chats. Amazingly we were never sued for having imaginary conversations.

Angelina happily posed for a picture with us in the bathroom. We had been given disposable cameras (this was before we were entrusted with digital cameras) just in case we didn't have Youngy to hand. Polly thrust one of our cameras into the hands of a stranger also queuing up for a pee and we all gathered around Angelina, who pouted perfectly for the picture.

I couldn't resist stealing a sidelong glance at Angelina as we posed. She really had the most sensual mouth I'd ever seen. And despite the slightly surreal setting of the ladies' loo, she had a glow of glamour about her that only true Hollywood stars possessed.

A few seconds later we had our picture. This was much easier than I had expected. The *Daily Mirror*'s editor, Piers Morgan, had told us during one of his frequent *Charlie's Angels*-style pep talks that he wanted as many photos of us with stars as possible, the bigger the celebrity the better. He wanted us to make an instant name for ourselves and in the process slap the showbiz world in the face. We would be rubbing shoulders with the A-listers from day one, and we'd show them that we meant business.

Angelina finished pouting at herself in the mirror and swept out. There was no time for any high-fiving as Cruise was sure to bound into the cinema like an over-excited Jack Russell puppy at any moment. We each took it in turns to open the bathroom door and peer out to see if Cruise was any closer to walking past us.

So much for our subtle behaviour. It wasn't long before a security man spotted the door opening and shutting. You could see that from his point of view we looked suspicious, what with our heads popping out every couple of seconds. Quite understandably he thought we were deranged stalkers. But it was only when Eva peered out and saw seven bodyguards heading our way that we realized how rumbled we were. A bulky female security guard barged into the ladies'. We later described her in the column as a cross between Rosa Klebb and Giant Haystacks.

Shit. We didn't have time to run to cubicles so we all pretended to look in the mirror and redo our lipstick for what must have been the fifteenth time that evening.

'Ladies, can I see your tickets please,' she barked at us.

We dutifully handed over our cinema tickets and assured her we weren't going to attempt to pop little Mr Cruise into our handbags and kidnap him, but the butch jobsworth talked right over us and told us to hurry up and sit down in the auditorium as the movie was about to start. We knew we had to take our time as we couldn't miss the big chance to meet Tom.

We ummed and aahed and stalled for time.

'I need to go to the toilet,' I said.

'Yeah, me too,' Eva said.

'Ooh, yes. I'm bursting as well,' Polly agreed.

We locked ourselves into toilet cubicles and pretended to use the loo. I've never been good at hiding my giggles in tense moments. I sat there with my hand clamped over my mouth, making strange whimpering noises as I tried to stifle my hysterics. The situation was just too bizarre. To make things worse, I could hear Eva trying to suppress her laughter too. Luckily she flushed her toilet just as a few snorts slipped out. I tried to cough extra loudly, but ended up making a very strange strangling noise.

I thought of the saddest thing I could in order to rein in my giggles. All that sprang to mind was my twelve-year-old Siamese cat dying. Not for the last time while working on 3am, I used the death of my elderly moggy in order to calm down. Poor Sheba, it worked every time.

The security gargoyle's eyes narrowed and she looked at us even more suspiciously as we slowly emerged from our cubicles and faffed about some more by the sinks, washing our hands as slowly as possible.

'Come on, ladies. Time to take your seats,' she ordered, her deep voice growing more high-pitched the angrier she got.

Unsurprisingly, she'd had enough.

Just as I thought a miracle might happen and Tom Cruise would see us file out of the loo like naughty schoolgirls, take pity on our forlorn faces and happily chat to us and pose for photos, the bodyguard handed us over to a male security man and instructed him to 'escort' us to our seats and keep an eye on us. We were now suspected of being some sort of security risk to the tiny film star. Us!

Our new guard couldn't believe his luck as he marched us into the auditorium and settled into a seat himself to watch the movie. Most of the time their job was to keep journalists and over-eager fans out of the way, not to sit and watch a movie at a premiere.

I was furious. So much for our big moment. Our debut at our first premiere had not gone according to plan. Piers would be outraged. I was scared of the kicking we'd get from him.

We squirmed about in our seats, looks of extreme distress on our faces. After five minutes of glaring at one another while the film started, Polly leant towards Eva and me. 'Fuck this. Let's get out of here,' she whispered.

As I learnt over the years, the last thing you want to do when something has gone wrong at an event is to think sod it and try to enjoy yourself. It's time to make a plan instead.

So we broke the news to our personally assigned bodyguard that we hated the film (it felt good to slag off the movie to someone working for a film company – pathetic, I know), and it heartened me to see the sadness in his eyes as he realized it meant he had to do some proper work instead of babysitting three journalists.

Swearing like schoolgirls at how the night had gone belly-up, we left the cinema and hailed a cab, instructing the driver to head to the after-show party, which was in a giant marquee by the Tower of London.

'This is our last chance to get him. If we fuck this one up then we're in the shit big time with Piers and Richard,' I said, stating the obvious.

'It's fine. We'll do it. There's no way Tom can say no to us. I mean, he actually can't say no to us – the prospect of us not getting the picture isn't worth thinking about,' Eva said nervously, with a laugh.

We had loads of time to fill before the bash started, so we walked into a wine bar across the road from the party venue, plotting our final assault on the star. The three of us knocked back several glasses of white wine each to steady our nerves. I soon learnt that alcohol was part of the whole game too. Not for me a cup of coffee to keep me awake – a glass of wine would do very nicely, thank you very much. No one felt hungry as we were too nervous to eat.

Several drinks later, we felt much more relaxed and ready for phase two.

At 10pm when the party was due to start, we ran across the road and tried to walk confidently towards the bank of security men at the party entrance.

'Invites, please!' barked a burly, bald monster.

We proudly thrust our laminated invitations at him. I got to know many of these security men well over the years on 3am. They worked at all the major film premieres and parties and mostly looked like *Crimewatch* extras, albeit ones dressed in tuxedos. Whether they did this to relieve themselves of the boredom of policing such events I don't know, but almost all of them treated the guests at these events as if they were crime suspects. Even if an achingly hip young woman dripping in expensive jewellery and decked out in the hottest gear off the catwalk had a party invitation in her hand, these bouncers would still scream like drill sergeants at her to get her invite out before ripping it from her hand.

'You're a bit early, ladies. At least you don't have to worry about drink in there,' guffawed one of them as he relieved us of our invitations.

This was my first premiere as a 3am girl and I was seriously impressed. The party organizers had certainly done their bit, and the inside of the enormous marquee was lined up with gorgeous serving staff holding trays laden with canapés which looked like miniature works of art.

Not that many people tended to stuff their faces with food at these types of parties, as I would find out. It was just not the done thing to be seen cramming your face with food, and invariably when I would subtly try and stuff the odd spring roll into my mouth, I'd dribble most of it down my chin and on to my top.

The drinks staff, who looked like models, offered us red frosted champagne glasses, each with a glass green vine wrapped around its stem. (I nicked one of those glasses that night to remember my first party as a 3am girl.) We each necked a glass, dumped it on a nearby table and picked up another glass.

'Let's stand by the snappers as they'll be the first ones to see Tom when he turns up,' ordered Polly.

We weaved our way towards a wall of photographers who had been invited to stand inside the party and take pictures of Cruise upon his arrival. Youngy was there and we told him that after he and the other photographers had finished hosing Cruise down (photographer-speak for taking picture after picture of the subject), we would leap on Tom and talk to him. Youngy was to start snapping away immediately, and hopefully in the photos it would look like Cruise was having a good old chinwag with his new buddies.

Youngy agreed and so we waited, crouching behind the photographers and growing increasingly nervous. What if the same security guards turned up and saw us? We'd be hauled off immediately. I knew we literally had seconds in which to do this, and it had to come off or we'd look like idiotic amateurs.

All of a sudden the PR people and party organizers who had been milling around simultaneously sprang into action and started talking nervously into their headsets. Cruise was close by. The photographers put down their canapés – they liked to tuck into the free food on offer until their wives would force them on diets at least twice a year – and took their stance just as a group of bulky men in black suits crowded the entrance. There in the middle of them – all 5 foot 7 inches of Hollywood megawatt smile – was Tom Cruise.

The photographers snapped away and he grinned as usual for the cameras. And then we went for it. We forced our way through the line-up of photographers and surrounded the actor. Eva flung her left arm around his shoulder and we all cooed, 'Happy Birthday, Tom', like love-struck schoolgirls.

Amazingly we weren't automatically rugby-tackled to the ground by his bodyguards, who just looked a little baffled.

'Oooh, thank you. That's soooo kind of you. You really shouldn't have. It's very thoughtful,' he said, as Polly thrust our birthday card at him and pinched his arm so that he'd look at her for the cameras.

'So how did you spend your birthday?' I asked.

'Well, me and a few friends went out. We just went to an Italian restaurant – nothing fancy.'

'And what did Nicole get you for your big day?' said Polly.

'Something filthy,' he replied, with a naughty grin.

We were momentarily thrown by his unexpected reply. Cruise never usually alluded to his sex life. It couldn't have been more perfect if we had made it up.

A millisecond later it was all over as we were finally dragged off him by his gang of minders and he was swept away. Youngy gave us the thumbs up and we crowded around his digital camera to check the photos. They were great, and Cruise looked like he was having a really good time with us.

Still, I realized I had yet to learn the art of placing myself right next to a celebrity for a picture. Not only was I not standing next to Cruise, but I discovered I wasn't facing the camera either. Eva had positioned herself perfectly to the right of Tom and he had one arm around her waist, while Polly had shoved her way to the left of him. She had cunningly offered to look after the birthday card all night so she could be the one to hand it to him, and indeed she was the one that he was talking to in the picture.

All you could see of me in that first photo of us all together was my back and a tiny bit of the side of my face, as I desperately tried to get close to Tom Cruise while nervously tugging at my black top. As much as I liked Eva and Polly, I was furious with them for beating me to it and distraught that I looked like such an idiot in the picture. But it was all my own fault. I would soon learn the power of using my elbows in these situations.

And at least we had a funny comment from Cruise and a photo with all three of us in it, even if it was just the side of my head. We were thrilled with ourselves. It was time to have a few more glasses of champagne at the party to celebrate getting through our first premiere together.

We had all learnt that this job was going to be a lot harder than we had previously thought. Everybody would always want a piece of whatever stars were there, and not only would we have to fight to gain access to these celebrities, we would also have to get them to pose for pictures with us and to give us a quote we could use in the column. We would have to keep an eye on every famous person there and keep an ear to the ground for any piece of scandal. Oh, and of course we would have to make sure we kept well away from those pesky security guards.

Compared with what was to come, our first premiere was a very gentle introduction to working for 3am. It did set a precedent: I was to find that hanging out in the toilets at parties was an essential part of the life of a tabloid journalist, and a great place to pick up gossip.

Eva, Polly and me

2. Dogs at Dawn

A few months previously I had been working on the *Daily Telegraph* for nearly two years when I received a call from the *Daily Mirror*. The showbiz editor of the paper, Richard Wallace, asked if I wanted to meet him for a drink. It was already known in the newspaper world that the current *Mirror* columnist Matthew Wright was quitting after five years to host his own Channel 5 show. Richard wanted to discuss the new gossip column they were launching following Matthew's departure.

I knew this was an incredibly exciting opportunity. At the time I was the deputy editor of the Peterborough column, the *Telegraph*'s slightly old-fashioned gossip section. I'd been doing the job for a year, and was feeling stifled by its fuddy-duddy approach to gossip news. My colleagues all seemed to be old Etonian Oxbridge graduates; I'd spent my university years watching *Beverly Hills 90210* and reruns of *Dallas* and *Dynasty*. They wanted me to dish the dirt on MPs, Lords and Ladies, and royalty; I was much more of an *OK!* magazine girl. When I referred to Robbie Williams in the *Telegraph*, I always had to describe him as a 'pop singer' as I couldn't assume our readers knew who he was. I couldn't even use the word 'toilet' because it was deemed too common.

I'd always wanted to work for a tabloid. You could say that it was in my blood. My father had edited gossip columns for the *Daily Mail*, the *Mirror* and the *Evening Standard* in the 1960s and the 1970s before becoming a feature writer and interviewer on the *Mirror* and then the *Daily Express*. Of course, it was all very different in his day. He seemed to write about real stars, whom he would interview in sumptuous mansions in Hollywood or at elegant parties in Mayfair and Knightsbridge. It was Groucho Marx at the Cannes Film Festival one day, Greta Garbo and Marlene Dietrich the next. He certainly didn't write about the Jade Goody types then. That sort of celebrity simply didn't exist. I personally couldn't wait to interview the Spice Girls and Rovers' Return regulars, so Richard's call was heaven-sent.

I met Richard in a bar which was comfortably far from Davy's Wine Bar, the drinking hole for journalists in Canary Wharf, and he talked in very vague terms about the new-look column they had in mind. I'd met Richard once or twice before, usually at Davy's after we'd both had a few after-work drinks. I also knew that his nickname was 'The Melting Snowman' due to his inability to remain upright if he got pissed and his tendency to spit and produce white foam which would froth out of the corners of his mouth after too many glasses of wine.

I told him what I had been up to on the *Daily Telegraph* recently, and how I had written an article about the TV broadcaster Desmond Wilcox who'd claimed he had been beaten by his headmaster at school for having a stammer. This was news to some of his old classmates, including a Church of England minister who had sent me endless letters refuting Wilcox's confession and accusing him of making it up. Wilcox furiously denied to me that he had made it up. A short while later, he fell ill with heart problems.

Richard clearly thought my career in gossip journalism had far from blossomed. 'You've got the easiest job in showbiz land,' he said, laughing.

The next day I was worried I hadn't done a good job selling myself and that I didn't have enough experience of writing about the big-name celebs of the day. I must have said something right, though, because a couple of days later I was summoned to an interview with Piers Morgan, the editor of the *Mirror*.

The *Telegraph* was in the same building in Canary Wharf as the *Mirror*, so I slipped away from my desk and, once on the ground floor, made a dash for the lift that would take me up to the *Mirror*. I was desperate not to be spotted by anyone I knew as I didn't want people at the *Telegraph* to know what I was up to.

Richard met me at the door to the editorial floor of the tabloid. 'Ah, Callan. Come with me,' he said with a grin before striding down towards Piers's frosted glass bunker. I kept my head down and scurried behind, hoping I wouldn't be recognized. Piers's office was at one end of the large, chaotic and messy open-plan editorial office, so it was easy for people to notice who walked in and out of his room.

I'd been introduced to Piers already, years before. After I'd graduated from university, I'd freelanced for eight months for gossip columns on a variety of national newspapers run by men who liked to hire keen university graduates, especially female ones, whom they dubbed the YHs – the young hopefuls. I was sent out to parties from day one and left by myself to learn on the job how to extract information from people, how to cope with free booze at book launches and film premieres, and how to deal with drunken politicians. At the end of what felt like one big party, I landed a place on the Mirror Graduate Trainee Scheme in September 1997.

Before I and the four other trainees were let loose on the various Mirror Group newspapers (we had to work in various departments on the *Sunday Mirror*, the *Daily Mirror* and its regional editions, the *People* and Live TV), we were given a tour of the Group's Canary Wharf offices. We were briefly introduced to heads of departments who were far too busy to even look up from their computers to grunt in our direction, but Piers had been friendly and welcoming.

'Hello, everyone. I'm Piers. I'm sure I'll see you all up here soon. Work hard. Get me lots of scoops,' he said, laughing, before walking off down the corridor.

The heads of departments had all ignored us, so we were all very impressed that Piers made the effort to say hi to us. I also learnt at the first meeting that Piers had an attention threshold of five seconds.

I was determined to make the right impression with Piers at my interview. I resorted to shameless tactics and turned up wearing a micro-miniskirt. I had learnt over the years that female gossip columnists had to use all of their assets to extract stories from people and to stand out from the ranks of male scribes from rival papers, so wearing a short skirt seemed the logical step to take.

I knew that Piers liked his journalists to be practically panting with keenness all the time, so I spent the entire interview almost leaping out of my chair with bubbling enthusiasm. 'I go out every night to parties and launches and premieres and events. I don't get hangovers. I don't pull sickies and anyone is fair game. Unless they're a friend of yours of course, Piers,' I said.

I'd heard that it was important to know who the boss's famous pals were, as writing about one of his regular drinking buddies would, I'd been warned, make for an uncomfortable ticking off. I knew I sounded like I was blatantly sucking up to him, but it was just the sort of thing I'd been told he liked to hear.

'That went well,' said Richard, as he steered me out of the office. 'I think he thinks you're bonkers, which is a good thing.'

A month later I had signed my contract with the *Mirror*. They still didn't have a name for the column and were very shady about the details of who else would be working on it, which did worry me slightly. But I knew that the positives would ultimately outweigh the negatives.

It was only after I had resigned from the *Telegraph* in May that the grand plan was fully unveiled to me. They'd kept quiet about it because they hadn't wanted any other rival tabloids to get in on the act first. I would be working with two other girls. One of them was Matthew's deputy on his column, Polly Graham, and the other girl was Eva Simpson, who was a showbusiness reporter on the *Daily Star*.

Piers and Richard had decided it was time for three female journalists to chronicle the antics of celebrities, from misbehaving megastars to naughty reality TV Z-listers. Until then, the front line of showbiz had been covered mainly by men. Matthew Wright and leader of the opposition on the *Sun*, Dominic Mohan, had been hard at it, writing about the likes of Madonna, the Spice Girls and soap stars for several years.

But then ladette culture exploded on to the scene. We were all glued to *Sex and the City*, in which women largely acted like blokes, drinking heavily and talking about their favourite sexual positions. The likes of Zoë Ball and Sara Cox were tearing up the London party scene and behaving badly. Who better to terrorize stars than three girls who could party with the best of them but remain sober enough to remember what the celebs had been up to?

Thanks to the insularity and incestuous nature of the showbiz tabloid world, Polly, Eva and I knew each other quite well. Luckily, we all got on fine. Tall, slim and black, Eva was feared by many. She had mastered the art of the steely stare and was frequently accused of giving evil looks to people. She usually wasn't, but it amused her that so many of our colleagues, PRs we dealt with and even some celebrities were scared of her. Polly and I were much louder, which was why her silence always unnerved people.

Polly was an old hand at the *Mirror*. The 5 foot 7 inch brunette had been Matthew's deputy on the showbiz column, so she knew all about the showbiz beat. She was fun, had a booming laugh and was a tough reporter. You didn't want to be on the receiving end of one of her blasts down the phone to PRs who had fucked up in some way.

Our brief was to leave all celebrities very afraid. The idea was that we would be out late at every premiere, every launch event, every after-show party, and every awards ceremony. And of course we'd have spies in the hottest clubs and bars around, so every celebrity's drunken move and misdemeanour would be reported to the nation. We were not to suck up to these celebrities' agents, PRs, publicists, lawyers or any of their entourage. If someone behaved like a prima donna to us, we were given the green light to name and shame them in the column. Our favourite stories? Celebrities fighting and fucking.

Two weeks before our launch date, Piers and Richard summoned Polly, Eva and I to one of the wine bars in Canary Wharf to decide on the name of the column. We spent most of the evening reeling off a list of predictable, clichéd names ('Gossip Girls', 'Showbiz Confidential'), until Richard then piped up, 'How about "3am"? It's short, it's snappy. It means that there are three of you and you'll be up until at least 3am chasing celebs and spying on them at parties.'

'Bloody brilliant, Dicky,' declared Piers, and that was that.

We christened ourselves with more wine before trotting off to

Davy's Wine Bar. Piers ordered vodka and tonics for us, and soon we were all sporting alcohol-flushed cheeks (Davy's didn't serve single measures). It was the first time I'd seen the editor drunk.

'So Eva,' he slurred at her, 'do you listen to hip-hop in your garage?'

'Fucking hell!' laughed Richard.

Polly and I winced while a stony-faced Eva simply raised an eyebrow at him. It wasn't the first time Piers would come out with some such faux pas. At times it was like having an embarrassing dad around. Especially when it came to his dancing abilities at the disgracefully drunken *Mirror* Christmas parties.

At last, in July 2000, Piers let us loose on the world with an entire page in the paper: 'Warning! It's 3am. The music's pumping, the lights are low, the Vodka Red Bulls are flowing. You're a superstar and you're misbehaving. You will not be alone. Our new gossip columnists will be there too.'

For three days the *Mirror* ran teasers in the paper about the new column, and on one of those days they printed the most embarrassing Q&A with Polly, Eva and me ever, so that the readers could get to know us a little better. Needless to say, most of the answers we had written had been heavily edited by Piers and Richard, who evidently already had in mind what sort of characters they wanted us to be. We joked that it felt like being in the Spice Girls. Piers decided I had to be the posh one, of course, as I had worked at the *Telegraph*. In the Q&A I also came across as a total tart: my fictional heroine was, apparently, Pandora from *Adrian Mole*, and the best party I had ever been to was 'any I can't remember in the morning. Same with boyfriends.' Even though I had a boyfriend called Tom at the time, my status was 'single, resolutely'. It was mortifying to say the least; I didn't like the idea that I was to be the column slapper.

I certainly hadn't suffered that sort of treatment at the *Daily Telegraph*. It was all so different from working on the broadsheet. For a start, I now spent most of my day working closely with two other girls. Of course, there were males also working in the showbusiness department of the *Mirror*, but they weren't like the

Telegraph lot who took politicians out for long, boozy lunches, went to polo matches and spent most of their time plotting to become Tory MPs or the next editor of the paper.

Secondly, everything was so unbelievably chaotic. The desks in the showbusiness department were laid out in two rows and were thoroughly untidy and definitely unhygienic. The fax machine constantly spewed out unread press releases, Styrofoam cups of cold tea and coffee with unidentifiable matter floating in them were strewn all over the place, biscuit crumbs covered every surface, packets of ketchup and vinegar were piled high, and everywhere you'd look there were notebooks filled with illegible shorthand lying about. How on earth did anybody know which desk was theirs?

And as for the careful filing away of cassettes from interviews, well, there was no such thing. We were all given Dictaphones with which to tape telephone conversations. That way, if someone disputed something we claimed they had told us, we would be able to open our gun-metal desk drawers and instantly find the relevant tape we were meant to have filed away in chronological order. It goes without saying that not one person who worked in that department was ever equipped with such organizational skills for the whole time I worked there.

There were teetering towers of CDs which music PRs sent to the department on a daily basis to review, scrunched-up day-old newspapers on the bright red carpet around our feet and piles of taxi receipts, restaurant bills and expenses forms on every desk.

'Bloody hell. This place is an absolute tip,' I said on my first day.

'Well, make yourself comfortable,' replied Richard.

His desk – next to mine – was the neatest of the lot. It helped that Sinead, our PA, sat next to him.

Any preconception that a tabloid showbusiness department would be even vaguely glamorous went straight out of the window on that first day. Without fail, ours was the messiest department at the paper, as well as the loudest. The banks of news reporters (whom the blokes in my department nicknamed the 'news bunnies') further down the room constantly glared at us angrily as they tried to have serious conversations with police contacts, recently bereaved families or the MOD. All they could hear was Richard or his deputy, Kevin, being rude to each other, laughing hysterically at their own jokes and calling each other c★★★s at the top of their voices.

The fashion department girls, who had the misfortune to sit next to us, were too horrified to look over in our direction. The men in our department were far more impressed by them and particularly liked it when young models arrived at the office to show the girls their picture portfolios. While they would never have dared to attempt to chat up any of the willowy fresh-faced models, they preferred to cry out, 'Corrrrrr' to each other instead.

The phones rang constantly. During my first few days there, I was taught that the correct way to answer a call at the paper was to say, 'Hello, showbiz!' in a chirpy, friendly manner.

'That way, if some reader has just witnessed a punch-up between two celebs in a pub or seen some married star with his tongue down someone other than his wife's throat and is nervous about ringing in with the story, you will be able to reassure them with your smooth, sympathetic phone manner,' instructed James, one of the reporters in the department.

Most people who would ring up 3am wanted to sell you stories. The rest were nutters who wanted to berate you for daring to criticize the likes of Gareth Gates and Michael Jackson (for some reason, the two singers' fans were the most vocal in contacting the paper and screaming obscenities down the phone if we'd so much as mentioned them in passing in the column). Because we were the new girls, the men in our department took great pleasure in putting these types of callers through to Eva and me. Trying to sound professional and not realizing at that stage that these were deranged stalkers who rang up regularly, I would end up getting stuck in long conversations with them before discovering they were in fact utter lunatics.

There was one particular woman who was rumoured to have spent time in a mental institution. She called repeatedly during my first week, sounding perfectly normal on the phone until she asked without fail, 'Are you going to write about David Bowie's long-running affair with me?'

By the time she called on day four, I'd reached the end of my tether.

'What you want to do is this,' instructed Kevin that day, taking the phone from me. 'Are you still alive? I thought you'd have done us all a favour by killing yourself by now. Try it again. Now fuck off,' he shouted down the receiver before slamming the phone down. 'And there you have it.' He smiled gleefully at me, proud of his unique technique.

Eva, Polly and I quickly slipped into working life together that first week. We spent every day and evening together, and as a result our working life crossed over into our social life. Our conversations first thing in the morning would usually go like this:

'I've got a cracking hangover today. I think I'm going to be sick. Can someone bring me back a bacon sandwich and a cup of tea from the canteen?'

'Don't talk to me; I'm in a vile mood today. Has anyone got any stories?'

'Aren't you wearing the same clothes as yesterday? Did you pull last night? You dirty stop-out! Who was it?'

We bonded very fast and our love lives became a hotly discussed topic among us. Our male colleagues loved to eavesdrop, especially when I talked about Tom, my boyfriend. By coincidence he worked on the *Mirror* too, his desk only a few feet from mine in the huge open-plan office, so naturally everybody loved to know what was going on in our lives.

In that first week, Polly, Eva and I underwent one of the many photo sessions we had to endure over the years so that the column sported up-to-date photographs of us. We all lost our sense of humour at that first photo shoot. Everyone was fussing about how their hair looked and as we had one hair and make-up woman to work her magic on all three of us, it took hours to do us all. Polly's long, thick, curly hair took so long to blowdry, Eva and I both lay down on the filthy sofas in the studio and took a nap. We had to go through five costume changes, including one where we had to wear matching suits like something out of a bad rip-off of Robert Palmer's 'Addicted To Love' video. By the end of the long and exhausting afternoon in the *Mirror*'s photo studio, we had stopped talking to each other.

After that we seemed to have to redo our picture byline practically every six months. All our colleagues thought we were terribly vain and that we were actually demanding that our pictures had to be redone. Honestly, nothing could have been further from the truth. I was a journalist, not a model (as no shortage of people were keen to point out), and I never found it natural standing in front of a camera in a studio. Trying not to blink for the billionth time and ruining the picture was torturous enough, without being told that I still looked awful in the photo. I always had so many layers of make-up smeared all over my face that Richard started calling me 'lady boy', a moniker he continued to use even after I'd left the paper. I had to be airbrushed on several occasions, which was beyond humiliating as I looked even worse in the 'after' pictures than I did in the 'before' shots. I had had a nose job when I was nineteen, but someone clearly thought my nose still needed some work as it was given an impromptu once-over during one of the airbrush sessions, leaving me with what appeared to be a pair of nostrils and nothing else.

Our first story in the column on 3 July 2000 was about how TV presenter Jamie Theakston and English actress Joely Richardson had become an unlikely couple. Up to then, Jamie had usually stuck to pop stars (he'd dated All Saints singer Natalie Appleton) and perky telly presenters, and yet here he was dating the impossibly well-bred and stylish Joely. We bought pictures from a paparazzo who had spotted the couple enjoying an intimate dinner in London and followed them out to the car park. We ran the story alongside a hilarious picture of Jamie and Joely looking dazed by the photographer's flash, which had gone off while they were mid-snog.

It was the perfect sort of story with which to launch the column. We wanted to warn celebs that no matter what they were doing and with whom, there was a new force to be reckoned with. That was the extent of our grand plan. I liked the idea of not lying about what celebrities were really like, sticking it to manipulative PRs and no longer allowing stars to set the agenda. I felt that our way was going to be more respectful of the reader. Everyone deserved to know what these people, who earned their fortunes from their fame, were really like.

During that first week we didn't have a clue how things would go. And we certainly had no idea that our column would spawn so many imitators – as part of our column we'd created a blind item I'd named 'Wicked Whispers', which allowed us to share a particularly outrageous piece of gossip without naming any celebrities, a formula quickly adopted by many rivals – or that we'd attract such controversy from celebrities, from the media sections of other newspapers and from websites such as Popbitch, who relished giving us a good kicking.

I couldn't believe how quickly the gossip columnists on other newspapers started to bitch about us. I didn't expect them to welcome the new column with open arms, but it was surprising to learn how threatening male journalists found us. The fact that the new unholy trinity of gossip consisted of women was hugely amusing to many of them and of course the first thing other gossip columnists and our celebrity victims attacked us for was our appearance. Within weeks of starting, we were christened with a host of new nicknames, one of which was 'Three Absolute Morons'. My personal favourite nickname was 'Dogs at Dawn' which was dreamt up by a group of photographers in reference to our late nights . . . oh, and our looks. But we never complained. It went with the territory, even if at times it felt like being back in the playground. At the end of the day we were gossip columnists, so we'd just have to shut up and deal with the fact that we were also being gossiped about and always would be.

We were instructed by Piers to throw a bash to celebrate the arrival of 3am on to the showbiz scene.

'It's going to be at Sugar Reef, which is really cool. It's where Posh and Becks hang out. All the top PRs and other important contacts will be there, and Piers too, obviously. We're not inviting any celebrities – that way we can't get slagged off if none of them turn up,' I said to my mother on the phone at work.

'It all sounds fantastic, darling. And what are you going to wear?' she replied.

What the hell *was* I going to wear? It was the day before our party, and I had completely forgotten that I had to make an effort to look vaguely glamorous. We had only been on the column for two weeks and the other reporters were spreading rumours that we had been given a clothes allowance. I bloody wished. Who did they think we were? TV presenters? We were writers like the rest of them.

I'd been too busy trying to blag as much free stuff as possible for the party to think about clothes. We'd been told we had a very small budget, and Eva, Polly and I had spent days on the phone striking deals. I was quickly learning that a lot of this job was about doing favours for favours. Did anyone actually like anyone in this industry? The answer was no, not really. Despite chummy drinking sessions and bonding nights out with PRs, agents and other contacts, it was all about what we could do for one another.

We had the VIP bar at the Sugar Reef in Soho for free, so that when the PR would ring up to tell us a celebrity had popped into the place we would repay him by including this information in our column. We had free booze supplied by Bacardi Breezer – in exchange for giving us crates of their alcopops, we would mention the drink in our story about our party and print the company's logo on our invitations. And there was I thinking my job was to dig the dirt and come up with dazzling scoops for our new gossip column, not to organize as many freebies as possible in order to save the newspaper money.

Polly organized the invites and we sent them out to PRs and contacts, praying people would come.

At 6pm on 19 July, two hours before the party was meant to start, Eva, Polly and I got changed in the unglamorous setting of the ladies' loo on the editorial floor of the *Mirror*. This was to become our regular changing room when we went to bashes straight from work. None of us had had time to shop for anything new, so we had relied on old favourites. I put on a purple sparkly Karen Millen skirt and backless black top. Eva wore a black top and cream skirt, and Polly wore a flowery skirt and an extremely low-cut top that drew attention to her generous décolletage.

We tottered to the Tube and talked excitedly about who we hoped would be turning up at the party, all three of us nervous we'd be the only people there.

An area downstairs at the bar had been roped off for us, and we marched around pretending to double-check everything was OK. Eva and I tried not to laugh. It was all a bit surreal, and we felt like we were kids hosting the school disco.

'I don't think we need to worry about whether anyone is going to actually show up. We'll get every ligger in town,' giggled Eva, who was pointing towards the door.

We needn't have worried. A full quarter of an hour before the party was meant to start there were already some thirsty-looking record company press officers pointing out their names on the security man's clipboard. We waved them in.

'Hi, guys. Where's the booze?' asked one of them.

We pointed to the trays of wine and beer. The PRs for Bacardi Breezer were still busy unpacking crates of the stuff.

Within half an hour the place was heaving and everyone was knocking back drinks. It was as if no one had been offered free alcohol in years. We had asked for bowls of thick-cut chips and cocktail sausages on sticks, but nobody seemed that interested in them. It was clearly going to be one long booze-fuelled affair. My mother and father arrived, and I hoped they wouldn't stumble across the growing number of people chopping out lines of cocaine in the loo.

Piers made his grand appearance at 9pm.

'Right, let's get a picture,' he announced, waving at Richard Young.

Eva, Polly and I gathered around Piers and we all held our drinks up. I was relieved when I saw the pictures later that I wasn't the only one who looked dodgy in pictures. Piers had an ever-so-slightly creepy leer on his face.

We had made a point of not inviting any celebs, but unbelievably a few tried to get in before they were turned away. Ex-*Hollyoaks* actor and *Celebrity Love Island* nutter Paul Danan and *Lock, Stock* star Nick Moran actually gatecrashed the bash, which made it even worse because it looked like we had asked them to turn up. One PR had brought along some girl band so that we could plug them. We did, and needless to say they disappeared off the face of the earth a few months later.

The *Evening Standard*'s Londoner's Diary gossip column also dispatched a reporter to gatecrash the party. Sadly for them, their keen, young and gangly writer was more interested in pitching his CV to a bored-looking Piers. In the end they ran a bitchy piece saying our party was so crap we only had cold chips and greasy sausages for our guests. I thought it was extraordinary that they had bothered to share this nugget of dreary information with their readers, who would have no idea what they were talking about. What did they care about the food we had half-heartedly ordered to help line the stomachs of showbusiness industry PRs?

Still, as Piers assured us, it was an indication of the fact that the other gossip columnists were all feeling extremely threatened by the new girls on the block. It was now time to deliver on the promise that the *Mirror*'s 3am would become the biggest showbiz column in the whole of the country.

Me, Bruce Willis and Polly

3. Fisticuffs

Our launch party may have been lacking any proper celebrities, but we'd all got into the spirit of things and had knocked back as many Bacardi Breezers as we could stomach. Eva and Polly had wobbled back to their respective Battersea flats late that night, and I had headed for Tom's. We were all drunk, but happy in the knowledge that we had officially been unveiled. Now all we had to do was meet some proper A-listers.

The next morning, despite cracking hangovers, the three of us were all set to meet George Clooney.

'We couldn't have picked a worse day if we'd tried,' I moaned when I arrived at work at 10am that Thursday morning. 'I've had a terrible night's sleep after yet another blazing row with Tom. My head is killing me.'

Polly was silent. Squinting at her with one eye closed in the hope that this would ease the banging in my head, I saw her furiously tapping away at her computer keyboard.

'You OK?' I asked.

'Yes. Fine,' she replied testily.

Great. I feel like shit, Polly is in the mother of all strops for no reason and Eva isn't even at work yet. We've only been going for two weeks. Marvellous start, I thought.

To keep my mind off my hangover and the thought that my fellow 3am colleagues were already playing up, I tried to think of ways to make our interview with George Clooney more exciting.

For a start it wasn't exactly an interview. We'd been promised five minutes with him in a hotel room at the Dorchester, on the condition that he could bring the director of his movie *The Perfect Storm*, Wolfgang Petersen, and his co-star Mark Wahlberg. We readily agreed to the edict of the film company's dragon-like head of press as, well, it was George Clooney and we would do anything for him.

The PR had already rung Richard that morning to warn him that Clooney was still up for meeting us but that he had the flu so wouldn't be on great form. Richard told us that that was PR-talk for 'George doesn't want to be interviewed by a tabloid but has got promotional commitments and has no choice in the matter so he's likely to be in a very bad mood'.

I knew drastic action was called for. Clooney was not renowned for his bad temper and wasn't precious like other Hollywood stars, so we were in with a chance to win him over in the whole five minutes we had with him.

I had actually met him once. Well, when I say 'met' I mean I was standing in the same room as him. I was covering the Cannes Film Festival for the *Daily Telegraph* and was having a few drinks at the exclusive Hotel du Cap, where all the megastars stayed. The bar at the ludicrously overpriced hotel – where, incidentally, you had to pay for everything in cash – was a great place to hang out. It consisted of two rooms with plump sofas and leather chairs and was crammed full of Hollywood types dressed in black tie, high-class hookers, unidentifiable billionaires and journalists trying to look nonchalant. At night, after the movie premieres, actors would pile in to slap each other on the back and bask in a golden glow of smugness.

Suddenly Clooney roared in and grabbed a bottle of Stolichnaya vodka from the bar. 'My name is George Clooney and I'm an alcoholic!' he joked as he pretended to down the bottle of booze.

I was thrilled to see the legendary George Clooney misbehaving like that. I watched as he was dragged on to the terrace outside the bar which overlooked the manicured gardens. He had been followed by Mariella Frostrup, who was now gyrating up and down beside him.

Tom, who was there with me, had bumped into the actor in the men's loo in the hotel basement only minutes before this scene.

'Hey man, I've left you a line of coke in there,' George whispered to Tom as he left one of the toilet cubicles.

Tom thought he had landed the scoop of the year. But when

he peered his head around the door, he saw there was nothing in there. It was one of George's notorious pranks.

So I was looking forward to seeing him again, and I wanted him to be on top form. I really wanted to get him something that would put him in a jolly mood. 'I'll be back in a minute,' I shouted at Polly as I dashed from my desk and made a run for the lifts.

I returned ten minutes later, having paid a visit to Oddbins in Canary Wharf. 'A little something for George,' I said, waving a bottle of Stolichnaya at Polly.

'Ah right, good idea,' she said.

There was no way I was letting the bottle out of my sight. This time I was determined to hand it over myself, so I had a chance to appear in the picture. Just at that moment, Eva staggered to her desk.

'Bloody hell, are you all right? What happened to you?' I asked. Eva was definitely in the realms of the unwell.

'Bleurgh. I feel so rough, man. I have never been so hungover in my life. I can hardly talk,' she croaked as she collapsed on to her chair and flung her head down on to her computer keyboard.

'Oh, dear. You do realize we have to leave in an hour to get to the Dorchester to meet George Clooney,' said Polly in her head girl-style voice.

'Yes, I know. And then I've got to get a train to Birmingham to go to the premiere of his shit movie. Why me? Why do I have to go? I just want to die. Ouch,' she mumbled, her forehead still resting on her keyboard. Eva couldn't put half as much booze away as Polly and I could and here was the evidence that she certainly couldn't handle hangovers.

Richard had indeed informed her a few days before that after interviewing George, she had to go to Birmingham where *The Perfect Storm* was having a premiere. And she'd have to cover the after-show party too, watching out for any scandal. I felt sorry for her. The poor girl looked like she was suffering badly, as if she was going to burst into tears. Watching Eva was my first lesson in drinking at parties: no matter what state we got into the night before, we'd have to be on the ball the next day. Not just because we had a column to write, but also because it was highly likely we'd be going to more parties in the evening.

This job was a lot harder than it looked. Yes, we got to go to lavish parties and meet some proper A-list Hollywood superstars. But we also had to be fresh-faced and ready to go all guns blazing at work the next day, hangover or no hangover. And then be prepared to do it all again that night.

Eva, who still had her jacket on, looked like she'd fallen asleep with her pounding head still resting on her keyboard. I promised myself I'd never get into that state. Or at the very least I'd hide in the toilet so my colleagues couldn't see how bad I felt.

'Right, ladies, go get 'im,' hollered Richard. He looked at Eva. 'You'll feel loads better once you see Swooney Clooney and you'll forget all about your hangover.'

Eva looked unconvinced. Or was she pulling that face because she was about to be sick everywhere?

'Have you eaten yet?' I asked as Eva, Polly and I left the building and made our way towards the Tube station.

'Ewwww. No. I think I'd vomit,' replied Eva.

'You've got to have something or you'll be sick. You've got to get a train to Birmingham and go out tonight,' said Polly.

'Yes, I know. I don't need reminding,' Eva muttered, rolling her eyes.

We arrived at Green Park Tube and walked to the Dorchester on Park Lane, where a lot of Hollywood A-listers such as Tom Cruise, Nicole Kidman and Elizabeth Taylor usually stayed.

We met up with Youngy in the lobby. 'Hey, girls. How are you?' he said brightly as he air-kissed us. He took a closer look at Eva. 'Bloody hell, girl, look at the state of you. What on earth happened?'

'She's slightly hungover,' I said as Eva narrowed her eyes and mumbled something threatening under her breath. She looked like she wanted to kill someone.

'Well, make sure you turn on the charm for George. I'm under strict instructions to get some great action shots of you guys larking about with him,' said Youngy after he'd stopped laughing at Eva. Her eyes narrowed even more.

We flung ourselves on a sofa and proceeded to make ourselves comfortable while waiting for the film company PR. We knew George would be running late, as no self-respecting Hollywood A-lister could possibly even conceive of being on time.

After twenty minutes of trying to cajole Eva out of her hangover from hell, we were finally summoned to a hotel suite to meet Clooney, Wahlberg and Wolfgang. I was still clutching the bottle of vodka, but once in the suite I decided to hide it under a table so I could present it to Clooney when the time was right. What a mistake.

Sweating and coughing up phlegm, the greying star shuffled into the room looking more like someone's sick dad than a Hollywood heart-throb. But he was still incredibly sexy and we twittered around him like blushing schoolgirls. Youngy took photos as we oohed and aahed as George told us about the nasty bug he'd picked up.

Before I even had time to think about my gift, Polly snatched it in a pincer-like movement and thrust it at George. She'd done it again! I was going to have to learn to move much faster in future.

He perked right up when he saw the bottle of vodka and happily smiled for the cameras. Unfortunately for me, I was snapped with my hands on my hips looking royally pissed off at Polly for getting in there first. At least this time I could be seen in the photos. Eva just looked rather dazed and as if she was about to be sick everywhere.

The film company PR didn't see the funny side of our gift at all. 'What the hell are you doing? What have you given him? Stop taking pictures. George, give me that,' she barked at us, like an angry teacher.

Although I could see why she was wholly unimpressed that her client would appear in a British tabloid clutching a bottle of vodka, I thought it merely added to his charm. She snatched it off him, leaving George looking very bereft.

I was still angry with Polly for muscling her way into the centre of attention with Clooney, but just then in walked Mark Wahlberg, who took my mind right off what had just happened. Wahlberg was even more gorgeous in the flesh than I had imagined, but he seemed to have lost his voice. 'I was out at Chinawhite and stayed up until six this morning,' he croaked.

Hangovers all round. Maybe Clooney was suffering from one too and was merely pretending he'd picked up the flu.

'We're feeling a bit fragile today as well. We had our launch party last night,' I piped up.

Clooney seemed more than happy to chat to us about alcohol. 'So you've all got hangovers, huh? Well, I know how that feels,' he laughed. 'I don't think I'm going to get up to any heavy partying in the UK this time around.'

Christ, I thought, he really must be sick.

We posed for a picture with Clooney, Wahlberg and the director, who, I'm ashamed to say, we completely blanked as we were far more interested in the fit actors in the room. We didn't even bother to make polite conversation with him. There didn't seem to be much point seeing as we had only a minute left with the stars.

Our time came to an end and George and Mark were marched out by the PR, who glared at us as she closed the door behind her.

'Right, let's ring the office and tell them what he said,' ordered Polly.

I didn't say anything to Polly about what had just happened. I didn't want her to know that she'd got to me by giving George *my* vodka. She was quick off the mark and I'd just have to learn from her.

Richard was delighted with the vodka story and the quotes, and Polly told him we had some great pictures of us with George.

'Get back to the office and write it all up. Every cough and spit,' he said, which became his catchphrase for wringing every single detail out of a conversation with a celebrity, no matter how innocuous.

Eva just stood there looking green and not saying much.

'Are you all right?' I asked her.

'No. I can't believe I have to go to Birmingham. I feel awful,' she whispered.

'You've got to eat something. Come on,' said Polly.

We accompanied Eva out of the suite and walked to the bar so we could make sure she ate.

'Get this down you,' Polly said to Eva after ordering her a plate of chips and a large freshly squeezed orange juice. Despite thinking that Polly was trying to outdo us from day one, I realized that she could be compassionate when she wanted to.

Eva nibbled at a chip.

I looked at my watch. 'We've got to go back to the office,' I said to Eva. 'Good luck with Birmingham, mate. Best idea is probably to get right back on it and start drinking again.'

'No chance. Don't even mention alcohol to me,' she replied meekly.

An hour later, Polly and I were sitting at Polly's desk, jointly writing the story up. Well, she was tapping away at her computer and I was making suggestions over her shoulder.

My phone rang.

'Guess what just happened? I'm so embarrassed.' It was Eva.

'Are you OK?' I asked.

'Well, I feel much better now, put it like that. I've just got on to the train. But when I arrived at Euston, I suddenly felt really dodgy and vomited all over the platform. It was disgusting. It was bright orange because of that juice and it had lumps of chips in it,' she chuckled.

Oh well, at least she was laughing about it.

Within the first month of starting at 3am I had already met Tom Cruise, Angelina Jolie and George Clooney. I was literally rubbing shoulders with the Hollywood A-listers – that is, whenever I managed to elbow my way to their side. I was stunned by the access we had managed to get to these big-name stars and how happily they larked around with us. When it came to publicity, it seemed that pretty much every celebrity was up for pretty much anything as long as their film, book or single was publicized, and together we formed a kind of unholy alliance where we would all get what we wanted. We were their necessary evil.

However, some stars were not quite as thrilled to take part in this unspoken agreement, especially if they had nothing specific to promote. Take Angus Deayton, for example, with whom we had our first celebrity fallout.

The column had been running for less than a fortnight when the former *Have I Got News For You* host took us to task over a story we had run on him. And he was the first star to learn that when someone tried to pick a fight with us, we would take things to pretty extreme lengths. Childish? Oh, definitely.

Deayton – who still presented the BBC Two show at that point, as his cocaine and prostitute shame had yet to be revealed – ordered his legal team to send Piers a letter complaining about a story we'd published. We had revealed that Deayton had made unreasonable demands during a trip to Paris thrown by Griff Rhys Jones and Mel Smith to celebrate the £62 million sale of Talkback Thames, the TV production company they partly owned at the time. A source involved in organizing the trip had revealed to someone in our showbiz department that Angus had caused her 'considerable inconvenience' by changing his travel plans at the last minute and demanding to travel first class in a specific seat on Eurostar, and to stay in a different hotel from the other guests who had been invited on the celebratory piss-up. He wanted to be away from the 'hoi polloi', apparently.

In the article we had also referred to Angus as short.

We wondered whether our comment about his height had tipped him over the edge. One of his aides rang up the *Mirror* to complain about the article and also pointed out tersely that Angus was at least six foot tall.

Richard and Piers rubbed their hands in delight. Here was our first celebrity target. 'Right, ladies, we need to start to dish it out to loser-boy Deayton. Time to rip the shit out of him about his height. Touchy boy!' guffawed Richard. He was on a roll. 'Let's start by asking the readers if they can help us out. Short of tracking him down with a tape measure, it's time to find out just how tall everyone thinks he really is.'

Richard had a fantastic way of hyping us up. It was a great idea.

A bit of harmless fun. And besides, surely someone like Deayton should be able to take a bit of gentle ribbing.

Two days later, we ran a request in the column asking people to contact us. 'Have you seen Angus Deayton? How tall do you think he is?' I soon learnt that *Mirror* readers loved to be included on quests of such national importance. We were deluged with emails, letters and phone calls from a countless number of people all putting him somewhere between 5 foot 3 and 5 foot 7.

'He's not exactly TV personality of the year, is he?' laughed Eva, as we giggled over yet another email from a reader telling us what a prat they thought he was. And a short prat at that.

Angus clearly wasn't as amused as Piers, Richard and the British public were by our teasing. A letter from his lawyers was shortly dispatched to Piers and to our legal department which contained denials about our original story and demanded compensation for the hurt and distress we had caused.

'Oh, bloody hell, we're in for it now. Is he serious? Hurt and distress?' I asked after Piers had come round to our department from his office and read the letter out to us. I was very nervous. This was the first time I had been involved in a legal dispute with a celebrity. But Piers and Richard were on our side. Luckily they were laughing the entire episode off. They clearly relished a fight of this magnitude with someone as unpopular as Deayton, and seemed to look forward to the legal tussle we were about to embark on.

Piers made several phone calls to cajole Deayton's aides into dropping the whole episode. But they didn't want to and said they were reporting the *Mirror* to the Press Complaints Commission, otherwise known as the PCC, an independent body who ensure British newspapers and magazines stick to the agreed Code of Conduct. They also deal with complaints from the public and from celebrities who feel they have cases against the press who breach the code. Angus had pressed the nuclear button and had dragged the big guns in. We were told in no uncertain terms that this was now war.

The night Piers had been sent the letter from Deayton's legal team spelling out his serious lack of sense of humour, Polly and I jumped on the Tube to go to Islington for the premiere of John Cusack's new movie, *High Fidelity*, an adaptation of Nick Hornby's novel.

As we were waiting to get into the cinema, Michael Greco, who played Beppe in *EastEnders* at the time and who knew Polly from when she worked on Matthew Wright's column, made a beeline for her. 'Hi, Polly, how you doing?' he grinned while leering at her boobs.

She made polite chitchat for a while before he slinked off into the cinema.

'He really fancies you,' I said.

She just grimaced. I told her Greco clearly had a thing for girls with big breasts. His most recent girlfriend was the glamour model Linsey Dawn McKenzie.

'Oh, shut up,' laughed Polly.

We decided to give the movie a miss. Sometimes we would actually stay and watch the film at a premiere as a way of filling in time before the after-show party would start. But mostly I preferred not to because if I did stay it meant that I wouldn't be able to go to the cinema with my friends, and I still wanted a social life. We strolled to the Elbow Room bar where the party was happening, and got stuck into the cocktails, waiting for the celebs to turn up.

A couple of hours later, the stars who had been at the screening appeared, joining a few more who had bypassed the cinema and headed straight for the party, where a never-ending supply of free booze and food was on offer.

'Bloody hell. Look who it is! Oh fuck!' I exclaimed, nudging Polly.

She turned around towards the door, where a scrum of people were elbowing each other out of the way to get to the free bar. There in the crowd, pushing their way through, were comedian Alan Davies and none other than Angus Deayton.

Polly and I moved further down the bar and stood in a dark corner, trying to suppress our giggles. The column had been running for less than two weeks and although our photos were on top of the page every day, we hadn't been recognized by celebrities yet. This was something which would soon change, but for then we were largely unknown, except to those Z-lister soap stars who wanted to be written about.

'Do you reckon he'd know who we were if we went up to him and started talking?' I asked Polly.

'God knows. Well, we certainly can't say who we are. We could just start chatting and see what happens,' said Polly.

Suddenly I had a moment of clarity. Those cocktails had seemingly sharpened my senses and I had an idea which, if it came off, would amuse Piers and Richard no end and would give us a piss-taking story to write up for the next column. 'I've got a much better idea. Where's Youngy?' I asked, looking around for our bearded snapper.

Polly stayed where she was while I rushed around the party, trying to locate Youngy. I found him by the entrance to the party where a few other photographers were waiting for more stars to turn up. 'Richard, we really need you now. Angus Deayton is over there and Piers is obsessed with him at the moment so Polly and I need to do a picture with him for the column. Piers will be ecstatic if we get a snap of him,' I lied.

Well, it wasn't exactly a total lie. Piers *was* obsessed with him now he was going to sue us. And if we managed to get alongside him in a photograph, Piers would be thrilled. I knew that if I told Youngy the whole story he would probably be reluctant to become involved. He was one of those photographers who all the celebrities adored. Not only was he a legend, he was also incredibly discreet and was always very professional. It was important for him to maintain these relationships because he often did private work for big-name stars when he wasn't covering after-show parties and lavish A-list bashes. I felt a little guilty, but the reality was I had a job to do. I was also keen to impress the bosses after failing to do anything other than stand with my back to the camera looking like a total fool at the Tom Cruise premiere.

'Sure. Take me to him,' Youngy beamed at me.

We walked back to where Polly was waiting for me.

'Right, let's find Deayton,' I said.

'What's going on?' Polly replied, looking bemused by the sergeant major-style tone in my voice.

'Well, I think there is a 50:50 chance he'll recognize us so we'll have to move very fast,' I confided to Polly as I pushed my way past revellers to get to Deayton.

'Move very fast? What are you talking about?' she asked, sounding perplexed.

I could see Angus Deayton still chortling and chatting away with Alan Davies by the bar. 'We can prove this height fiasco once and for all,' I replied, unable to keep my eyes off him. If we pulled this one off, it would be just the sort of story Piers wanted us to run in the column.

'How?' Polly asked, starting to sound a little bit irritated.

I looked at her and grinned. 'We just pretend we're fans, ask him if we can have our photo with him, we stand either side of him and then Youngy can snap away,' I whispered. 'Hopefully Deayton won't wonder why a couple of giggling fans have a famous photographer to take their picture, but he might not take long to work it out, which is why we'll have to move fast.'

'Er, right,' said Polly, sounding a bit dubious as to why I was getting so excited about having our picture taken with Angus Deayton.

'But once we have the picture in the bag, guess what we can do with it in the column?' I asked.

'What?' Polly said.

'We blow the picture up really big and we get the sub-editors to draw height charts on the photo, so we can prove that he is short! Look at him, there's no way he's over 6 foot!' I babbled excitedly.

Polly clapped her hands. 'That's hilarious! We both know our own heights so we can work his out in no time. We can get lines drawn on the top of our heads to show he's only at best an inch or so taller than us, if that,' she said, getting excited about the idea.

I checked that Youngy couldn't hear us discussing our devious plan, and saw that he was deep in conversation with a colleague. I called him over. 'Right,' I said to him, 'we're going to go up to

Angus now to ask him for a picture. Piers said you were a total genius for the way you did those photos of us chatting to Tom Cruise. He really wants more action shots in the column, so just go for it when we start talking to him, OK?' I instructed.

Youngy nodded, and Polly and I made our way towards Deayton. I was nervous, but I knew that there was no point standing around trying to build up courage or stalling time by having another drink. Anyway, I tried to convince myself, it wasn't like we were being heartless tabloid harpies. We were just having a laugh with him. Surely he'd eventually see the funny side!

'Hi, we're huge fans, can we have a quick picture with you?' asked Polly, putting on the sweetest smile she could muster.

Angus turned towards us but barely looked us in the eye. 'Oh, if you really must,' he sighed.

What a charmer. I couldn't believe how unfriendly he was to two girls he thought were admirers. No wonder his 'legions' of so-called 'fans' had failed to ring us or write to us at the *Mirror* begging us to lay off him. At least he hadn't recognized us.

We stood either side of him, but at that precise moment, the ludicrousness of the situation hit me and I started to laugh uncontrollably. Polly then started giggling too while Youngy snapped away.

Alan Davies, who had been observing our encounter, wanted to join in the fun and games. And didn't he just. 'You girls are too tall for him,' the *Jonathan Creek* star told us. He tried to push our shoulders down so we would appear shorter next to Angus, who was doing his best to put on a suave smile for the camera. But we had what we wanted.

'Thanks,' said Polly, with a smile, and we moved away as fast as we could. Youngy followed us and showed us the images on the screen of his digital camera. Incredibly, the usually morose star looked happy to be with us in the picture. And he appeared to be around our height too.

Youngy wandered off to take some snaps of a sozzled Rhys Ifans who was falling about nearby, and Polly and I celebrated our coup by ordering two more cocktails. Just then we saw Deayton walking briskly away from a female journalist we recognized from a rival paper who was in hot pursuit of him.

'You're not one of those 3am girls, are you? I hate them,' we heard him sneer at her.

The next day I arrived at work half an hour early. Richard was always in at 9am, a good hour before the rest of the department turned up. I was so excited about what we'd done the night before I wanted to tell him as soon as possible. To be honest, I also wanted to get in there with Richard before anyone else did. Polly was a sharp operator and I was learning quickly that I'd have to employ the same tactics she used and be just as pushy. It was something I was having to pick up on the spot. This job was just too important for me, and I didn't want to mess it up.

I knew that Youngy wouldn't have sent his photos in yet as he worked late into the night covering the parties. He usually sent his snaps over to the picture desk around mid-morning, and we would then all decide between us which celebrity snaps we'd use in the next day's column.

I sat down at my desk and started flicking through a magazine in the most nonchalant way I could. 'You'll never guess who Polly and I saw at the *High Fidelity* party last night,' I said to Richard, trying to sound casual.

'Who? Callan, why are you being so cagey? Come on, spit it out,' he laughed, narrowing his eyes at me. There was no fooling Richard, ever.

'OK, OK. We did a picture with him and he was smiling away and everything, and he looked really happy to be seen with us. Obviously he didn't have a bloody clue who we were,' I said, teasing him a little longer.

'Who the hell are you talking about? Just tell me!' Richard banged his fist against his desk in mock anger.

'Angus Deayton!' I shouted, jumping up and down in my chair.

'You're joking! That little shit. Piers will love this. Well done. Well fucking done.' He laughed and spun around in his chair. 'Love it. I fucking love it.'

Luckily, so did Piers and we ran the picture in the column with a height chart drawn on it to indicate that I was 5 foot 8½ in my high heels, Polly was 5 foot 7½ and that Angus was therefore a 'towering' 5 foot 9.

The headline ran: 'Have we got some short but hilarious news for you, Angus'. We did make light of the situation and ended the article by appealing to his better nature, referring to him as 'dishy' and as our old friend: 'Come on, Angus, old chap, regain that sense of humour and remember our 3am maxim: if you can't take it, don't dish it out . . .'

Strangely, for someone who merrily ridiculed every famous name on *Have I Got News For You* week after week, Deayton didn't take too kindly to having the piss taken out of him. He failed to be won over by us and seemed even more furious than before. The humourless presenter insisted on sticking to his guns and pressed on with his case against us, claiming to the PCC that the original story about his behaviour on the trip to Paris was 'unfair' and a breach of its code of conduct.

A year later, in August 2001, he lost his battle with 3am. The PCC made the decision that it could not criticize our coverage as we had not breached the code. A spokesman ruled: 'We understood his irritation at the suggestion that he was "obtuse" but the woman was entitled to say she had been inconvenienced, and that came across in the story.'

Deayton wasn't the only enemy we made in that first month. He was shortly joined by Noel Gallagher, who also took offence to us the month we launched the column.

We'd run a short story about his wife Meg Mathews and at the end of the piece we'd made a passing comment about the Oasis star, who at the time was on holiday and attracting the attention of the paparazzi. We wrote that the monobrowed Mancunian had been 'unwisely sunbathing nude in the garden of his Ibizan villa'. Some might have said that was a fair enough point to make. But who'd have thought the surly singer and guitarist was such a sensitive little soul?

A few nights later, I was at Tom's flat watching TV, exhausted from a week of covering parties, drinking to excess and struggling to hide my hangovers and remain bright-eyed and bushy-tailed at work every day. Tom wanted to go to the pub. All I wanted to do was lie on the sofa of his Stockwell house and feel sorry for myself. Luckily, he took pity on me and he agreed not to force me to go anywhere that night.

At 10pm my mobile rang. Showbiz journalists – as with the rest of the press pack – have to be contactable 24/7 so that the office can get hold of them at any time. This meant I could never turn my mobile off, even if I was away for the weekend or on holiday. Some of my fellow showbiz contemporaries at another newspaper were ordered never to travel on the Underground, as it meant they would be out of contact for a short while. Now that was tough.

My mobile phone screen showed that the caller's number was withheld, which meant it was probably someone at the *Mirror*. 'Hello?' I answered cautiously. I knew this wasn't a good sign – it rarely was when you received a call after 10pm. The first editions of the other papers came out around 10.30pm, so if I received a phone call at that time it meant that another newspaper – usually our big rivals the *Sun* – had a showbusiness story which we had missed and I would be bollocked and asked to chase it up and see if it was true. This usually entailed ringing up the PR of the celebrity in question. Ninety-nine per cent of the time the article was correct, so I often had the torturous job of writing up the story that we had missed and that wasn't an exclusive any more.

You also had to take into account that if the PR denied the *Sun*'s scoop, it didn't mean it wasn't true. There would be two reasons for this: either the publicist didn't want the story coming out or, as was usually the case, the PR had colluded with the other paper and confirmed the story off the record for whatever reason but denied it on the record until they wanted to admit it. Either way I would receive a kicking from the bosses.

So I braced myself and prepared to put on my most professional-sounding voice to speak to either Richard or whoever it was on their shift on the night news desk.

'Hi, Jessica. Sorry to bother you on a Friday night,' Chris Hughes, one of the news reporters, said hesitantly.

I was a bit taken aback by this. The news desk – or indeed anyone else at the paper – never usually apologized for ringing. Something was up.

'No problem. What's the matter?' I asked brightly, trying not to sound too anxious.

Chris had been a showbiz reporter before moving on to news a year or so before, so he knew what it was like covering the celebrity beat. He was a good laugh and hung around with the blokes in my department – who usually ribbed him constantly for wanting to be a serious news reporter – so I knew he'd be upfront with me.

'Erm, well, er, I don't know how to put this,' he stuttered.

'Oh, bloody hell, Hughsie, what's going on? Am I in trouble?' I implored.

'Well, not exactly.' He started laughing nervously. He wasn't helping matters at all.

'Right, OK. Well, we've just had a call from a news reporter at the Oasis concert currently taking place at Wembley Stadium,' he explained.

'And? What's happened?' I asked, trying to coax the information out of Chris. This was turning into a very frustrating conversation.

'Yes, right. OK. So anyway, um, it seems Noel Gallagher just made a comment about you and the other 3am girls. Mid-concert. In front of the sold-out stadium. Eighty thousand people,' he said, clearly getting into his stride.

'I get the point, Hughsie. A lot of people. What did he say?' I could tell it wasn't going to be good.

'Well, they'd just finished a song and then Noel said that "3am" stood for "three absolute mingers". And that you're fifteen times uglier than Matthew Wright.'

It was a tumbleweed moment. There was a silence. I didn't know what to say, and neither did Hughsie.

'Hello? You still there?' he finally asked.

'Yes, I am. Bloody hell. Did he really say that? What a nutter,' I whispered.

'Yeah. You guys must have really pissed him off. What did you write about him?'

'Um, just that he had been sunbathing naked in his garden. And had been papped. We didn't even say what a gruesome sight that must have been. I think we said he had unwisely been caught with his kit off, but that was it. Talk about over-reacting!' I said. We had upset the poor little flower so much, he had felt compelled to share with the tens of thousands of Oasis fans his views on our physical appearances.

'Anyway, thought you should know. Richard will think it's hysterical no doubt, nice guy that he is. I guess that's your column for Monday sorted then. Bye!' said Chris.

Tom was looking at me, perplexed. 'What was all that about? You got a kicking for missing a story? Bad luck, kiddo. You really can't be having anyone at the *Sun* beating you when you've just started at the *Mirror*. Doesn't make you look good at all,' he kindly pointed out.

'Oh, shut up. Noel Gallagher is onstage at Wembley Stadium right now and just called me and Eva and Polly mingers and said we're fifteen times uglier than our column predecessor, Matthew Wright,' I said, a little dazed by what had happened.

'What? You serious? What an idiot. Bloody funny though. You better make sure you write a story saying what an ugly bastard he is. Ha ha. Poor kiddo! You're a minger! Minger!' Tom laughed.

He was clearly tickled by this. I ignored him while he continued to chant 'Minger!' and danced around the room as he did so. I rang Eva on her mobile.

'Hiya, what you up to?' she asked. Hearing her bright tone, Hughsie clearly hadn't broken the news to her yet.

'I'm at Tom's,' I replied.

'What is that noise in the background?' she asked.

Tom was still on a repetitive loop like a toddler who had just learnt a new word and was alternating between laughing his head off and calling me a minger. 'Oh, be quiet, I can't hear Eva,' I snapped at him.

'Ooohhh! Stroppy girl. Just because you're a minger,' he guffawed.

I marched out of the room and sat in his kitchen.

'You guys having another lovers' tiff?' Eva laughed.

'Oh, he's just being an idiot as usual. Listen, I've just had a call from Hughsie. You'll never believe this. Someone from the newsroom is at the Oasis concert and they just rang up the news desk to tell them that Noel Gallagher told the audience "3am" stood for "three absolute mingers" and that we were fifteen times uglier than Matthew Wright. I know some singers find it hard to think of witty one-liners to entertain their fans between songs, but this is taking banter to a whole new level.'

Eva was as stunned as I was. 'What an arse! What the hell did he say that for?' she asked.

'It's got to be in retaliation for us saying he'd unwisely been photographed sunbathing naked in his garden in Ibiza,' I replied. 'I so wish we'd written what a hideous sight that must have been. Noel roasting his dangly bits in the sun. Gross.'

'Yes, I know. We were incredibly restrained. Well, he's going to learn the hard way now, isn't he? If Angus Deayton got it bad, that's nothing compared to the bucket of shit we're going to heap all over Noel. *He*'s the ugly one!' stormed Eva.

Even I feared for Noel now. When Eva was on the warpath, that was it. She was capable of being so laidback one minute she was practically comatose, but when she went nuclear it was time to put on your tin hats and hide.

'He must be really upset by us questioning his attractiveness for him to go to the effort of calling us mingers halfway through his concert set,' I said.

That evening I realized just how powerful the column could become. And that I'd have to grow some very tough skin to put up with jibes about my looks. Coming from Noel Gallagher, it was easy. I knew we were going to make enemies, especially after the Angus Deayton incident, but not for one minute did I realize it was going to happen again so quickly.

Unfortunately for us, we didn't get quite the revenge we had envisaged.

Richard was on the rota for that Sunday (we all took it in turns to write the column on our own on a Sunday), and he had concocted what he described as 'a fucking great idea'. He wrote up the lead story for that Monday's column, inviting readers to take part in a phone-in poll and vote for who they thought was uglier – Noel Gallagher, Matthew Wright or us. Richard was friends with Matthew Wright, and took every opportunity to be rude about him.

I was mortified. It was obvious who was going to win. Oasis fans would no doubt agree with Noel and we'd had no shortage of calls from readers since the column had been launched telling us what a bunch of dogs we were. I could just picture the glee with which some of the more disturbed members of society would take part in voting for 3am.

It was indeed a massive defeat for us. We were officially uglier than Matthew and the least attractive Gallagher brother.

When Polly, Eva and I arrived at work on Tuesday, we insisted the phone lines be checked for sabotage in case our friends at the *Sun* had been told to repeatedly hit that redial button and vote for us. But alas, there was no sign of that. Our readers did indeed share Noel's sentiments and had decreed we were the ugliest.

'Sorry, ladies, but your public has spoken. You are mingers,' cackled Richard.

I knew I couldn't take it to heart. I was now a tabloid gossip columnist and as we had patronizingly pointed out to Angus Deayton in the column, if we couldn't take it, we shouldn't dish it out. So we reported the results of the poll.

With the headline 'Ugly Truth About Noel' we ran the following story, which was sprinkled with what Richard referred to as his 'showbiz razzle dazzle':

After Noel Gallagher's attack on 3am, our phone poll to discover who you thought was ugliest – the beetle-browed Oasis part-timer, our long-forgotten predecessor Matthew Wright or us – provoked an interesting reaction. Initial voting yesterday morning was a clear two horse-faced race between Gallagher and The Gurner. Hundreds phoned their lines while just six saddos called our number.

But after midday – coincidentally the time both Matthew and Noel get up – there was a mysterious shift in fortunes with a concentrated dialling of our vote line.

As you can see from the results, the two gargoyles clearly decided a pincer movement was necessary to establish us as the most repulsive.

3am: 65 per cent.

Matthew: 4 per cent.

Noel: 31 per cent.

Predictably, there was no apology from Noel, married to the famously gorgeous Meg Mathews.

At least he can now retire to his Ibizan holiday chalet in the full knowledge that at least he's not as ugly as Chris Moyles.

And so Chris Moyles, the Radio 1 DJ, was to become our next fan. He was clearly feeling left out – we had devoted many column inches to our fight with Noel – and wanted some publicity too. We were informed one day that month that Moylesy had gone on air, bless him, and said we had 'fallen out of the ugly tree and hit every branch on the way down'. Tom was even more amused by this. So was the rest of the office. Piers and Richard in particular loved it.

'You know what they say, girls – all publicity is good publicity. At least you're being talked about,' said Piers that afternoon when he strolled down to our department to see what all the laughter was about. He chortled away, but instead of joining in I looked away. Not because I was upset, far from it. It was because I had been subjected to an uninvited sight. He had an unnerving habit – no doubt a technique he considered to be a good man-management skill when talking to women in the office – of standing with one foot on your desk when speaking to you. This meant that when you turned to answer him, your head was unfortunately level with his crotch.

'To hell with Moyles, I reckon we don't give him so much as one sentence of abuse in the column,' I said. 'I reckon he's doing this for the publicity. He's gagging for us to turn round and slag him off as that'd give him some publicity in a national newspaper along with something to bore his listeners with on his radio show as he lays into us.'

Noel Gallagher wasn't using us for publicity. He just hated us. We reckoned Moyles wanted his name in the papers.

So we decided to ignore him, for now.

If we thought Angus Deayton, Noel Gallagher and Chris Moyles were rude, we'd seen nothing yet. It was mid-August, traditionally known as silly season. The entire nation was on holiday. No one bothered with launch parties, big premieres, important award ceremonies or any sort of interesting bash as all the celebs were sunning themselves in St Tropez or Ibiza. Although this was a tricky time for us, it was in fact heaven for PRs. They knew that we had space to fill on the column every day and bugger-all stories – there were only so many pieces about yet another soap star burning his buns on the beach in Marbella that we could run. So we were overjoyed when a PR for Planet Hollywood, Jonathan, told us that Bruce Willis, one of the part-owners of the restaurant chain, was jetting into London that weekend to make an appearance at the Piccadilly Circus burger HQ. We were invited to be the only journalists to meet and interview the *Die Hard* star.

It was a Saturday night. Emma, an old friend from university, was staying with me that weekend. I had made plans which I now had to cancel. I was getting used to the rule that we were permanently on call. Weekend plans I made with friends were regularly scrapped at the last minute as I'd be sent to a party or a club. Most of the time we would get advance notice from Richard, but there were plenty of occasions when we'd be sent somewhere without prior warning. Not that I would utter a word of complaint.

I convinced myself my friends would understand. These were people I had been to school and university with, and none of them worked in journalism. They were a bit perplexed that I seemed to be dashing around London most nights and surviving on very little sleep. But they all got a kick out of seeing my picture in the paper and enjoyed teasing me. Not that any of them actually bought the *Mirror*. In fact most of them couldn't remember which paper I worked for. They certainly liked to help keep my feet on the ground.

Polly had made plans for Saturday night too, but Jonathan told us that we were more than welcome to bring our pals along to the restaurant – we could have a few drinks with them before our chat with Willis.

Emma and I, and Polly and her friend, turned up at 7pm. We were ushered into a roped-off VIP area.

'Hello, hello!' Jonathan greeted us chirpily. 'Right, I think Bruce might be a teeny bit late so I'll get the champagne in and you and your friends can have a few drinks while we wait.'

We got stuck into the champagne and waited. And waited. And waited. 'Um, Jonathan, do you know how long he's going to be? Where is he? At dinner?' I asked the increasingly flustered-looking publicist.

'I am so sorry. He's got caught up in traffic. You know what it's like in the West End on a Saturday night,' he replied, forcing a strained smile out. 'I'll get you more champagne!'

Polly and I exchanged glances.

'I don't think he knows where the hell Bruce is,' hissed Polly. 'For God's sake. I've got better bloody things to do than sit in Planet Hollywood on my Saturday night.'

Drinking champagne while waiting for a non-existent Bruce Willis to turn up wasn't part of the equation for either of us. But we carried on waiting until it got to 8.30pm. Bruce was an hour and a half late. We were officially bored.

'Jonathan. Oi, Jonathan – what the hell's going on?' Polly shouted at the frantic PR who was dashing around the VIP area with his mobile phone attached to his ear. He was whispering nervously into the mouthpiece. He turned to our table.

'Oh please, don't get angry. I'm so sorry. He really is on his way. He's just downstairs. He and his friends got a bit lost on the way,' he said.

'Yeah, right. He got lost coming from his Park Lane hotel down the road in his chauffeur-driven car? I think not,' I muttered under my breath.

Then in walked Willis, surrounded by an entourage of sycophants and burly blokes with earpieces. He was kitted out in jeans, a cowboy hat to hide his bald head and a far too tight Planet Hollywood T-shirt which showed off his man boobs. Jonathan proceeded to talk to Bruce and some of his aides.

'Let's just flirt with him. He's meant to be a bit of a charmer anyway. We'll get loads out of him,' Polly said to me.

She seemed to know what she was talking about and as she was far more experienced than me in the job, I took her word for it. Flirting with a big Hollywood star seemed like a great idea. This was the sort of story Piers wanted us to put in the column – us getting in there with celebrities. He'd be impressed by our piece.

'Right, ladies, if I can get you to sit down at this table, then I'll bring Mr Willis over and we can get going,' instructed Jonathan brightly.

Polly and I got up from where we'd been sitting, left our friends to neck the remnants of the champagne and followed Jonathan to the middle of the VIP area where there was a table laden with plates of burgers, chips, ribs, coleslaw and huge Planet Hollywood-emblazoned glasses of vanilla milkshakes and Coca-Cola.

There were three chairs in a row on one side of the table. Jonathan guided me to the one on the right and asked Polly to sit on the one on the left. This meant Bruce would be sitting between us. It had all been set up so it would appear that we were enjoying a leisurely dinner with Willis at his restaurant. A photographer hovered nearby while Jonathan dashed off again to try and catch Bruce's attention, but he was far too busy with his friends.

'This is a bit cringey,' I whispered to Polly.

'Oh, it'll be fine. They just want maximum publicity for Planet Hollywood. And the photos will look amusing as Willis will look like he's having a fabulous time being charmed by us over burgers and fries,' she replied.

Or not. I leant out of my chair and craned my neck to see what was taking Bruce so long. I could see that he clearly hadn't been told about this interview. He was narrowing his eyes in our direction while one of his aides was pointing at us and whispering in his ear. He didn't look too thrilled to be joining us for a soggy onion ring.

Jonathan was by now tugging at his shirt collar and trying to give me a convincing smile and a thumbs-up sign to indicate that everything was going according to plan.

'This is a bloody shambles. I don't think they've even told Willis he has to talk to us,' I said to Polly.

'He hates the press anyway, especially the British tabloids, so no wonder they decided to leave it to the last minute,' she replied.

As we patiently watched the cold burgers on our table congeal some more, Bruce started making his way towards us. Jonathan fluttered nervously around him like an agitated moth. 'Bruce, this is Jessica and Polly from the *Mirror*. Girls, this is Bruce,' he said in his most professional-sounding voice.

'Hi, how are you?' cooed Polly, who then launched into some Olympic-level eyelash-fluttering and hair-flicking.

'Hi,' he mumbled in our general direction.

He then plonked himself on the chair between us. Realizing that he'd be practically rubbing elbows with us, he then quickly moved his chair back by about 12 inches so there would be no physical contact between us.

Not a good sign.

He eyed me suspiciously before turning to Polly and giving her the same cagey once-over.

'So, Bruce, good to see you in London. Would you ever think about moving here?' I asked in the most enthusiastic voice I could muster. It was hardly the most Paxman-esque question, but I was learning on the job that you had to ease these Hollywood types in. I was also doing him a favour. Most American stars when asked if they'd like to buy a London pad answered yes, even if they could think of nothing worse, as they knew it would garner them huge headlines and endear them to their British fans.

Bruce was having none of it though. 'I hate your weather,' he muttered in my direction.

That would be a no, then.

Polly and I exchanged a nervous glance and she leant forward on the table, pushed her arms together and gave her cleavage an instant boost. Not even that nifty move endeared her to Bruce, who refused to look her way.

'So, how was Brad Pitt and Jennifer Aniston's wedding?' I twittered. Things were not going according to plan, so I decided to plunge straight in with a question about the recent nuptials of the then Hollywood A-list couple du jour.

Bruce looked at me pityingly, shook his head and made a big show of examining his watch. He shifted in his chair and snarled, 'You've got 90 seconds. Starting from now. 90, 89, 88, 87.'

Thinking he was joking – quite why I thought Willis would choose this moment to reveal that he did have a sense of humour after all, I don't know – I looked at Polly and started to laugh. 'What present did you buy Brad and Jen then?' I continued.

But Bruce clearly wasn't having a laugh. He simply continued with his countdown and proceeded to recite the numbers over me as I tried to engage him in friendly banter. '86, 85, 84, 83, 82,' he continued, getting louder. Well, at least he knew how to count. Finally, after reaching number 75, Bruce got bored and announced, 'Right, I'm off.' He dragged himself up from his chair and marched out of the VIP area back into the main part of the restaurant.

'Did that just happen?' I asked Polly.

Polly and I remained at the table, too stunned to move. It was the fastest interview we had ever conducted. We watched Willis move from table to table where ordinary diners were trying to enjoy their dinner. He kept giving them high fives.

Jonathan crept towards us, looking like he wanted to commit suicide on the spot. It wasn't the type of interview he had been expecting and he knew by the looks on our faces that the publicity for Planet Hollywood wouldn't be either. 'I can't apologize enough. The least I can do is get you some more champagne,' he whispered, close to tears.

Before we had time to answer and tell him just what he could do with his champagne, he hollered to a passing waiter, 'Hello, hello, waiter! Can I get more champagne!'

Polly and I got up from our fake dinner table and made our way back to our friends who'd been watching the proceedings and were looking utterly shell-shocked.

'I can't believe he just did that,' shouted Emma in her booming Brummie accent. 'I hope you tear him to pieces.'

'Too right,' I replied.

Jonathan came over to us, clutching the champagne. 'You're not going to be too hard on him, are you?' he implored.

I was fuming. 'What the hell do you expect? You ask us if we want to do an interview with him, we give up our one night off of the week and he's not only incredibly late but incredibly rude to us. All he said to us was that he hates the weather in London before counting down from 90 to 75. Which bit of that would make for a fascinating interview? There's no other way we can write this up, Jonathan,' I said, totally exasperated that he was still trying to put a PR spin on it.

Jonathan bit his lower lip and said nothing.

Just then we saw Bruce climb up on to the bar, getting a leg-up from his mates. The next thing we knew he was being handed a microphone. 'Hey, everyone. I'm Bruce Willis. Thanks for being at Planet Hollywood. Enjoy! I love you guys. I love London,' he shouted to wild applause from the tourists who couldn't believe their luck that the film star was actually there.

'Oh, please. I want to be sick. And it's not just this disgusting champagne that's made me feel ill,' said Polly, rolling her eyes.

Jonathan went scurrying off to Bruce and his people, who were by now back in the VIP area necking some drinks. I didn't know what Jonathan said to them, but we noticed that soon they were surrounding him and listening intently to every word. We sat in our corner watching them. What was going on now?

Suddenly Bruce got up from his table and marched up to us. 'Can I have a private word with you two?' he asked.

Polly and I tried not to snigger, got up and followed him to an empty table. The three of us sat down.

'Look, I'm sorry if I was rude. I want to talk properly to you girls. You look like lovely girls. It's just that I hate the whole celebrity thing. So what are you doing later tonight? I'm going to a Bon Jovi concert at Wembley, but why don't you meet me later at the Met Bar? I'm going to be doing the DJing there. Bring your friends,' he said, talking at a hundred miles an hour. Without even waiting to hear our reply, he winked at us, put on his most winning smile and sauntered confidently back to his entourage. His mates slapped him on the back and escorted him out of the restaurant. His job was done.

Polly erupted. 'Is he having a fucking laugh? I can't imagine anything worse. He obviously thinks he's won us over by forcing himself to be nice to us. Well, mate, you really didn't try hard enough. Come on, we're going,' Polly shouted in the direction of her by now utterly inebriated friend.

Jonathan was looking much perkier. 'Well, there we go. Wasn't he nice once he got going? I explained that your column is very important and that you are very famous journalists and he said he was going to invite you to the Met Bar. Won't that be fun?' he asked.

'Er, no, Jonathan.' I couldn't help but laugh at his cheek. 'I can't see Piers wanting us to write something flattering after we have been subjected to one of the most awful interviews we've ever been put through. No offence to you, though.'

Jonathan sat down and looked pained again. 'Fine. Will you give me a ring tomorrow and give me the gist of the damage?' he asked.

That Monday we ran a half-page piece on our 'date' with Bruce entitled 'Try Hard – Moody Bruce Finds it a Struggle to Charm Us'.

When I went to New York three months later to visit my brother who lived there, I was invited to the opening of the new Planet Hollywood in Times Square. One of the other London PRs was there and he instructed me to wait by the entrance inside as Bruce wanted to say hi.

'Yeah, right. This is going to be fun,' I said to my brother, Jamie, who I had brought along so that he could witness the spectacle.

This time, as Willis sauntered in, an aide whispered in his ear and pointed at me. He was steered towards me by Robert Earl, the billionaire British businessman and founder of Planet Hollywood. Robert shook my hand vigorously. 'Hi, Jessica. I'm Robert. Bruce, you remember Jessica?' he said.

This time Bruce had clearly been briefed. He was on his best behaviour. 'It's *so* nice to see you again. I had *so* much fun when I saw you girls in London. I can't wait to return and hang out with you all.' Bruce oozed sincerity.

And with that he was off, surrounded by his entourage.

Me, Guy Ritchie, Vinnie Jones, Polly and Eva

4. Shameless

The column had pretty much taken over my life. I had been working on 3am flat out since we launched at the start of July. I didn't mind, because I was loving my job. Every day was different. I couldn't wait to get into work every morning and report back with outrageous tales about the celebrities I had interviewed or spied on the night before. Piers sauntered over to our desks every day to hear our stories and was full of advice about how to be the best diarists in the business. In actual fact we soon realized that his tips for the top were more of an excuse for him to reminisce about his time spent as a gossip columnist.

'I remember when I used to run the Bizarre column on the *Sun* . . .' he would invariably begin his monologues.

Eva, Polly and I would exchange looks and raise our eyebrows.

Despite the fact we spent virtually all of our time together, it was obvious that the three of us weren't going to become the best of friends overnight. But Eva and I did strike up a very close relationship from day one. We were both in the same position: we were the new girls.

Eva and I had a lot in common, particularly where blokes were concerned. We were both in long-term relationships, and we were both helplessly watching them race towards the final furlongs. Handily for her, Eva's boyfriend had nothing to do with our occupation, and she could come into work every day and forget about the row she'd had the previous night. I felt I had it a lot worse. Tom's desk was exactly twelve metres away from mine.

We'd met on the Mirror Graduate Trainee Scheme and had been going out for three years when I started working as a 3am girl. Our fiery relationship was already in its dying stages, but my new job was the final nail in the coffin. Not only did Tom now have to endure endless banter from Piers and Richard about how

I would be out late every night trying to fight celebs off, he also had to put up with the loud, laddish and vulgar behaviour of his girlfriend and her new colleagues in the showbiz department.

Most of the people who worked on the paper saw our department as juvenile, unprofessional and just plain irritating. And it didn't help that Piers spent lots of time sitting at our desks laughing with us. It must have been particularly infuriating for Tom. He was a hard-nosed, serious news reporter, and hearing me giggling at my co-workers' jokes all day long and watching me troop off to the pub at lunchtime, only to stagger back to his flat in the early hours of the morning completely drunk, was not particularly amusing to him.

But it was an unfortunate incident a few weeks into my job that led to the final breakdown of our relationship.

Eva, Polly and I were instructed to attend the Party in the Park for the Prince's Trust on a rainy Sunday near the end of July. The big story at the Hyde Park event was Victoria Beckham's duet with Dane Bowers on their single 'Out of Your Mind'. It was her first single outside of the Spice Girls. Piers was a big fan of Posh, and we were more or less instructed to like her and write something favourable about her performance.

We knew we just had to meet her, but as soon as we arrived we were ushered into the press tent along with all the other journalists. We knew there was no point staying there – at events like that all you got in the press tent was what was known as the 'rat run'. That was when all the media – print, radio and TV – were lined up, and those performers who could be bothered to come backstage and talk to the press were whisked in to yabber at us excitedly and give us all the same nugget of information they hoped would make it into the papers. By the time yet another perky wannabe boy band had bounded in to garner some headlines, most of the press had got bored and sloped off for a drink or a change of scene.

So we made it our mission to head straight for the VIP area. It was the only place to meet Victoria anyway. We knew we wouldn't miss anything vital in the press tent: there were various freelancers and radio journalists who made a good living from selling us juicy soundbites they'd got out of celebs, so we knew our backs were covered.

Journalists weren't technically allowed into the VIP marquee at the all-day concert, but, luckily for us, the performing stars' PRs were desperate for coverage and they led us into the forbidden tent. We spotted Dominic Mohan from the *Sun*. That was the way it was: you couldn't let in one of the tabloids and not the others or the PRs would have some pretty arsey journalists on their hands.

'Right. Let's find Posh's PR, Alan, and tell him we're here. He'll bring Victoria over to us so we can have a picture taken with her and get a few words. The single is out in a couple of weeks, so she'll be on her press charm offensive,' instructed Polly.

After making a few enquiries, we were told someone would come and fetch us. We would watch Victoria perform her duet and then we'd get to meet her. So we had an hour to kill, and while we waited we rang up our copytakers with stories we'd landed so far. The *Mirror*'s copytaker women always made me laugh. We would read out our story over the phone to these highly skilled, middle-aged typists who would just love to comment while we were mid-story. This usually happened when we were on deadline and in a mad panic.

'Did she really say that to him? Well, I never. I never warmed to her, you know. And what did he say back to her?' I heard this more than enough times.

'I'm on deadline! Can I tell you the ins and outs afterwards?' I muttered through clenched teeth on a few occasions.

We had to be polite as we depended on these women if we didn't have laptops with us. I for one never filed my stories to the paper on a laptop anyway. I much preferred doing it the old-fashioned way on the phone. I just didn't trust my computer not to crash while I was at the end of an article. I'd seen that happen to far too many people and watched them look nauseous and gradually lose the will to live. To me, it was so much easier to ring up a copytaker, try and decipher my shorthand scribbles and then be done with it.

Once Eva, Polly and I had finished filing our fascinating titbits of scandal about who had demanded what backstage, we filled in time observing all the other people in the tent. The so-called VIPs consisted of record industry bigwigs, PRs, a smattering of *EastEnders* stars, backing singers, dancers, hangers-on and corporate sponsors. It was all a bit grim because it was chucking down with rain outside and everyone was crammed into the sweaty tent, stuffing their faces with the freshly barbecued burgers and sausages, and downing the free booze. So it came as a relief when Caroline McAteer, one of Victoria Beckham's PR team, led us outside to watch Victoria perform. It had been a long day and we'd seen some instantly forgettable acts, but Posh and Dane were one of the highlights of the afternoon and we were looking forward to seeing them.

Caroline was a no-nonsense Northern Irishwoman whose looks were certainly deceiving. She was small, extremely slender and only a couple of years older than me, but boy was she tough. I knew she had a fearsome reputation and that generally there was no love lost between her and most journalists who encountered her. I had actually already dealt with her when I was at the *Daily Telegraph*, and luckily we had not fallen out. Mind you, it wasn't as if the *Telegraph* were in the business of running contentious stories about the Spice Girls, so I'd never been a target for her infamous wrath.

She was renowned on the *Mirror* for her 'It's not true, it's not a story' catchphrase. Caroline denied practically every story anyone in my department ever had about the Spice Girls, or about Posh and Becks, whom she also did the PR for. It got to the point where the blokes in my department would spend entire afternoons doing their impressions of Caroline. 'No, it's not true, it's not a story. David Beckham did not do that. Anyway, David Beckham who? There is no David Beckham. He is a figment of my imagination,' I heard them joke on many occasions after Caroline had denied yet another of their stories.

Most of the time she would deny the most innocuous stuff, such as Becks buying Posh a new ring for her birthday. And maddeningly, the story would later be revealed to be true in many cases. She was a PR who liked to be in constant control of the information that was out there about her clients.

But Caroline was a good laugh once you got her out of the 'them and us' PR mentality, and I was to spend many a fun lunch with her. She would also prove to be great company when I hung around at parties and awards ceremonies, where we would gossip together about other journalists, PRs and celebrities. And she would always be amusing about Posh's latest celebrity best mate, whom she usually wouldn't approve of.

We watched Victoria and Dane perform. I had been expecting the worst and as Caroline was with us, watching our reactions, I was all ready to plaster on my most fake smile and lie: 'Wow, that was amazing! She's fantastic! We'll back her all the way!' But she was really quite impressive. And amazingly so was Dane Bowers. He had been known as the cuddly one from boy band Another Level and it was definitely a strange pairing, but they had managed to pull it off and it was a great R&B track.

We trooped back into the VIP tent while Caroline slipped backstage to find Victoria. We were soaked. We hadn't thought to bring a single brolly between the three of us. We had left our flats that morning in glorious sunshine, but now it was like a monsoon outside. A typical British summer's day.

'This is bloody grim. The ends of my jeans are trailing in the puddles. Yuck!' I howled at Eva, who was looking distinctly unimpressed too.

'It's disgusting. We're going to look awful in the photographs,' agreed Polly. Suddenly she let out a cry. 'Shit! We haven't got a photographer,' she said.

We looked at each other. What were we like? We'd seen Richard Young taking pictures from the front of the stage and knew that he was probably roaming around inside the VIP tent and snapping away at the stars off-duty. It was rammed inside and we knew we'd never find him, so I whipped my mobile phone out and dialled his number.

'I can't get through to him. There must be thousands of people all using their mobiles here today and it's clogged up the network,' I said.

We looked around us. There was no way we would track him down in time. Alan, who ran the PR firm which represented Victoria, had instructed us to wait inside so that he could introduce us to her. They would be here soon. Besides, if one of us left to find Richard, then it would be sod's law that Victoria would appear and the others would get to meet her, have their photograph taken by another photographer, and whoever had disappeared to track down our snapper would be left out. I certainly wasn't going to volunteer. I looked at my two colleagues. Neither of them were exactly desperate to find him either. We just didn't trust each other enough. And Eva and I certainly weren't going to go off together, leaving Polly to meet and greet Victoria on her own.

So we all stayed put. And then I remembered something. I felt around in my bag. Yes! I thought to myself. I had packed a throwaway camera before leaving my flat that morning.

'Look what I've got!' I exclaimed, waving the camera around.

'Oh, nice one, mate,' Eva said with a smile.

Perfect timing. Alan, Caroline and Victoria Beckham were making their way towards us. We were introduced to Victoria. She had met Polly in the past and they embraced like old friends. The showbiz air kiss really was alive and well and not just something out of *Absolutely Fabulous*.

This was the first time I had met the Spice Girl. I could see instantly why Piers liked her so much. She was a consummate professional. Friendly, quick-witted and savvy, she chatted away to us and I was really impressed.

'You were great,' I gushed.

'Thank you,' she said with a gracious smile, and proceeded to entertain us with a few stories about some backstage shenanigans that had just taken place.

'Do you think we could do a photo with you?' I asked.

'I'd love to,' she replied.

Embarrassed at our lack of professionalism – the *Sun* would always have their showbiz photographer Dave Hogan on hand at events like this – I handed my battered camera over to Alan. Thankfully he refrained from ribbing us about our lack of digital technology and suppressed a smile when I told him to just point it at us and take the picture. Who used cameras like that any more? The 3am girls, clearly.

To be fair, the reason why I had one in the first place was because sometimes it was handy to pretend to an A-list star that you were just a fan. But there was no escaping the fact that when introduced to a big celeb and trying to do an impromptu interview, it was downright shameful for us not to have a photographer there.

As Eva, Polly and I gathered around Victoria for the picture, I made damn well sure I was right next to her. Alan wanted to whisk her off to meet some other journalists, so we had only one shot at this. We all smiled while he snapped us and I immediately pocketed the camera so I wouldn't lose it.

We were very close to deadline, but it was too late to get the camera picked up by a courier to whisk back to the office for processing. The picture would never make it into tomorrow's column. We'd have to wait until the next day to have it developed.

The next morning we told Richard about our encounter with Victoria Beckham in time for his editorial conference, which was when all the heads of department would discuss their main stories for the following day's paper. First thing every day Richard would question us about whatever gossip we'd picked up from the night before. It was handy when you actually had something already in the bag before you got into work; otherwise you'd spend a pretty tense moment before the conference ringing contacts and scouring your emails for a story, a quote, a rumour, anything at all to give Richard. It was either that or you'd receive a bollocking.

On this occasion, it was clear we didn't have much of a story on Posh – she was such a pro she'd given nothing personal away – so the focus of the piece would have to be on the picture.

'It'd better be a good one,' warned Richard.

As soon as I could I legged it down the office to the picture desk and handed over my camera. The department consisted of an odd collection of men. Ian was the bald picture editor who had the shit ripped out of him daily by pretty much all the executives on the paper for going on caravanning holidays. His deputy was a wisecracking, cuddly scouser called Greg who did stand-up comedy in his spare time. I'd only been there for a few weeks, but I'd got to know the big personalities and I'd quickly found out how to handle them. On this occasion I decided to bypass Ian and Greg. I was so desperate to see the photo I thought I'd apply some pressure on a junior I'd never seen before to jump the queue.

'We need it asap. It's for tomorrow's column,' I said a little too grandly, trying ever so slightly to intimidate him. The new boy looked at me blankly. 'It's a picture of us with Posh Spice at Party in the Park yesterday. We only had one chance to get the picture so we only have one shot of us,' I explained patiently. 'I hope it comes out OK.'

The guy still seemed a little spaced out. This was not looking very promising. I was so desperate to see that picture I felt like throwing a hissy fit, but instead I tutted loudly, turned on my heel and marched back to my desk.

He was to get the last laugh.

A couple of hours later, another bloke from the picture desk skulked towards Polly's desk. 'Got your pictures developed for you here, Pol. Think there are a few snaps in there that the guv'nor wouldn't want to see in the column,' he sniggered.

Immediately, I had a sense of foreboding. I watched as, looking confused, Polly snatched the plastic folder away from him and started to look at the photos.

'Oh my GOD!' she shrieked. 'Er, Jessica, I think these are yours.' She threw the folder towards me.

'What's the matter?' Eva asked. 'Do we look terrible or something?'

There on the top of the pack was the Victoria Beckham shot. This time I was next to the star herself, and I was facing the camera, which was a good start. But I had managed to blink at the exact moment Alan had taken the picture. I looked like I had nodded off next to Posh, while Eva and Polly were beaming away in the shot. I had succeeded in closing my eyes at the critical moment and looked like a total twerp in it.

'Well done, me,' I muttered under my breath.

Yes, it was another terrible photo but I didn't understand why Polly had reacted in such an extreme way. Then I looked at the second picture and realized why. It was a picture that I had taken a few weeks before and had clearly forgotten about. A photo that had nothing to do with work, shall we say. In no time at all, word whipped around the office that I had handed in my camera containing a close-up of Tom in the shower. I had done it to piss him off when he was running late for work one morning.

Another lesson learnt – never hand in your personal camera to be processed at the office.

'You are a total twat!' Tom shouted at me later that night. He'd managed to contain himself all day, but as soon as we were in the privacy of his own flat he'd exploded at me for making him a laughing stock among all his news reporter colleagues.

'It's not like I did it on purpose! As if! Don't you think this is highly embarrassing for me too? I've just started at the *Mirror*,' I said, trying to reason with him. But my gaffe seemed to have opened up the floodgates.

'It's so bloody unprofessional. Everyone at the paper knows and everyone is laughing about it. I'm furious with you. It's weird enough having you working in the same office as me, but now I have to deal with this sort of behaviour! Honestly, it's just not on.'

Protesting that it wasn't my fault didn't seem to get me anywhere. He was adamant that I had embarrassed him on purpose and refused to accept that it was a genuine mistake. I was just as humiliated. I had only been at the *Mirror* for a month and the entire office now knew I had taken naked snapshots of my boyfriend in the shower. It was hardly an auspicious start. I thought he was being very unfair.

'Will you stop being so unreasonable? You're being completely over the top. I'm really sorry, but it's a bit late now to bollock me like I'm some sort of naughty child. I really think you're overreacting about the whole thing. Can't we just forget about it and move on? I hate this, Tom. Please, can we stop fighting?' I pleaded.

'No, we can't just forget about it. I bet you and the other girls were all having a good laugh, weren't you? If you feel like I'm treating you like a child, it's because you've behaved like one,' he retaliated.

This was doing my head in. Why couldn't he just understand that I was genuinely sorry it had happened?

Hours later, after giving me the silent treatment, he finally seemed to have calmed down. 'So,' he said, trying to sound casual, 'um, er, did Polly or anyone else mention how good I look naked?'

It was not a good week for me. To make matters worse, Richard had rewritten the caption that went with the Victoria Beckham photograph. It now said that I had dozed off after having been spotted earlier that day 'smoking a funny-looking cigarette'.

'Great! Not only do they want me to be the token posh girl on the *Mirror*, and the column slapper, I'm also the 3am stoner,' I moaned to Eva. 'Why me? You get to be the scary, tough bitch one. Why are they trying to turn me into Patsy from *Absolutely Fabulous*?'

'It is a bit harsh. But very funny. At least you didn't get a bollocking for messing up the picture,' she laughed.

My colleagues and our readers all thought I was spending time at events smoking joints and nodding off in photos. And my boyfriend had lost the plot with me for handing in a camera containing compromising shots of him. Could things get any worse?

Indeed they could. That weekend Tom said he wanted to have 'a chat'. I knew what was coming. After a tense meal in a nearby restaurant, he drove me back to my flat. He parked the car and turned the engine off. He turned to speak to me, and I braced myself.

'Jess, I just think this isn't going to work any more. You and me – we're more like brother and sister, don't you think? We'd get on better if we were, er, friends, no?' he stammered. He hadn't used every cliché in the book, but he'd come pretty close. 'All we do is fight. I just want a more peaceful life.'

I burst into tears.

'Are you going to be all right, kiddo?' he asked, wiping his own tears away.

'Oh yeah, just great. I've just started my dream job, I'm working my arse off and now I've been dumped. Just marvellous,' I replied.

We'd talked ourselves into silence.

'Is that it? Three years for nothing then?' I asked, my tone a bit bitter.

'Oh, don't be like that, kiddo. I haven't dumped you. You feel the same way too,' he said.

I went ballistic. 'Will you just stop calling me that?' I shouted and jumped out the car, slamming the passenger door.

I knew he was right. It wasn't going anywhere any more and we were spending all our time falling out with each other. Our temperaments were very alike and both of us wanted to be the centre of attention in the relationship. And neither of us liked to back down or say sorry after an argument. Added to that was the fact that the stresses and strains of 3am meant I wasn't seeing him as much as before, so when we did meet up there was even more pressure to have a good time. I had to agree with him, but it still hurt.

It wasn't easy having to see him the following morning in the office, but it was comforting in a way to see that he looked about as miserable as I felt.

'Can I speak to you in the toilets?' I emailed Eva first thing. 'Meet me in there.' I looked over at her and she nodded at me, looking concerned. I slipped away from my desk and headed for the ladies' loos that were further down the corridor, away from the prying eyes and ears of the rest of the department. I stood by the sinks – where we were to have many *Cagney and Lacey*-style moments over the years – and waited for her.

She appeared at the door and closed it behind her. 'What's going on? Are you OK, mate?' she asked.

I burst into tears again. 'I've broken up with Tom. It's been on the cards for months and months but he finally called it a day this weekend,' I blubbed. 'Talk about great bloody timing. As if I don't have enough on my plate with starting here on 3am.'

'Oh, mate, I'm so sorry,' she said sympathetically, handing me some toilet roll. 'If it's any consolation, I broke up with David last week.'

I stared at her. 'Why didn't you say anything?' I asked.

Eva was the height of discretion when it came to her own private life, or those close to her. If you had a problem or a big secret, you knew it would be safe with her.

I knew she'd been having problems, but hadn't had even the vaguest clue that her four-year relationship had hit the skids so badly. She was a consummate actress.

'Well, I just wanted to deal with it on my own. Sod 'em both,' she laughed.

'Yeah. Sod 'em,' I giggled, blowing my nose on the rough toilet paper and patting my red-rimmed eyes in the mirror. 'Well, we're both single now. Polly's single too. I guess Piers and Richard finally have their wish. There's no need to rush back home at the end of the night now. We really will be gallivanting around town,' I laughed.

'Too right, mate. And you know what? We're both Aries girls, aren't we? And Tom was a Sagittarius, wasn't he?' she asked. I nodded. 'So was David. We need to stay the hell away from Sagittarius blokes. They are just wrong, wrong, wrong for us. Bunch of tossers.'

I never really paid much attention to star signs, but the way I was feeling at that moment in time, crying in the toilets at work, I couldn't have agreed more. If only I had listened to her three years later when I embarked on my next – and most catastrophic – long-term relationship with yet another Sagittarian from the media world.

For the moment, though, I moved out of my house in Stockwell. I'd never really liked living in that area, and now there was no point living near Tom when I wouldn't be hanging out with him any more. He really wanted us to remain friends, but I'd asked him to give me time and space to get to grips with it all. So I moved back in with my parents in Chelsea until I could find somewhere else.

Wannabe celebs will do pretty much anything for maximum column inches. I knew that before I started the job. But on occasion I was also surprised by the conduct of some of the biggest names in the showbiz world when confronted by a journalist.

On the eve of the premiere of his movie *Snatch*, on 22 August 2000, Guy Ritchie invited us to interview him hours before he would take to the red carpet with Brad Pitt and Vinnie Jones, the stars of the movie. The Brit director's other half, otherwise known as Madonna, had given birth to their son Rocco eleven days before. Naturally we were keen to ask him about the baby, but suspected the subject was off-limits.

Ritchie's PR had hired a suite at the Dorchester, which was rapidly becoming our second office, and we were instructed to arrive there at 5pm for our twenty-minute meeting. It was skirting very close to deadline time, but we had no choice in the matter. We also knew that Dominic Mohan, the showbiz editor of the *Sun*, would be interviewing Ritchie after us, so whatever information we got out of him wouldn't hold until the next day. We would have to file our interview straight to the office as soon as we'd finished with him. We would then go to the premiere.

Polly had met Ritchie at the premiere of his first movie, *Lock, Stock and Two Smoking Barrels*, and said he was pretty much game for anything in order to get his film publicized. There had even been an 'impromptu' punch-up at the premiere itself. Not that anyone questioned whether the fight was real or not – it gave everyone something to write about, which was exactly what the film's PR had hoped.

Eva, Polly and I hopped off the Tube at Green Park and made our way via the back roads to the glitzy hotel. Once there, we squeezed ourselves into the tiny lift and were whisked up to the suite where Guy was waiting for us.

'Hi, ladies. How we doing?' It was Youngy. He was waiting for us outside the suite door. We took turns to kiss him hello just as the door opened, and Guy's PR, Kris, invited us in. Even though Ritchie was a young Brit, I was expecting a team of Hollywood aides dashing around inside, bodyguards and flunkies screeching into earpieces. He was Mr Madonna after all. But as we walked into the sumptuous suite, all we found was Guy and Vinnie Jones sitting on a sofa.

'Guy, Vinnie – this is Jessica, Polly and Eva from 3am,' said Kris.

Wow, I thought. Ritchie was much taller and broader than I had expected. I knew he was obsessed with karate but bloody hell, his arms weren't half muscly. I had to stop myself from grabbing his biceps for a quick squeeze. He had bleached blond hair, a cheeky smile and a glint in his eye, which clearly spelt trouble. We were all instantly smitten with him.

To see Vinnie there, however, conjured up very different emotions. We knew he particularly despised *Mirror* journalists. Several years before, he had taken a chunk out of the nose of a *Mirror* reporter he'd taken an instant dislike to. We'd agreed beforehand that, should we be introduced to the former hardman of soccer, we would be extremely polite to him. Best to keep him on side, even if he did make us feel terribly uncomfortable.

Five gilt-backed chairs had been arranged in the middle of the room. Guy shook our hands, flashed a flirty grin and sat down in the middle. Vinnie sat behind him.

I was taking no chances and threw myself on to the nearest chair next to Guy. I was determined to be photographed hanging off his broad shoulders, and this time my eyes *would* be open.

Most stars only wanted to talk about whatever it was they were promoting, and on occasions like this, where we were actually allowed a private interview with a celebrity, we would be given a list of topics that were no-go areas. But Kris hadn't warned us off any subjects.

There was clearly one topic hanging in the air. We didn't try our usual and more obvious approach of easing him in with some flattering comments about how much we loved the movie. We hadn't even seen it. We went straight in for the kill.

'So, Guy, congratulations on your baby!' cooed Polly.

Ritchie looked at us, cocked his head to one side, and flashed a heart-melting little-boy grin.

'Oh, all right then,' he said, and pretended to sigh dramatically. He put his hand into his back pocket and whipped out four Polaroid pictures of his son. It was immediately apparent in the first photograph that Rocco was only a few minutes old in the photos. The girls and I sat there wide-eyed and speechless. We had literally just sat down, Polly had asked him one question and here he was showing us his pictures of his newborn son. In the space of a minute we were looking at the first photographs of Madonna and her British boyfriend's baby.

'It's the best thing that ever happened to me. I still can't get over it.' Guy beamed while staring proudly at his son.

'Oh, he's gorgeous,' I simpered.

Vinnie peered at the photo over Guy's shoulder, oohing and aahing his agreement. So far so sweet.

Then Guy showed us the next photo, and we were speechless all over again. Here was yet another deeply private snap he had taken. This one was of the Queen of Pop herself lying in bed without a scrap of make-up on, her greasy hair tied back, wearing a baggy white vest and a grubby tracksuit and cuddling their son. She'd have been livid if she'd known that Guy was showing three tabloid gossip columnists personal photos of her post-labour. Clearly we now had our headlines.

Youngy snapped away at us cooing over Guy and his baby photos. I had manoeuvred myself so that I was literally rubbing shoulders with him.

'Hey, Guy, do you fancy turning one of those pictures around so I can take a snap?' asked Youngy, only half-joking. Rocco had yet to be unveiled to the world and our photographer knew he'd be sitting on a goldmine if he managed to reel off just one frame.

Guy glanced up at Youngy, shook his head and held the pictures protectively against his muscly chest. 'No chance, mate,' he laughed. So there was a limit to how far Guy would go. Presumably he knew he would have had a giant bollocking from the missus.

All Guy wanted to talk about for the rest of the interview was Rocco, who we learnt had been born three weeks prematurely in LA. He'd been about to go and play poker with Brad and Vinnie, but instead he went straight to the hospital.

'When I first held him he felt so light, it was scary. But not as scary as cutting the umbilical cord. Your hand is shaking and you think, "I care for this thing more than anything else in the world," and there you are holding a pair of scissors and they're all saying, "Go on, cut it."'

How lovely. But Guy didn't notice we were squirming. Staring at the pictures of Rocco swaddled in a blanket, he looked totally mesmerized by his son. 'I think he looks like me,' he continued. 'But he looked a bit Greek when he first came out. I was worried for a moment!'

He was so relaxed and happy that it really felt like no subject was off-limits now. As we got him talking about the film, he even started joking about the huge royalties he had to pay his superstar girlfriend in order to use her hit 'Lucky Star' in the film. 'She hurt us for it. I thought I was going to get it for free, but I didn't,' he told us.

Kris intervened at this stage. 'I'm sorry, but your time's up,' he instructed.

We said goodbye to Guy and wished him luck for the premiere that night. Vinnie still hadn't said more than 'ooh' and 'ahh' and we even got a forced smile from him when we said goodbye.

We filed out of the suite and squeezed ourselves into the lift with Youngy in tow.

'Well, that went well, didn't it!' exclaimed Youngy.

'Boy, didn't it just. He's amazing. How fit is he?' I swooned.

'Yup, not bad at all,' agreed Eva. 'I really didn't expect to see those photos. I knew he'd say a few words about the baby as he does have a film to promote after all. And he's very friendly.'

'But bloody hell. Pictures of Madonna looking rough and cuddling her newborn baby! She'll go mental at him!' said Polly.

'Oh God, don't! Photos of Madonna hours after giving birth! Oh wow!' exclaimed Youngy, doing some calculations in his head.

We got out at the ground floor and Polly rang Richard at the office to tell him about our unexpected interview with Ritchie. Eva and I could hear him screaming down the phone in excitement. We were told to file immediately as we were bang on deadline. We told Youngy, who legged it to his car which was parked nearby so he could send the digital pictures straight over to the picture desk from his laptop.

Polly, Eva and I huddled together on a sofa in the lobby of the hotel and tried to remember what Ritchie had actually said to us.

'I can't believe how big his arms were. He's like Popeye,' I said, eyes glazed.

'Oh, Jessica, just get over it,' snapped Polly. 'What else did he say about Rocco?'

Eva rolled her eyes and giggled.

We recalled all his quotes and tweaked our article until we were happy with it. We hoped that Piers would be so impressed with the story he would instruct Richard to take it off the column and put it on a news page, which he sometimes did if we had a big scoop.

Polly rang up the copytakers with our story and then spoke to Richard to say we had filed the story. 'He says Piers loves it and it's the lead story in tomorrow's column,' she informed us, and she snapped her mobile phone shut and put it back in her bag.

It wasn't the front page, but it was still good news that Piers liked it enough to make it a lead story.

We had some time to kill before the premiere started, so we headed for the Radisson Edwardian Hampshire hotel just off Leicester Square. This was the place where the showbusiness journalists who covered premieres all hung out after the stars had arrived so they could file their copy in peace, away from the screaming crowds of fans who had been barricaded for hours behind metal barriers, hoping to catch a glimpse of their favourite actors.

We knocked back a drink each and then made our way to the cinema. There were thousands of fans. It was hardly surprising considering Brad Pitt – fresh back from his honeymoon with his new bride, Jennifer Aniston – was the star attraction of the night.

He played a gypsy bare-knuckle fighter in the hit film and had adopted an impenetrable Irish accent for the part. I was hoping he'd still be in character when he arrived at the premiere. Brad Pitt with an Irish accent would be almost too much for a girl to cope with.

We had been assured he would be making an appearance at the after-show party at a club called Rock on Embankment. But you couldn't always count on such promises. Sometimes the bigger stars would turn up, pose for the cameras and then head out to a private members' bar where they could relax away from the gaze of the public and the media.

If we saw a big star, it was always better to just grab them then and there in case we didn't get the chance later. And we just knew Brad, like Tom Cruise, would be trailed by gorilla-sized security men. If you were Jennifer Aniston, you'd persuade your other half it was a good idea to bat the girls away, wouldn't you?

So we hung around with the other journalists in the lobby of the cinema, waiting for Brad to turn up so we could get some quotes off him, and leer at him. A whole load of celebrities arrived. Kelly Brook, who was dating *Snatch* star Jason Statham at the time, stole the show by turning up in a *very* revealing pink slashed Julien Macdonald dress. Luckily she had knickers on or the photographers would have had unappetizing shots of, well, let's just say the title of the premiere was apt for what she almost had on show that night.

After more celebs, including Mel C, Vinnie Jones and Lulu, arrived at the cinema, Brad finally made his appearance. Like all Hollywood stars, he was keen on making an entrance. First he treated the screeching fans outside to a Tom Cruise-style walk-about, signing endless autographs and posing for pictures with hyperventilating women.

'Come on, Brad, time to make us faint!' shouted out a short female showbiz reporter from the *Daily Star* who was standing next to me in the foyer of the cinema with the other journalists. 'Get your arse in here!'

Eventually Brad sauntered into the lobby. He was much shorter than I had imagined – I thought he'd be a strapping chap. Why did all these American A-listers turn out to be much more diddy in the flesh. But he was still taller than Tom Cruise. And while Cruise had flashed that megawatt smile at all and sundry, Pitt wore what looked like a stoned expression on his face. He had played a brilliant stoner in *True Romance* and was wearing that same goofy grin now.

He made his way towards the radio, TV and print journalists, who had forgotten about remaining professional and unfazed by the presence of a Hollywood star and were all clamouring to get near him.

That's when I noticed that he didn't have any entourage with him. Guy Ritchie was waiting for him in the lobby, but apart from him there were no bodyguards, agents, publicists, flapping PRs or hapless flunkies.

'We've got to get him now. Youngy is just over there,' I said excitedly to Polly and Eva.

They agreed. It was the perfect opportunity.

'Richard. Richard!' shouted Polly, trying to get Youngy's attention. He was far too busy taking photos of Brad as he answered questions from the press. 'Oh, for God's sake, Youngy!' hollered Polly. Never try and get the attention of a photographer when he's taking a picture, especially when his subject is Brad Pitt.

We got right behind Richard. 'Youngy,' hissed Polly. Richard finally turned around. 'We need to get a picture with Brad. As soon as he's finished the press line-up we've got to intercept him before he goes into the cinema. There's no point waiting for him to turn up to the party. We want to do it here and we want to do it now,' instructed Polly.

I loved her when she spoke like that, but only if it wasn't to me.

'OK, fine,' mumbled Youngy.

We stood inside the cordoned-off media area waiting impatiently for Brad to finish telling the panting press (the male journalists looked as impressed by him as the female ones did) how great married life was and how he was sad that he had to leave his bride in LA as she was busy filming episodes of *Friends*.

Finally he finished and instead of being steered straight into the cinema, he stood chatting outside the auditorium with Guy Ritchie. The film publicists, who had just arrived, were trying to gather all the male actors from the film so the photographers could do a series of pictures of them in a group shot.

Here was our moment.

'Hi, do you mind awfully doing a picture with us?' asked Polly.

Her accent always became increasingly posh when she talked to American actors. When I talked to Hollywood stars I employed the same trick, hoping that hearing a journalist talking with an accent out of an Enid Blyton book would make them forget I was a tabloid reporter.

'Sure. Go right ahead,' he grinned.

There then ensued what was now becoming the usual skirmish. Polly stuck herself to Brad's right-hand side and I managed to squeeze myself on to his left while Eva was left hovering next to me. Or, to be precise, she was left batting away the security guards, who thought we were lunatics harassing Brad. At the bottom right-hand side of the photo that we ran in the column two days later, you could see the meaty hand of the security goon who was trying to push us out of the way.

Luckily we were all smiling at the camera and, amazingly, I had my eyes open. Brad, on the other hand, was looking in entirely the wrong direction. In fact, when we all huddled around Youngy to inspect his photo in the digital viewer on the back of his camera, we were appalled to see that Brad looked more like a waxwork than a human being. Oh well. At least we knew we had stood next to him. I had even put my arm around him and hadn't resisted giving his waist a quick squeeze. It was a once in a lifetime chance, so I'd thought I might as well cop a feel while I could.

I rang Richard and he said not to bother filing any copy as we'd be running the Guy Ritchie baby-photo story in the column the next day. He told me we should save anything from the premiere – unless something major happened, like Brad Pitt collapsing, getting assassinated or snogging Lulu – to write up at work the next day for Thursday's paper.

For once we decided to watch the film before heading over to the after-show party. We knew there'd be the inevitable scrum to get into the VIP area where our fellow showbusiness journalists would be stalking Brad. What did the media expect to see him do there? Take drugs? Try and pull? As if. But we knew that we'd all have to stay at the party until Brad left. Here was a major Hollywood star and we'd be tracking his every move.

As expected, there were hundreds of people waiting outside the club by the time the movie was over. Luckily the film's PRs were on the door, and the team from Freud Communications were incredibly helpful. Their job was to ensure the movie was publicized. And unlike in-house film company PRs, who seemed to actively enjoy waging battle with the press, the Freud lot were fun, useful and gave us what we needed. Spotting us gasping at the horror of the crush of people trying to get into the party, a few of the Freud boys told the beefy bodyguards at the door to let us in without queuing. Life was so much simpler when we didn't have to fight to get into a party.

'Get yourselves downstairs. There's loads to drink and the stars are turning up soon,' one of the PRs said with a smile after we'd thanked him endlessly for letting us skip the queue.

It was rammed in the basement of the club. This premiere party was nothing like the *Mission: Impossible II* party. The basement of Rock was a long narrow corridor with a few roped-off areas, a large staircase and a small bar. It couldn't easily accommodate the hundreds of people swarming about. Even the serving staff were finding it difficult to do their job in there. The cocktails on their trays kept falling over and spilling everywhere.

'Good job we already did the picture with Brad at the cinema,' I shouted over the din to Eva and Polly.

It was a pretty grim party. We were squashed up against other fed-up hacks with nothing to do but knock back cocktails as we waited for Brad to arrive.

Suddenly, I noticed a commotion at the top of the staircase. There, fighting his way down the stairs, with a bouncer smaller than himself leading the way and another the size of a WWF wrestler bringing up the rear, was Vinnie Jones and a group of friends, including his wife.

'Well, there's our celeb for the night. The incredibly friendly Vinnie Jones!' I cheered.

The bouncers pushed people out of the way so that Vinnie and his pals could make their way to the roped-off VIP area, which was the smallest I'd ever seen.

'What are they going in there for? They'll be squashed up against each other. And besides, who's going to bother Vinnie bloody Jones?' asked Eva.

We watched as Vinnie, decked out in a *Bugsy Malone*-style wide pinstripe suit, made himself comfortable. We were even more surprised to see his two bodyguards remain by his side.

'Have you seen? He needs *two* bodyguards even when he's just having a drink! He looks like he's permanently having to calm himself down. Maybe he's got the bodyguards with him so he can headbutt them instead of the press. Or anyone else for that matter,' I said.

While we had been distracted by Vinnie's strange display, we had failed to notice that some of the other stars of the movie had slipped into the party. Maybe they didn't want to be noticed and therefore weren't flanked by needless security staff. Guy Ritchie and Brad Pitt were necking drinks by the bar, on their own, with no entourage.

We weren't the only ones to spot them. Seconds later, word spread and Pitt had female reporters hurling themselves at him and stamping on each other's toes to get near him. He was utterly oblivious to all of them, and continued chatting to Ritchie. Very soon, the women became impossible to ignore as they accidentally on purpose pressed themselves against his torso. He was soon surrounded, but, being the utter gent he clearly was, politely talked to everyone who asked him a question. Ritchie just chuckled away next to him, finding the unfolding chaos hysterical.

'Sod this. We may as well get among the crush ourselves!' I yelled to Eva.

Actually, deep down, I wasn't a massive Brad Pitt fan. Sure, he was cute, there was no denying that. But he was a bit too chiselled and his body was too slight for me. I preferred the bulkier George Clooneys of this world. Brad was the type of man my gay friends would coo over. They would be furious that I had been in his presence.

But I wasn't going to allow the opportunity to come into contact with Brad Pitt's behind pass me by. It would be rude not to. And I could get to know Ritchie a little better too. So what if I'd just been unceremoniously dumped by Tom – time to have some fun! So Eva and I dived into the crowd. Elbows out, we shoved our way to the front of the baying mob. By the time we got there, Guy had disappeared.

'So, Brad,' Eva shouted into his face while I positioned myself as close to him as I could so as to be within licking distance. Any vestiges of dignity had sailed out of the window a long time ago. I was sure Piers would understand. In fact I assured myself he'd approve of me frisking Brad Pitt. All in the name of work, of course.

'Yes?' he replied, turning his gaze to Eva, who, for the first time ever, visibly wilted.

'What colour is your wife's toothbrush?' she asked.

'What?' I looked at her, baffled. What the hell was she asking that for? This was hardly the time to remind him he had a bride.

'Blue. Like her eyes,' he replied, that grin not wavering for a second.

'Ahhhhh,' answered the chorus of women who were still surrounding him and hanging on his every word. Even Eva and I sighed too. What a romantic!

Being the good sport he was, Brad continued to charm Fleet Street's finest by encouraging us to get hitched. 'Married life is great. I really recommend you try it. I really miss her and wish she could be in London with me,' he informed us.

Chance would be a fine thing, I thought. Eva had just come out of a long-term relationship. I had just been dumped. Polly was in the throes of singleton shenanigans.

Much as we were enjoying getting love advice from Brad Pitt, there were so many women trying to talk to him we decided to let him be. We entered the tiny VIP area, where Kelly Brook was showing off her change of costume.

'I had to change out of that last dress. I was showing a bit too much off in the cinema,' she giggled.

Brad was resolutely refusing to sit in the VIP area. He was happily getting pissed at the bar with his mates from the movie. We didn't want to talk to Vinnie and there was nobody else of any interest. We grabbed a few more cocktails and waited for something exciting to happen.

'Hi, girls,' boomed a voice.

We looked around. It was Guy Ritchie. Things were improving by the minute. As lovely as Brad Pitt was, in my eyes Ritchie was a much more manly-looking man.

'We loved the film,' I piped up.

'Thanks,' he replied.

Then, leaning forward, he suddenly whispered in my ear, 'You've got lovely eyes.' And then he promptly disappeared into the crowd.

I was stunned. I knew I had to say something, but I couldn't think of anything apart from, 'So have you!' which I shouted at him.

Eva looked at me like I had just said something rude about someone's mum. 'What the hell are you talking about?' she asked.

'Did you hear what he said to me? He said I had lovely eyes! Bloody hell. I'd have him over Brad any day,' I said.

'Oh, shut up. He did not,' said Eva, prodding me in the ribs.

'He bloody did! Oh God, did I sound like a real prat when I shouted after him?'

'Yup, you did,' she laughed.

The rest of the night was pretty much scandal-free. Vinnie Jones stayed in his VIP enclave, which, once Kelly Brook had gone home, only consisted of himself, his wife, a couple of mates and his ludicrous bodyguards. Brad seemed to enjoy the bar so much he got behind it and started serving people. The novelty of Brad Pitt serving pints soon wore off and around 2am the crowds started thinning out. We had our picture with him and enough quotes to pad out our column.

We couldn't leave until Brad did. He was having too much of a good time and clearly didn't want to return to his empty hotel room. In the end he had to be escorted from the bar: the organizers needed to shut the party down as it was the end of the night, which meant all the journalists could call it a day too.

In the taxi on my way home I thought again about how much fun I was having in my job. Bruce Willis aside, I was thoroughly enjoying meeting these Hollywood superstars. It seemed the bigger they were, the less ego they had. British stars could certainly learn a thing or two from them. There was Vinnie Jones with his bodyguards, who no one wanted to talk to, and Brad Pitt with no entourage, who was happy to let screaming women chat him up. What a star!

Polly, Eva, me and the boys from Westlife

5. Spice World

Life on 3am was more exciting than I had imagined. Meeting stars and getting access to parties and premieres was part of my day-to-day life. Little did I know that we were about to have our biggest celebrity fallout. Our spats with Deayton and the like were nothing compared to the evening we were about to spend with the Spice Girls.

It was hardly surprising that we were constantly compared to the girl group. 3am was a manufactured gossip column put together by not one but two Svengali figures, Piers and Richard. Eva, Polly and I had been allocated very distinctive personalities for the column, albeit without us having been consulted (I was now getting used to my posh slapper label). And, just like the Spice Girls, we'd been put together with instructions to shake things up and be mouthy and opinionated. That last brief was easier than we had imagined: we'd only been going for four months and we'd already had run-ins with plenty of celebrities.

On 7 November 2000 we came face to face with the Spice Girls themselves for the launch of what would turn out to be their final album, *Forever*. They were going head to head with Westlife with their record releases, and both bands had decided to hold parties on the same night, sparking the inevitable articles about which would be the better party.

We'd been invited to both events, and decided to head for the girl band's party at the Red Cube club in Leicester Square first. Caroline McAteer had assured us we would get a few words from the pop stars and a picture with them too. We would then race over to the Westlife bash at the nearby St Martin's Lane Hotel, where we'd also been promised time with the band.

We'd all really liked Posh Spice when we'd met her at Party in the Park, but we had yet to meet the other girls. We had always supported them as they were on our list of celebs we had decided were very 3am and who deserved our backing. Some of the other newspapers had been giving Sporty Spice Mel C a kicking around that time for putting on weight, calling her Beefy Spice, but we hadn't attacked her for that. We'd agreed it was out of order for us to poke fun at other women struggling with their weight, especially if they had issues. Everyone knew that Mel was on antidepressants and struggling with an eating disorder. Mel had even admitted that she was taking Prozac via her PR when Eva had confronted him about it, a story that made the front page of the paper. While our male bosses would have liked us to get in on the act, we resisted. We were more than happy to give someone a pasting for wearing a bad outfit or for being caught on camera looking drunk and ropey, but to attack someone for looking a bit curvaceous in their bikini was not on.

As we approached the Red Cube we were buzzing with excitement and looking forward to the evening ahead of us. What a great night it was going to be, chatting to the Spice Girls and then hanging out with Westlife. Westlife were one of our favourite bands at the time. They understood the nature of the press game and were always incredibly polite. They knew how to be friendly and enjoy a few drinks with the media, and you could always count on Bryan McFadden to take the drinking too far, get sloshed, misbehave and come out with some brilliant quotes.

'We'll get loads of great soundbites tonight for the column. Should be fun. I've always wanted to meet the Spice Girls!' I said enthusiastically to the other two.

The crowds outside the club were screeching far louder than at the Tom Cruise premiere. Caroline ushered us to one side and told us that the girls were due to arrive any minute and that we could do a photo with them at the entrance and get some words from them about their chart battle with Westlife.

We stood inside the entrance with Youngy, who had his camera at the ready to snap us with the band, and watched as Posh, Baby, Scary and Sporty arrived and played up for the banks of screaming photographers positioned outside the club. Victoria

Beckham and Emma Bunton had really gone to town with their outfits and were wearing risqué low-cut tops. Posh was decked out in a green see-through shirt with a green and pink bra on show and a matching micro-miniskirt; Emma was wearing a gold tuxedo with her jacket open and a gold bikini top on display. They pouted away. These two knew what to do to get on to the front pages.

As for Mel B and Mel C, they were refusing to smile and instead pulled vulgar expressions. Mel B was wearing a sequinned high-necked top and trousers and was doing her usual lairy trick of sticking her pierced tongue out for the cameras. Mel C had made no effort whatsoever and was dressed down in a scruffy dark sleeveless top and trousers. It was like watching two separate bands, so different were their demeanour and their appearance.

The two Mels walked into the club first. They took one look at us and stopped dead in their tracks. Before Caroline even had time to introduce us they let rip.

'Who the fuck let them in here? I'm not doing anything with the fucking papers. They can all just fuck off out of here,' sneered Mel C.

Mel B was similarly pleased to see us. 'What the fuck are those sluts doing in here?' she snarled, before pushing past us and heading straight for the VIP area. Mel C stormed off after her.

There was a stunned silence.

'Er, what the hell . . . ?' asked Eva.

Had they really just called us 'sluts' and told us to 'fuck off'? Judging by the look on everyone's face in the general vicinity, I hadn't imagined the brief encounter we'd just had. Caroline seemed mortified. Posh and Baby, who'd walked in after Mel B and Mel C and overheard them, appeared even more horrified. They knew instantly that as their bandmates had been less than welcoming to us, we wouldn't exactly be writing about how much we hoped the Spice Girls would beat Westlife to number one.

Emma Bunton tried her best to gloss over what had just happened and loyally attempted to cover up for her surly bandmates. 'Sorry about that, girls. But they haven't seen their mums for a while and they were probably in a rush to see them,' she explained sweetly.

Posh Spice didn't bother trying to make up lame excuses for us being called 'sluts' by Scary Spice. 'I'm so sorry about what just happened. Don't ask me why they said that. I've got no idea,' she said.

It was decent of her to even try to apologize on their behalf.

Victoria and Emma apologized again and gave us 'please don't crucify us' smiles as they disappeared hand in hand into their roped-off VIP area, where their friends and families were waiting for them. Youngy shook his head and looked appalled.

After a brief pause Caroline opened her mouth to also try to smooth things over. 'I'm so sorry. Let's go find them. There's no way they should speak to you guys like that,' she said firmly. She also knew what was coming: a pretty nasty story about her most important clients.

'To be honest, I don't really see the point,' Eva snapped, rooted to the spot.

'No, no, come with me. Let's go find them,' insisted Caroline, leading the way to the VIP area.

I turned to Polly and Eva. 'Brilliant! This is absolutely brilliant!' I whispered excitedly to them. 'If they hadn't said that, we'd have had the most boring story to write up tomorrow. We've just been called sluts by the Spice Girls!'

'I know,' Polly giggled. 'It's fantastic! I always preferred Westlife anyway. This way we've got a really good reason to back them. We may as well follow Caroline to the VIP area. You never know, we could be lucky and get a glass of champagne chucked in our faces.'

'We can but hope,' I agreed.

Eva still looked like she wanted to rip someone's head off. Anyone's would do. When Eva was like this the usually bolshie Polly would stay away from her, but I knew her better and had worked out that if you teased her then you could usually cajole her out of her mood.

'Mate, this is great news,' I said to her. 'Don't think of it as utterly humiliating. We can really go to town on Mel B and Mel C in the column from now on. Piers wants us to make celebrity enemies. Well, we've got some great ones now! The two surliest members of the biggest girl group in the world officially hate us! Let's go and see what else they have to say about us.'

We all knew by now that if a celebrity was rude to us – as Bruce Willis had been – then we could write a much funnier article than if they'd crippled us with courtesy. One of our initial aims with 3am was to strip back the gloss and the glamour and reveal exactly what the stars were really like in person, and if they were vile then all the better. We loved to write a juicy salacious story. Those who didn't appear to have a bad bone in their body would struggle to get much of an appearance in the press.

Rachel Stevens was a case in point. You couldn't have met a nicer pop singer. But that was it: she was plain nice, nothing else. When S Club split up and Rachel went solo, the small Londoner and her aides went on a full-on press offensive to win us all over so we'd back her when she released her singles. But it was very hard to write about her. She didn't throw rock-star tantrums, didn't pull inappropriate men, didn't get drunk and vomit over herself and didn't take drugs. Quite simply, she was too sweet.

To make life more difficult for us, Piers had a crush on her. He would love to 'jokingly' manhandle her when he saw her at public events such as the *Mirror*'s Pride of Britain Awards. He would insist that we write about her, but we couldn't just run a blatant plug for her new single. There had to be more. I lost count of the number of times I pleaded with her PR for a nugget of gossip or a hint of scandal.

Rachel once insisted on coming to the *Mirror* to let us interview her. What we were unaware of was her phobia of lifts. But such was her determination to be friendly with the press, she eventually made it up to the twenty-second floor of our building and by the time she arrived she was in total hysterics. Her two aides had to stop her entire body from shaking and wipe away the tears before she could even think about having her photo taken in the office. I never worked out why she put herself through that, especially since she had nothing of any interest to share with us once she had calmed down.Pop star gets scared in lift was hardly front-page news.

Basically, it was far better to have celebrity enemies than celebrity friends. It made for far better copy. Which was why I was relishing our fallout with the Spice Girls. So much for their proclaimed Girl Power.

Eva, Polly and I followed Caroline to the VIP area where the frostiness between Victoria and Emma on the one side and the two Mels on the other became all the more apparent. Baby and Posh Spice were with their friends and families, but Mel C and Mel B were keeping well away. They were tucking into the free booze on offer and didn't seem to want to lower themselves further by insulting us again.

'You know what, Caroline,' said Polly, 'thanks for trying but we're going to head to the Westlife do. There's not much point hanging around here for much longer.'

Caroline knew there was no point in trying to convince us to stay, and we legged it as fast as we could before the two girls suddenly underwent personality bypasses and decided to say sorry. The last thing we wanted was for Scary and Sporty to apologize. That would have totally ruined the story.

'Guess it would be too much to hope for the Westlife lads to call us a bunch of ugly slags,' I joked as we walked the short distance to St Martin's Lane Hotel.

'Oh, no. They're always soooo nice. The best we can hope for is Bryan getting pissed and trying to punch someone,' said Polly, waving crossed fingers.

'I always preferred Westlife anyway,' said Eva, who was finally coming round to the idea that it was good to be insulted by stars.

We arrived at the hotel and made for the Asia de Cuba restaurant, where there was an endless supply of far superior cocktails and nibbles than there had been at the decidedly ropey Spice Girls party. This was more like it. We hit the drinks and chatted to record company PRs, who were working hard at getting us drunk.

The band appeared an hour later and were their usual charming selves, greeting all the showbiz reporters like old friends and making sure our glasses were constantly filled too. We posed for a picture with all five of them. This time we didn't have to worry about who stood where as there were plenty of them to go around. The fact that we towered over most of them – apart from Bryan, who was a strapping lad – made the photo look very amusing.

The band had just notched up their seventh number-one single that weekend, putting them on a par with The Beatles. Not that their spectacular feat had gone to their heads. They were still the down-to-earth Irish boys they had been since they first appeared on the pop scene.

'Congratulations, guys! We hope you beat the Spice Girls to number one. You deserve it. We've just been at their album launch, and Mel B and Mel C went mental at us and called us sluts!' explained Eva.

Kian Egan, one of the singers, was appalled by her revelation. 'They should show some respect. If I ever get like that, then that's when I know it's time to give all this up,' he told us.

Bryan didn't hold back. 'I can't believe they said that to you. It was Mel B, wasn't it? She has a big gob and doesn't know when to keep it shut,' he hollered. 'They're just jealous because you 3am girls have more class.'

As great as it was being insulted by celebrities, it was heartening to be complimented too. I was well aware that the Westlife boys couldn't have cared less that the Spice Girls had insulted us. But they knew that if they played good cop to the Spice Girls' bad cop, then they'd get our backing in the paper.

We didn't mince our words in the column when it came to the Spice Girls versus Westlife battle. Mel C was her own worst enemy that night anyway. She'd necked back the drinks and was pictured being helped out of the party and into a waiting car while giving the one-finger salute to the photographers outside. Piers stuck the photo on the front page of the paper and we split the column into two, Girls V Bestlife, backing Westlife for number one. They beat the Spice Girls in the album charts that Sunday.

But we hadn't heard the last from Mel C.

Three weeks later we were given tickets to a Madonna concert at the Brixton Academy in South London. It was her first concert to be broadcast live on the Internet, and the 3,000 tickets were strictly for competition winners, members of her fan club and her celebrity friends. We'd been given two very precious tickets, but luckily Polly was away on holiday and so we avoided a very ugly argument in the showbiz department.

Eva and I were thrilled, although Eva was much better at hiding her excitement than I was. I'd never seen Madonna perform live before, so I was acting desperately uncool in the office. The cherry on the cake was being given access to the VIP area – we were assured there'd be plenty of stars there.

'Go and have fun, girlies. Remember we need the review asap. It won't make time for the first edition, so ring it through to the copytakers as soon as you can and top it up at the end when the gig's over,' instructed Richard while we were getting ready to leave the office for the gig.

Fighting off the temptation to see how much we could sell our free VIP tickets for to a tout outside Brixton Academy, Eva and I made our way to the upstairs part of the venue. So far the only famous faces we'd spotted were Natalie Appleton, Donna Air and Sara Cox. Standing at the top of the stairs waiting to see who else appeared was our arch-rival from the *Sun*, Dominic Mohan.

'All right, girls. Hoping to get to Madonna tonight, are you? A nice little picture for your column?' he asked.

I didn't blame Dominic for trying to wind us up. Some of the blokes in our department took great pleasure in trying to rile him and would regularly send him faxes at the *Sun* calling him boss-eyed and generally taking the piss out of him. Unhelpfully they would sign the faxes 'From your friends at 3am xxx' Luckily Dominic knew it wasn't us.

Just then, Mel C raced up the stairs, eyes blazing. Funnily enough, she didn't look at all chuffed to see Eva and me. She just glared at us, sending 'just don't think about trying to talk to me' vibes. She could be pretty intimidating when she wanted to be,

Sporty. We didn't dare say anything, but Dominic was having none of it. He tried to turn on the charm.

'Hey, Mel. How are you?' he asked in an over-friendly manner.

'I don't want to talk to you,' she replied stroppily and pushed past him, her boyfriend Dan Williams following close behind.

'Well, that went well. Last time she saw us she asked, "Who the fuck let them in here?"' I told Dominic. 'A pleasure as always.'

Eva and I made our way into the VIP section of the Academy, talking about Mel C. It was still a bit of a mystery why she'd taken an instant dislike to us as we hadn't written anything negative about her before the *Forever* party. But now we'd described her behaviour at the party in our column, we weren't too surprised that she didn't want to be friends. Nor did we particularly want to beg her to be nice to us either.

Madonna was mesmerizing live and it was difficult to believe she was really forty-two. The biggest cheer of the night occurred just before she launched into 'What It Feels Like for a Girl', when she said, 'This is to all the pop bitches out there. Including myself!' Everyone was still roaring their approval when she ended the concert with her hit 'Music'.

Eva and I rushed to the ladies' loo. We huddled together by the sinks and wrote the review together as fast as we could so we could file it in time for the next day's paper. Eva marched over to one of the less disgusting-looking cubicles, put the toilet seat down and sat on it so she could ring up a copytaker and read the review over. I motioned to Eva that I was going to ring Richard outside.

Just as I pushed the door open, in walked Mel C. She saw me and stood in front of me, blocking my way out.

'Hey, you. I want to talk to you,' she barked, her face right up close to mine.

Shit, I thought to myself, she's going to kick my head in. I could see Dominic hovering outside the toilet – he'd obviously been stalking her for a quote or something – and knew he'd overheard Mel because he looked wide-eyed with shock.

'Right. Yes. Of course,' I stammered. So much for me learning how to be a thick-skinned, tough tabloid reporter. I was visibly wilting under the uneasy glare of Sporty Spice. How humiliating to be shown up in this way in front of my biggest rival.

'Let's make peace – I don't want to be your enemy,' she said, still standing in the doorway and offering me her hand.

I shook it straight away. 'Of course. We've never been nasty about you,' I said hurriedly, sounding desperately needy.

She walked over to the sinks and I followed her back in, closing the door behind me. I didn't want Dominic to be privy to the rest of the conversation. Mel C had suddenly decided I was her best friend. For the next fifteen minutes, she and I stood there as other celebs such as Donna Air and Sara Cox came in, washed their hands and reapplied their lip gloss, pretending not to overhear as she poured her heart out.

'No one knows me at all and everyone seems to have had their go at slagging me off. But no one knows what it's really like to be in my shoes. I have cried about the things people have said about me. I have been in tears when I've been called fat and a lesbian. It's hurtful, and no one but me really has a clue about my life,' she revealed.

I just stood there nodding away while she spoke.

'Like any woman, I'm not happy that I've put on a bit of weight, but no one has the right to criticize me so unpleasantly about it.'

The ladies' loo was now thinning out as people prepared to go home, but Mel was in no mood to stop talking. In fact, she wouldn't stop. She really wanted to talk about how the insults and the Fat Spice jibes had driven her to despair. She continued to tell me about how she had been struggling with depression and what it was like when other newspapers had labelled her Beefy Spice after she'd been snapped on holiday in the Caribbean that May with her female personal assistant, Ying Yau.

'That just devastated me. I cried and cried. I knew I wasn't as slim as I used to be – but they didn't have to kick me when I was down. I'm not the first girl to go on holiday with a female friend. What did I do wrong?' she asked me, looking as if she desperately wanted me to understand that she was just a normal human being.

I would have comforted her, but I couldn't get a word in

edgeways. And anyway she was coming out with some amazing stuff. I didn't want her to stop, I just had to make sure I could remember it all.

Eva finished on the phone and walked over to us. All this time she'd been sitting in her toilet cubicle filing our review down her mobile, trying not to be distracted by Mel. For all she knew, Mel could well have been explaining to me the painful torture she was about to inflict on us, her least-favourite journalists in the world. Eva had been hurrying the process up so she could join us and listen in on what was going on.

'Hi,' she said to Mel.

'Hi,' Mel replied. She was still on a roll. 'To many people, I'm sure my life seems terribly glamorous. But I suppose I am living proof that fame and wealth don't necessarily make you happy. I just wish people would be nicer to me. I can't believe the amount of abuse I get. I am just a young girl at the end of the day, and I just want to get on with my music.' And with that she shook our hands, said goodbye and walked out the loo with her head held high.

I had the biggest story of my 3am career so far. Mel C had spoken for the first time about her struggles with fame, depression and being labelled a fat lesbian. I could just see the headlines.

It was also the first time that it was brought home to me that my job wasn't just about getting into petty spats with celebrities, revealing which star had been snogging who and posing for cheesy photographs with famous people while being elbowed out of the way by my colleagues. I was dealing with people who actually had feelings beneath their showbiz personas. Naturally I had always known this, but I had somehow brushed it under the carpet. Mel C's outpouring had been so honest and revealing that it made me stop and think.

I felt genuinely sorry for her. Unlike a lot of celebs, she hadn't realized she had been photographed in a bikini on holiday. It was true she'd looked bulkier than she had in the past, but as she herself had admitted, she had been struggling with a cycle of binge-eating and starvation for years. I could see why she didn't like journalists at all.

'Bloody hell,' was all I could say to Eva.

'What else did she say? I thought she was threatening you and was dying to get off the phone so I could plough right in,' replied Eva.

And then my journalistic impulse kicked in with a vengeance.

'I've got to write this down before I forget any of it,' I said. I got out my notebook and pen and began scribbling it all out in my illegible shorthand. 'Oh, bugger it, I'll never be able to read this back,' I muttered under my breath, and got my mobile out of my bag. I rang up my direct line at work and recited back as much of the conversation as I could remember into my voicemail.

Eva listened in and when I hung up she just stood there looking incredulous. 'Bloody hell. No offence, mate, but why the hell did she tell you about her struggles with life? You're not exactly a therapist, are you! Dominic is going to go mental when he reads that!' she laughed.

The next day I got into work and breathlessly recalled the incident to Richard.

'Fuck me, Callan, excellent work. I want every cough and spit. Email me the best quotes now,' he shouted as he jumped up from his chair and legged it to the other end of the office to the picture desk to find photographs that would go with the article.

I rang up my voicemail and tape-recorded the message I had left myself the night before, so I could replay it and write down the juiciest quotes for Richard to read out in the morning conference.

Piers was thrilled with the story. The next day the headline on the front page read: 'My Hell. Mel C's astonishing 30-minute confession to our 3am girls from this loo at the Madonna concert'. He splashed a huge picture of Mel C's head alongside a photo of the sinks inside the bathroom where she had collared me at Brixton Academy.

We'd made the front page, but my joy was slightly dampened by my realization that I was probably making an unhappy celebrity even more miserable. I would never forget Mel C's outpouring. It had been one of the very few honest conversations that I would ever have with a celebrity. She'd taught me a lesson: it wasn't all a game for every celebrity. Some of them didn't want to live their lives under the scrutiny of the press. As I was to find out, this was something I would often overlook in my keenness to land juicy scoops.

Piers was extremely happy with the column and I did feel that thus far we were succeeding in fulfilling our brief of exposing celebrities and shaking things up. Eva, Polly and I worked well together and shared a similar sense of humour, so the job was fun too. My love life was in a shambles, but at least my working life was great. I was constantly thanking my lucky stars that I'd left the *Telegraph*, and felt that I'd really landed on my feet.

Unfortunately for us girls, a month after our Mel C encounter, Piers promoted Richard Wallace to head of news and we lost our mentor.

'Sorry, ladies. Your Uncle Dicky's off,' Richard confirmed to us one day after weeks of rumours about his possible uprooting to the news department.

We watched in anguish as he moved his things to the other end of the office, and his deputy Kevin O'Sullivan stepped into his shoes to become the new showbusiness editor and our direct boss.

Eva and I in particular knew we'd miss Richard a lot. He was the one who had headhunted us from our previous newspapers to join the *Mirror*. We felt he'd been very supportive and had helped us a great deal in developing the style and tone of 3am. Kevin's reputation preceded him: brash, quick-witted and a hilarious writer, he could be painfully scathing about anyone – from celebs to colleagues – for no reason other than he felt like it and thought it was funny. We knew that his offensive sense of humour sometimes bordered on the downright evil.

One of his very first ideas for the column was that we should regularly hint that Cat Deeley and her friend Edith Bowman were lesbian lovers, as they were frequently pictured out together. We protested that this was totally untrue and that it was a bad idea writing these lies because we'd have to face both women at parties all the time. But Kevin overruled us, and told us that the fact we'd be bumping into them at celebrity bashes made the whole story even funnier. Every time I saw Cat's PR, Simon Jones, I would apologize to him profusely for our innuendos about his client's sexuality.

'Oh, don't worry about it,' Simon would reassure me. 'She just thinks it's funny.' And then he'd add, 'Kevin's a bit odd, isn't he?'

Kevin was not exactly renowned for his women-friendly views. He loved winding us up, calling us 'useless c***s'. All it did was unite Eva, Polly and myself like never before. That said, he couldn't bear the thought that he was disliked by his reporters, and when we were at our angriest with him, he would try to tell jokes and make us laugh. Eva always managed to remain steely and unmoved, but Polly and I regularly failed and would crack and join in with him.

All in all he was a tough cookie, but we quickly located his two sensitive spots. The first was his dog, Stan, who he had rescued from the aftermath of an earthquake in Los Angeles. The second was his hair, which he took great pride in. He lost his legendary sense of humour when we presented him with a gift-wrapped box of Just For Men hair dye on his birthday that year.

We ended the year with another spectacular celebrity fallout, and this time I didn't feel like making amends one bit.

Jude Law had invited the media to the launch of a theatre company he was setting up with his then-wife Sadie Frost and pal Ewan McGregor. Polly, Eva and I turned up at the small press conference at St Martin's Lane Hotel at 2pm to get a few words from Jude and a photograph with him. As we had been invited along, we expected that the *Talented Mr Ripley* star might for once deign to speak to the tabloid press from whom he usually stayed well away.

Joining journalists from other newspapers, we waited for the threesome to make an appearance in the hotel's lobby, famous for its oversized and over-trendy furniture. Half an hour later, a stroppy-looking Jude, a haughty Sadie and a thoroughly pissed-off Ewan finally made their grand entrance. They posed for the photographers there, barely managing to squeeze out the merest hint of a smile between them.

'Oh, great. They look in fabulous moods. I can just see them dying to talk to us,' I whispered to Eva.

Jude Law whipped out a scrap of paper and read out a statement about their new theatre company. McGregor gave monosyllabic answers when asked about any productions they were currently working on. Sadie was asked to do a TV interview but shook her head and refused to utter a single word.

'What the hell is all this about? Why did the moody buggers invite us all to a press conference when they don't want to play ball?' Eva said to me.

I'd been staring at Law and hadn't really been listening to what was being said. I was looking at his head. For the first time I noticed how big it was. It was far too large for his body. He had, I decided, a lollipop head.

All the showbiz journalists were looking round at each other and shrugging their shoulders. It was the strangest press conference I had ever been to. Why bother holding one if you don't want the publicity? It was time for another tactic.

'Can we do a picture with you?' asked Polly, putting on her most angelic-sounding voice.

'Absolutely no way. I'm not going to be pictured with them,' Jude said to his wife, pointing at us.

We weren't exactly feeling the love in the room. And then, all of a sudden, Jude, who'd been looking at the assembled journalists like he was going to catch something off us, cut the strained conference short by claiming he was needed for a reshoot of a film in Germany. That very minute. And with that, Jude, Sadie and Ewan all strode out of the hotel.

'Sod this. Let's chase them,' Eva announced, running after them.

Polly and I followed Eva on to the street.

'Oi, Jude! Oi! Can we have a quick word with you!' hollered Eva.

None of them looked back. Eva was absolutely livid, and determined to spell out to Jude the error of his ways.

'What's your problem? What's the point of having a press conference if you don't want any bloody publicity? We've got better things to do than slog all the way across town for this shit.' And still they ignored us.

'Oi!' she shouted again.

Evidently Jude wasn't so keen to hear her point of view and instead jumped into a black cab along with Sadie and Ewan. But he didn't know Eva the way we did. Refusing to give up, Eva ran up to the taxi.

'Oi! You miserable fuckers!' she shouted, as Ewan tried to shut the taxi door in her face.

'Eva! You'll get yourself knocked down. It's not worth injuring yourself for Lollipop Head Man,' I hollered, trying to make myself heard over the din of beeping horns. The traffic had been building up, obstructed by Eva standing in the middle of the road and attempting to hijack the taxi, and the waiting drivers were not best pleased.

'What a waste of time. We've got nothing to put in the column now,' snapped Polly as Eva finally admitted defeat and walked back towards us, muttering angrily to herself.

On the Tube journey back to Canary Wharf we plotted our revenge on the peculiar little man.

I came up with a plan. 'The best way to get our revenge is to ridicule them. They knew they had to publicize that theatre company but clearly didn't want to have to actually mingle with the press. Perish the thought. So let's refuse to give them the publicity.'

Half an hour later we were in the lift on the way up to the paper at One Canada Square.

'Kevin will relish the idea of giving Jude Bore a right kicking,' quipped Polly.

'What a good name for him – Jude Bore! He'll go mental. He bloody is though,' said Eva.

'I can't see this heart-throb thing at all,' I agreed. 'He's got a concave little body. And Sadie had a spot on one of her boobs.'

Kevin had been waiting for us. 'So how did it go with that pretentious bunch?' he asked when we reached our desks. 'Did you get a nice picture of you pretending you're best of chums with them?'

'No chance. They were the moodiest people I've ever met and refused to talk to anyone, let alone do TV or photos,' Polly replied. 'So we want to hammer the hell out of them. Well, Jude Law especially.'

With Kevin's approval, we ran a large blank space in the column the following day and wrote a caption alongside it stating that we would have run a picture of the actor but as he had refused to pose for photos we'd been forced to leave the area empty.

A few weeks later we received a call from a woman called Meena who said that Jude and Sadie had hired her to be their publicist. 'Why are you guys so mean to them?' she asked Polly.

Polly pointed out that they had started it by being so moody with the media for no reason, despite asking us all to attend their press conference.

'It's not very nice to say that Jude is losing his hair,' Meena persisted. She then changed tack. 'Sadie wants to start afresh with you guys. She's got an after-show party for her FrostFrench collection at next month's London Fashion Week and would love you lot to come to the show and then to the party. And you can do an interview with her there, as well as photos. Jude will be there and will do pictures too,' she said.

It seemed a little bit of ridicule went a long way with some stars who took themselves way too seriously. We'd only been taking the piss in the column, and now they were pulling out all the stops to win us over.

I was away on the night of the party, but when I came back Eva and Polly gleefully filled me in on how it had gone. After watching the catwalk show, they'd been accompanied by Meena to the after-show party and immediately introduced to Jude and Sadie.

'Sadie was really friendly and chatty,' Eva told me. 'Can you believe she actually thanked us for coming along? What a joke! We'd only mildly taken the piss out of her and Jude and suddenly she was all over us.' She shook her head and laughed. 'But it really killed Jude. He looked like he'd far rather eat his own head than have to even breathe the same air as us. Sadie made him say hello and forced him to join her in the picture with us. It was as if someone had just strangled a kitten in front of him, he looked that upset. I reckon we could have a right laugh with him and just take the piss in the column whenever we can. Just so I can picture that pained, constipated expression on his face.'

I feared for Jude. Once we all decided someone took themselves far too seriously, then there wasn't much chance of us chronicling their achievements and writing favourably about them. It was far more fun to rip the piss out of Jude, his receding hairline and his oversized head.

Extraordinarily, a few years later he came seeking my advice on how to deal with the press in the aftermath of his affair with his children's nanny and his break-up with fiancée Sienna Miller. We refrained from calling him Lollipop Head on that occasion. Just.

Jordan and me

6. Planet Jordan

After eleven months in the job I took a much-needed holiday, backpacking around Bali with an old university friend who'd just split up from a very controlling boyfriend. In between swimming in the sea and visiting temples, I gave her daily pep talks on the benefits of being single, and even managed to sound convincing. Indeed, she seemed to get the grip of things when a warship of American marines turned up for two nights of shore leave in the party town of Kuta.

I came back to work and regaled the others with tales of how I had done my bit for Anglo-American relations on holiday.

'Nice one, Jessie. Did you have a spit-roast on the beach?' asked James, the showbusiness news reporter. He was always asking me probing questions about the finer details of my romantic life since my split from Tom.

I had only been in the office for a couple of hours when Kevin told me I was being sent on a foreign press trip. 'You're going to the Laureus World Sports Awards in Monte Carlo next week. They're the Oscars of the sporting world and some big name stars are going. You're expected to get some pretty big scoops over there,' he informed me. He looked me straight in the eye and lowered his voice. 'Piers is in a bit of a bad mood at the moment. He's pretty pissed off with everyone at the paper – there hasn't been a big sensational story for ages and we need to come up with the goods.'

Shit. I was still in holiday mode in my head and wasn't quite ready for this. I was going to have to work my butt off out there. But I was also looking forward to covering the event, which I was told was a two-day whirlwind of parties and dinners. International sports stars were the main guests, but some models and actors were always invited, and I'd heard there were often a few scandalous stories. I knew I would have to join in and immerse myself in the champagne-fuelled mayhem.

Infamously, a few years ago a celebrity had dived fully clothed into an outdoor swimming pool at the hotel where the after-show party was taking place. So far so what, but when a photographer started snapping away at her as she hauled herself out of the water, she took it as a cue to hitch her designer frock up to her waist and shove a few fingers up herself.

The pictures were never published. It would have been possible to run them by pixilating the rude bits, but the pictures remained locked away in the safe of the photographer. He must have had his reasons: he'd probably decided it was in his best interests to protect the star, and that if he didn't embarrass her by flogging the snaps, she'd grant him a few favours in the future. Why do someone over for a short-term gain when you could build up a mutually beneficial relationship that could last years instead? Fingers crossed there'd be similar frolics at the awards next week.

Sunday afternoon, four days later, I disembarked from my EasyJet flight at Nice airport and made my way to the baggage carousel to locate my overstuffed suitcase. I was going to be in Monte Carlo for three nights and had been booked in to stay at the world-famous Grand Hotel, which overlooked the sea. There was no point getting too excited about staying there, however, as there was no way I'd have the time to bask in the Mediterranean sun. I knew I was going to have to rummage around for gossip like crazy. Even if I did have a spare half-hour to take a dip in the rooftop pool, the thought of Piers's displeasure should I not bring any stories back with me was too unbearable. I made a mental note not to allow myself to get tanned out there. If I came back to the office with any sort of healthy glow, I'd be accused of sunbathing the entire time instead of out hunting for scoops. I was here to fill the column with tales of celebrity misdemeanours and scandalous tittle-tattle.

I jumped into a taxi, glad to be out of the office and heading to Monaco, where the sun was shining. It was going to be hard work, but at least I wouldn't be staring at my computer screen in blustery Canary Wharf.

Once I'd checked into my hotel I immediately rang Derek, the showbiz reporter on the *Sun* who was also covering the event, on his mobile. Although we were rivals, we got on well and enjoyed catching up and sharing titbits of information and gossip. It was the same with most of the other showbiz reporters. We were all hugely competitive with each other, but as we spent more time together than we did with our friends and family, we felt like we were part of a small community, and hung out with each other a lot.

Mind you, it could feel like being back at school sometimes, only with alcohol, cigarettes and drugs. Not necessarily sex – strangely enough, there were very few sexual shenanigans, though not through lack of trying in a few cases. One showbiz reporter from another paper once offered me a month's salary to let him into my bed. I declined. This was a married man who had injured his foot after tripping over in the shower of his local brothel in north London.

Derek wasn't arriving until Monday morning, the next day. So I called Toby, the PR in charge of the whole event, and we met for a quiet dinner that evening. Over pizza and wine I quizzed him about which celebrities would be attending the actual awards ceremony on Tuesday. It was Toby's job to battle constantly on our behalf to track down a definitive list of confirmed celebs. He knew for sure that Catherine Zeta-Jones and Michael Douglas would be there. But that didn't guarantee me a good story. In fact, if anything it meant no story at all. They were huge stars but they didn't actually ever get up to anything untoward. Well, not that the press ever found out about anyway.

'Anyone made any outrageous demands?' I asked, biting into a slice of Margarita.

'No, not really. I have heard that Jordan is joining Dwight Yorke, who's coming over with a whole load of Manchester United players. That might be fun. Just make sure you mention Laureus World Sports Awards all over your articles or I'm in for it,' he implored, plying me with more red wine.

After dinner we went to a small drinks reception.

'I'm not promising there'll be any A-listers there, but you never know,' said Toby.

I'd arranged to meet Sam there, a TV and radio presenter who wrote a party column in the *Mirror*. Blonde, gorgeous and bubbly, she was immediately noticeable and I had no problem locating her. She was there with her movie-producer boyfriend, and while Toby went to get the drinks we surveyed the room. I could see Youngy nearby, camera at the ready. Then I saw the food.

'This is meant to be a small-scale party?' I asked Sam. A huge table was laden down with bulging prawns, smoked salmon, caviar, oysters, champagne, wine and cocktails. I instantly regretted having stuffed my face with pizza. I felt hugely out of place as well, in my Karen Millen dress. I was used to attending showbiz parties in London, not suave events in Monte Carlo. And this was just a warm-up party.

'There's David Ginola. I'm sure he'll be good for a chat,' giggled Sam.

Reluctantly, I started making my way towards him, making signs at Youngy to follow me. I'd heard that Ginola was very pleased with himself, and as I chatted to him he turned out to be just what I'd expected. He happily agreed to a photo with me and we made polite chit-chat until a beautiful brunette sidled up to him. I moved away and pretended not to listen to them flirting with each other.

'I'm bored and cold,' she moaned.

Flicking his ludicrous locks, Ginola didn't miss a beat and pouted at her. 'Well, let me take you somewhere much more fun and then we can go for breakfast afterwards,' he simpered.

So this was his legendary 'charm'! All I wanted to do was get away. Hiding my smile, I turned and spied British Olympic star Daley Thompson. The double-gold-winning star had made no effort to dress up for the night. While everyone else was in suits or cocktail dresses, Daley was in sweaty-looking tracksuit bottoms and a T-shirt. The man obviously just didn't do the smart look.

I remembered reading an article earlier in the year that said he had left his wife of fourteen years for a much younger woman. He hadn't talked about his marriage split or indeed the new woman in his life, so I thought I'd give it a go to see if he'd open up.

I had learnt pretty quickly that there were those famous people who talked to the press, and there were those who'd rather eat their own arm than reveal anything about their personal life to a journalist. It seemed as if he fell into the latter camp, so I decided not to volunteer the fact that I was a reporter. I also decided to drag Sam over with me to talk to him. I figured that I stood a better chance of flattering him and getting him to inadvertently tell me something interesting if I had another girl with me, especially a gorgeous blonde one.

'Hello, I'm a huge fan of yours. You looking forward to the awards?' I asked.

He grinned back at us, giving us his full attention. Piers and Richard may have had a point when they decided that girls should handle the *Mirror*'s gossip coverage: male celebrities on the whole responded well to obvious flirtation. I knew Daley was a renowned womanizer. Despite being married to his school sweetheart, he'd been seen on several occasions with other women, notably wining and dining the model Marie Helvin, and partying with a 21-year-old, with whom he had had a long affair. He might well fall for my plan of a two-pronged attack, I thought to myself.

Daley duly chatted to us while we simpered at his jokes.

I decided to go for the kill. 'So where's your girlfriend?' I asked, fully expecting him to tell me she was at home or somewhere else at the party.

'I'm here on my own. I don't have a girlfriend any more. I'm old, free and single. It felt a bit odd at first, but now I'm loving it,' he replied.

I tried not to show any sort of reaction on my face. Could he really have broken up with the thirty-year-old woman he had left his wife and kids for only six months before? If that was the case, then I had a strong story on my hands.

I clung tightly to my glass of champagne and continued to laugh at his jokes with Sam until a friend of his came over to talk to him. I hung around a while longer but wanted to get a good night's sleep, so I said goodnight to Sam, her boyfriend and Toby, and made my way back to my hotel.

On the way I reflected on Daley, and on the fact that I hadn't told him I was a journalist. I didn't really feel guilty about not telling him who I was. If he had asked me then I might have admitted it. I hadn't lied to him, I reassured myself. Anyway, he couldn't really take the moral high ground. After all, he was the one who had cheated on his wife, and he was clearly revelling in his newly found single status.

The next morning I woke to glorious Mediterranean sunshine. I gave in and had breakfast on the terrace on the top floor of the hotel. I may as well make the most of it, I reasoned with myself. And besides, the sun wasn't strong enough to tan me so I would still be returning to Canary Wharf looking pale. I'd just have to make sure I had minimal sleep to give me that battered look which said I had been too busy tracking down celebs to bother with bed.

Back in my hotel room, I rang Kevin to tell him about Daley Thompson splitting from his mistress.

'Great. File it over. It'll probably make a news page,' he said.

After writing up the story and ringing it over to the copytakers, I lay down on my bed and slowly entered the paranoid state that all reporters suffer from after filing what they think is an exclusive. What if someone else had got the story? I was slowly realizing that being out of the office on a foreign assignment meant the pressure to land big scoops was even bigger than when in the office. The company had splashed out hundreds for me to fly to Monaco and stay at a top hotel. There was no way I could let any of them down by coming back with no exclusives.

My jumpiness wasn't helped by the fact that the rest of the newspaper correspondents had arrived. In fact, everyone was walking around rather nervously, keeping tabs on one another to make sure no one was secretly working on a big story.

I got hold of Derek on the phone.

'Hi, Derek. How are you? What time did you land? Where are you? Do you fancy meeting up? Let's ring Toby and find out what's going on tonight and if he has our tickets yet.'

Derek was just as tense as I was. Although we had been invited to cover the two-day event, we weren't sure we'd get our tickets to the awards ceremony. The organizers of such occasions never made it easy for journalists to get the precious pieces of card that got us into all the parties. Why did they have to make it so hard? If they wanted us to give the awards publicity, why couldn't they just give us the invites? It was a constant battle to get in anywhere.

After several hours of hounding Toby and frantically wondering if I was ever going to land any more stories out in Monte Carlo, I was finally given a ticket to the star-studded gala at the Monte Carlo Beach Hotel that night.

'This is the big one,' said Toby, handing it over to me. 'There's a VIP area but I haven't got any passes, so you'll have to blag your way in. Everyone's going tonight: Catherine Zeta-Jones, Michael Douglas and loads of supermodels. Oh, and Jordan and Dwight Yorke are definitely coming.'

My ears pricked up at the mention of Jordan.

In 2001 she was Jordan, the hellraising ladette, not Katie Price, the clued-up married mother and successful businesswoman she is today. The contrast between her then and now couldn't be more extreme, almost like dealing with two different people. At the time she was dating Manchester United striker Dwight – she was to become pregnant with their child, Harvey, shortly after – and had a reputation as a shambolic pisshead party girl. I had never met her before, but had written up stories around pictures the paparazzi had taken of her falling out of taxis, clubs and parties. We'd enjoyed writing about it in our column. She was the perfect target for 3am – drunk, underdressed and gobby. I was expected to get enough stories that night to fill the entire column the following day, and I was pinning my hopes on Jordan.

Kick-off time was 9pm. I rang up Sam to tell her I'd meet her there. She and her boyfriend were enjoying a romantic late afternoon wandering around Monte Carlo. I felt a pang of jealousy that she had someone to share her life with and couldn't help but feel a bit lonely in my large hotel room. I had broken up with Tom ten months before and had hardly had the time to mope about my non-existent love life, which in a way was a good thing.

But at times like these, when I could imagine what could have been, I did wonder whether I was in denial.

Getting ready for the big party that evening, I wondered whether my love life was going to permanently suffer due to my career. I had been set up on a disastrous blind date with a management consultant called Paul in October, which had ended up with me being sick at the bar after too many tequila shots and no dinner. Strangely the chap had come back for more and we'd had another two dates, but I had no inclination to see him when I was sober.

'Do you ever have a night off the booze?' he asked me on our third date.

'Well, I have a very hardy constitution and have to be capable of drinking a lot in my line of work. So no, not really,' I replied.

He turned out to be a bit of a health nut and was in training for the New York marathon. I never saw him again after that. I guess going on dates with a woman who could drink a man under a table doesn't do a lot for a guy's ego.

Which is exactly what happened when I had a date with a financier before Christmas. We went out for dinner and then went back to my flat. I had moved into a new place near Gloucester Road Tube station following a short stint at my parents' flat. There I proceeded to continue to drink while Richard completely passed out on the living room floor.

He commented to mutual friends that he was astounded at the way I put away alcohol. And I don't think he was very impressed.

'I can totally see why journalists end up going out with other journalists,' I said to Eva one day in the office. I hadn't heard from the financier since he had keeled over on my living room rug. 'All the men we meet who aren't in the newspaper world are total wimps when it comes to boozing. They can't keep up and it does nothing for their self-esteem. I totally scare them off. Please don't say we're going to have to end up with journalists.'

Eva laughed. 'Oh, no. Please no. There's no one worth fancying. And that's the ones who are taken. Look at the single ones. All total freaks!'

'Do you think they say the same thing about us? They must

wonder why we're single. Being a gossip columnist isn't exactly doing wonders for our livers. Or our love lives,' I replied.

We may have been laughing about the situation but neither of us was actually joking.

Tom meanwhile had moved on too and had started going out with a friend of a friend of his. He had made a big deal about telling me and insisted on taking me out for a sandwich one lunchtime to inform me that he was in a serious relationship. In fact, he'd sent me an email when he was in Nepal on a story to tell me he was 'stepping out', as he put it. I hadn't replied as I couldn't believe he had actually emailed me about it. I had told him after we broke up that unless I asked, I didn't want to know about his love life. That didn't seem to stop him though, and he was adamant that I should know all about it.

We sat on a bench by the shops in Canary Wharf.

'So have you been seeing anyone?' he asked while I pretended to be deeply fascinated by my Pret A Manger tuna baguette.

'Actually, yes. I've had a few dates with a bloke called Paul,' I replied, leaving out the bit about me chundering on our first date and the terrible nights out we'd had since.

'Oh, right. When did this happen?' he asked. I detected a slight hint of arsiness.

'October. He went to university with my friend Sarah, and she set me up with him,' I explained.

'When in October?'

'Jesus Christ, Tom. This isn't a competition about who pulled first since our break-up. I'm glad you've found someone nice who gives you all the time and attention you need,' I said.

'For fuck's sake, kiddo, you don't have to be so sarcastic. Honestly.'

'I'm not being sarky, I mean it! She doesn't work in newspapers so you don't have to spend your entire time talking about work. She sounds like she's great for you.' I tried hard not to sound whiny. OK, so I wasn't the most thrilled person on the planet that he had found a replacement for me so soon, but I did still care for him a lot and he'd had the decency to tell me. Even if I didn't want to know.

We left it at that and changed the subject.

Putting on a black lace top and a black skirt and some vertiginously high heels in my hotel room in Monaco, I told myself to stop thinking about my crappy love life. After all, being single really did help when it came to covering parties. I had no one to rush back home for and could flirt away with celebs without feeling guilty. And that night I was to experience a whole new type of flirting, all in the name of work.

I left the hotel at 9pm and hopped into one of the many chauffeur-driven cars waiting outside the hotel.

There were about forty photographers waiting alongside TV crews outside the Monte Carlo Beach Hotel for the A-listers to turn up. I waved my invite in front of the sadistic-looking French bouncers outside, and was surprised to find they didn't rip my invite off me like their British counterparts. It was still relatively early and I guessed the stars wouldn't be here for at least another hour, so I had a wander, taking note of where all the toilets, the VIP area, the bar and the exits were. All very useful to know while dashing around chasing celebs.

The venue was completely amazing. There was an outdoor Olympic-sized swimming pool, surrounded by at least one hundred waiters and waitresses dressed in black tie and carrying trays of champagne, a cinema-sized screen by the pool, coloured lasers in the sky, trees decorated with hundreds of lights, huge speakers everywhere, sound systems rigged up and cushions scattered all over the place. They really raised the game in Monte Carlo when it came to parties. I had never seen anything quite like it.

'Bloody hell. What is this place?' I said out loud.

Toby, the PR, was standing nearby, looking and sounding frantic.

'You all right, Toby?' I asked.

'No, course I'm not bloody all right. You try keeping all the British photographers in check. Do you think they're ever happy? Course they're not. Ever. And I'm dealing with the Laureus lot too. Can't stop,' he shouted over his shoulder, dashing off.

I moved closer towards the VIP area, which was to the right

side of the pool. There were more than twenty tables set up for dinner, with waiters and waitresses lined up and ready to serve the elite guests. I knew I'd have to get in there somehow. Judging by the size of the surly security men standing by the obligatory sets of velvet ropes and patrolling the swanky place, it was going to be a challenge. But I was up for it. I didn't really have a choice anyway.

The guests started arriving, all immaculately turned out. Most of the women looked freshly Botoxed for the night and wore sleek designer frocks and stilettos. No one here did flat shoes, that was for sure. They were all beautiful. It was like being at a conference for Amazonian supermodels. The female athletes among them were easy to spot, as their bulging biceps burst out of their sleeveless frocks.

I walked back to the entrance of the party and tried to look inconspicuous so the security men wouldn't ask me to move inside. Youngy had turned up and was waiting there too so he could be in prime position for snapping the stars. I waited next to him so I could jump on any celebs and get the pictures over and done with early on instead of trying to stalk them later.

It struck me for the first time how odd it was waiting to do pictures with stars without Eva and Polly. At least I knew for sure I'd be in the frame alongside the celebs in question this time. But it was definitely much lonelier on my own.

Suddenly a succession of flashbulbs lit up the balmy evening.

'*S'il vous plaît!*'

'*Par ici!*'

The French photographers were screaming, whipped into a frenzy.

'Who is it, Youngy? Who is it? Can you see?' I leaned on his shoulder and jumped up and down to try and catch a glimpse.

'No, I can't. Oh, hang on. It's Michael Douglas and Catherine Zeta-Jones. Get ready. Catherine is coming in!'

I knew she'd be flanked by bulky bodyguards and that I had a two-second window to get this picture, which I was desperate for. I had long admired the actress. For some reason a lot of people at work couldn't bear her and didn't like her fierce ambition, nor the fact she'd had an array of very unlikely boyfriends, from John Leslie to Mick Hucknall to Michael Douglas. I'd always thought she was pure Hollywood old-style glamour. You'd never see Catherine on the pages of *Heat* magazine picking her spots, wearing no make-up, popping out to the shops in a grubby chav-tastic tracksuit or falling out pissed from a club. This was a woman who had gone from ITV's cosy telly drama *The Darling Buds of May* to doing some pretty impressive acrobatics in a sexy catsuit and snogging Sean Connery in *Entrapment*, and starring in the swashbuckling *Mask of Zorro*. I thought she was great. I especially liked the way she insisted on taking her Hollywood superstar bloke back as often as possible to her hometown of Mumbles in Wales.

She swept in wearing a low-cut silver and gold couture number, dripping in blinding diamonds and looking like Hollywood royalty.

'Catherine, I love your dress!' I gasped as she came within a few feet of me.

Celebrities are used to being – and expect to be – flattered on their appearance at all times. It was worth a punt to blatantly suck up to her, even if it meant embarrassing myself in front of the male British journalists who were chasing her inside and hovering nearby trying to get a quote. She smiled at me.

'Why, thank you,' she replied in a strange accent, which could only be described as the bastard love child of Ruby Wax and Inspector Clouseau. What had happened to her Charlotte Church-style lilt? And with that she moved past me, with Michael Douglas trailing behind.

Luckily, Richard had secured a shot with Catherine and I grinning at each other in the same frame. We looked like we were best pals catching up on gossip. I was thrilled I had a photo with her, but what I needed now was a story to go with it. The actress and her husband had been ushered into the VIP area, and I knew I had to get in there no matter what.

I spotted Toby hovering by the ropes. 'Um, Toby. You know the VIP area . . .' I started to say.

'Don't even go there, Callan. I told you I haven't got any passes to get you in there. Just try and talk your way in,' he replied, before rushing off again.

There was no chance I'd get in there. Not only were the bouncers massive, they were all French, which meant it was impossible to talk my way in. Usually I would try to stroll into an exclusive roped-off section of a party like this one, having pretended I had merely wandered out by accident and lost my VIP pass. If you acted brazen enough and wore a slightly superior expression on your face, as if it was your birthright to be in the VIP area, you were usually allowed in unquestioned. But on this occasion I reckoned the French security men would have laughed in my face. I was wearing a Hennes top and a Zara skirt. Not exactly a look straight off the catwalk of the Paris fashion shows. And next to all that Eurotrash lot, I looked like an underdressed student trying to blag her way in.

I had two choices. The easiest one was to join the other showbiz reporters back at the entrance and hang out with them for a while. But I knew all we'd do was moan to each other about what crap stories we were going to write while downing too much booze, scabbing cigarettes and whingeing about our lot in life.

The second was to persevere in trying to get into the VIP area. That had to be the favoured option. Piers had drummed it into us that we were not to hang around with the rest of the press pack, that at 3am we were to do our own thing, hunt our own stories down and stand out from the crowd.

I skulked around to the side, and just then the huge screen on the wall near the pool flickered into life. The guests stopped talking and turned to watch. At the same time the pool sprang into life and synchronized swimmers with plastered-on grins began doing a silly-looking routine.

Out of the corner of my eye I could see waiters and waitresses walking into the VIP area via another route. I peered at the side of the screen and saw that if I ducked under it quickly I could slip through an unmanned side entrance for serving staff into the exclusive area.

Everyone was distracted by the lovelies in the pool and by the montage of sports stars on the big screen, so I dashed into the side entrance of the VIP section. I got in unnoticed.

'Hi there. Lots of good people here, aren't there?'

I jumped and looked round. It was Youngy.

'What? How did you get in here?' I asked.

'I was invited to come in,' he replied, shrugging at me as if I was the biggest dimwit he'd ever met.

Of course. Youngy was a class above most other photographers and was on first-name basis with all these stars.

We stood and observed the celebrities around us. The likes of Rachel Hunter, Heidi Klum, Helena Christensen, all looking like creatures from another planet, were chatting politely to friends and batting away the trays of canapés.

'Look, there's Michael Douglas. I've got to have a photo taken with him. Please, Richard. Can we try?' I implored.

'OK, then. But let's be quick about it. Prince Albert of Monaco is about to arrive any minute.'

We made our way towards him.

'Mr Douglas, I'm a huge fan. Can I have a photo?' I asked in the most upper-class accent I could muster in order to get his attention.

He didn't look round. But Catherine sure did. And this time she wasn't flashing me a kindly smile. How could I explain that I wasn't some barking-mad fan who was trying to get off with her wrinkly other half?

'Hello? Mr Douglas?' I quickly tugged the back of his jacket before Catherine could give me another death stare. I reckoned that if she lost her temper she'd drop that ludicrous accent for a thick Welsh one full of expletives. I didn't want to risk finding out whether I was right.

I soon discovered that the *Fatal Attraction* star wasn't ignoring me. He seemed to be suffering from a hearing problem. While Youngy snapped away, I tried to make polite but loud conversation with the actor in the hope of getting an interesting story. I knew he'd been expected as the star attraction at a celebrity golf tournament earlier in the day, but that he hadn't turned up. I tried to probe deeper, but Michael seemed to be having an entirely different conversation with me.

'Why weren't you at the golf? You would have won!' I said, trying to smarm up to him.

'What? My girlfriend? What about my girlfriend?' he asked me, looking baffled.

'No, not girlfriend. Golf! Golf!' I shouted back at him, looking and sounding as if I was attempting to converse with a deaf elderly relative.

Michael just looked even more puzzled. 'What? What?'

I gave up. Youngy went off to shoot Prince Albert and I stood for a minute on my own, wondering what to do next and missing Eva and Polly. I was beginning to feel very out of place, surrounded as I was by these freakishly tall supermodels.

'Oi, you! Why are you always so rude about me?' I heard a voice screech behind me.

It was Jordan. The pneumatic model was wearing cream trousers and a matching top that barely contained those infamous breasts. Her blonde hair extensions were straggly and knotted, her dark roots showing badly, and her lips looked plumped out of all recognition and were smeared with coral lipstick. She looked like a real-life cartoon character.

Some Eurotrash women standing nearby looked her up and down and pulled sneery expressions as if someone had put dog poo under their surgically upturned noses. Thank God, I thought to myself. Someone who is even more out of place than I am. And who is likely to liven the night up.

Dwight Yorke was standing next to her, looking smart in a beige suit and open-necked chocolate-coloured silk shirt. He was drinking from a glass of champagne and grinned at me. I shivered inadvertently. He may have looked more stylish than her, but boy did I find him pug ugly in the flesh.

'What? I'm not mean about you,' I replied.

I knew exactly what she meant, but I didn't fancy having a showdown with Jordan in the VIP area of an A-list bash in Monte Carlo. Especially standing so near to the swimming pool.

'I'm going to get another drink. I'll get you girls one,' said Dwight before moving swiftly away from us.

Jordan looked me straight in the eye. 'You are. You lot are always mean about me. Why? I haven't done anything to you,' she said, thankfully a bit quieter this time. I noticed she looked genuinely hurt. She wasn't being confrontational for the sake of it. She suddenly seemed very vulnerable. I instantly felt sorry for her and regretted that we had taken the piss out of her so much in the column about her drunken tumbles at parties.

'I've never met you before and this probably isn't the most ideal way to get to know each other. But there really wasn't any other way to write about you when we were offered photos of you drunk and falling over,' I explained.

She bit her bottom lip and looked like she wanted to cry. So much for the tough bitch act she put on, I thought to myself.

'Well, now you've met me and you can see I'm not a horrible person.'

She seemed to make a decision about me there and then.

'Look, I'm 'ere on my own with Dwight and he's got his mates with him. I really could do with a girl to chat to. So do you want to hang out?' she asked. She was like the new girl at school who was asking to sit next to someone in the canteen.

So we each necked a glass of champagne and chatted while Dwight talked to David Ginola and one of the Formula One team bosses Eddie Jordan.

'Thank goodness you're here. Everyone's staring at my boobs. Are my nipples showing?' she asked, readjusting her wisp of a top.

When I replied that they weren't showing, she looked slightly put out. It looked as if I had given her the wrong answer.

'If he wasn't here, I'd be 'avin' a right wild time. If it was just me and the girls, it would be mental!' she hollered.

Dwight looked utterly oblivious to her. I couldn't quite work their relationship out. They weren't tactile with each other at all. In fact, they spent most of their time studiously ignoring one another.

'I've booked a Club 18–30 holiday in Rhodes this summer for

me and the girls, but he doesn't know yet. He'll go mad. But it's going to be mental.' She grinned, downing yet more champagne.

I soon learnt that almost everything in Jordan's world was 'mental', including her seven-month relationship with the £25,000-a-week soccer star.

'I know he sleeps around,' she said sadly, as we watched Dwight eye up Rachel Hunter. 'But that's just men. They're all the same, you know. If women hand it to them on a plate then they bloody well take it. But I do my own thing and try not to let it bother me too much.'

It seemed to me that she was bothered. Jordan was all of twenty-two then, but she'd already had her ups and downs with men. And she was quick to get the details of her forlorn love life off her eye-poppingly large chest. Jordan had met me for the first time half an hour ago, and even then she'd berated me for painting her as a wild, drunken party girl. But in no time she was opening up to me about the true nature of what it was like to go out with a footballer.

'Well, why do you stay with him?' I asked. 'Does he make you happy?'

She shrugged and took another slurp of champagne. Dwight wandered back over and she excitedly told me it was her birthday the following day.

'But I never ask you for anything, do I?' she said, poking Dwight.

The mute footballer blanked her and instead eyed up some passing Eurotrash beauty.

'All I want from him is a cuddle and for him to say happy birthday,' she continued, looking at him misty-eyed. I really began to feel for her now. He was totally uninterested. So she tried another tack. 'But I wouldn't say no to a sex aid!' she guffawed.

He looked over the top of her head, still ignoring her presence.

'Come on, let's go to the loo,' she said, pulling me by the arm. Dwight looked relieved to be out of her grip and I trotted after her. We walked inside the hotel and past a room where a disco was going on.

'Ooh, let's go in here now that Dwight isn't around,' she pleaded.

Standing by the dance floor and surveying the scene was ER actor Eriq La Salle, who played Dr Peter Benton. Jordan bowled straight up to him.

'Hiya, my name's Jordan. It's my birthday tomorrow.' She sounded like a little girl, albeit one with 32GG boobs.

'Well, I'd better give you a birthday kiss,' he smirked, grabbing her head and giving her a long smooch on the lips.

I should have looked elsewhere, as it seemed indecent to stare, but I couldn't help it. They were practically licking each other's faces. So this is how celebrities pull, I thought to myself. They finally stopped kissing, to my relief, and Jordan let out a big Barbara Windsor-style cackle.

'Ooh er. I hope my boyfriend didn't see you doing that. Mind you, he fucks other women all the time!' she said by way of explanation to the actor, who looked more than a little surprised.

We tottered back outside where the other guests were tucking into plates of oysters, sushi and pasta and watching the fencing and high diving display on the screens. It was now 1.30am and I was getting tipsy. I knew I had to remember everything Jordan was saying to me. It was difficult to slip off to the loo to jot it all down, as she seemed reluctant to let me out of her sight. When I wanted to actually use the loo, she insisted on squeezing into the cubicle with me. She clearly couldn't be on her own for a second. I would have to take the booze a bit steadier.

'We're going to Jimmy'z nightclub. Please come with us,' Jordan slurred to me.

Shit. So much for taking it easy. But there was no way I could say no. Jimmy'z was a famous club where the drinks were notoriously expensive. It was as cheesy as hell but it was where all the celebs piled in, flashing their wads of euros and trying to outdo each other by showering the dance floor with vintage champagne.

I left with my new friends – but not before Youngy took a photo of me with Jordan – and got into a taxi with them. Dwight got into the passenger seat in the front while I squeezed into the back with Jordan, Eddie Jordan and a friend of his. It didn't take long for the model to wriggle her way on to Eddie's lap, and she giggled as he pulled her top down to make a closer examination of those famous boobs.

'I'm going to do *Playboy* in two months' time. I can't wait,' she trilled.

We soon arrived at the club. We fell out of the car and pushed our way to the front of the queue, and went inside. I followed the others to the bar and Dwight unrolled a thick wedge of banknotes and bought us all glasses of wine. He looked relieved that someone was keeping Jordan company so he could go sharking around the club with a couple of dodgy-looking mates. Jordan and I watched him as he wandered off with them.

'Look over there. He's chatting up some girl. I think he wants to have sex with her. Where are they going? Can you see him? Come on, let's find him.' She sounded panicked.

How could anyone possibly think the life of a glamour model was fun? Going out with a footballer – one with such a playboy reputation as Dwight's – was hardly a laugh a minute, I could see. Jordan spent most of her time worrying about what he was up to. And for good reason. I was mortified for her, as he was blatantly trying to pull other girls in front of her.

She seemed to be in a state of paranoia the entire time. And when she wasn't asking me where he was and what he was up to, Jordan was divulging deeply personal aspects of her doomed relationship. I had just met her that night, and I was a tabloid reporter! She was too trusting by far, and I was already feeling pangs of guilt for what I was going to have to write up about her in the newspaper. But this was my job.

'Maybe he's jealous of me and that *ER* bloke?' she asked hopefully, sloshing white wine down my front.

'Um, I don't think he saw you talking. You know, I'd say the same to any of my mates at home . . . why the hell are you going out with someone who makes you so desperately insecure?' I asked.

She peered at me and didn't reply. She didn't seem to know what to say.

I spent the next two hours being dragged around the club by Jordan, chasing after Dwight and trying to catch him out. By 3am I was drunk and exhausted. An evening on Planet Jordan had knackered me, and I wanted out. I had enough to write about by now. But it wasn't about to end yet.

I was standing by the bar, watching the Euro-types dance badly, when I became aware of someone sliding up to me.

'Do you like black men?'

It was the first question Dwight had asked me all night, apart from whether I fancied another drink.

'I beg your pardon?' I replied. Jordan was standing nearby, busy picking at her split ends.

'I have a friend I'd like you to meet. He's around here somewhere,' he said, scanning the packed dance floor.

'What for?' I had a horrible feeling Dwight wanted to set me up with one of his slimy mates. I may have been privately lamenting my single status earlier that day, but this really wasn't what I had in mind.

Dwight leant in. 'How would you like a threesome with me and my mate? We are going to a party on a yacht now. Come with us. I promise that you'll really enjoy yourself.' He smirked, a lecherous grin spreading across his face.

'Oh, I promise you I really would enjoy impaling myself on my biro more,' I almost said. But I didn't. I was sickened but I also knew I had to keep him talking further to get more mileage out of what had rapidly changed from a couple of lines about Jordan and Dwight's dysfunctional relationship to a much bigger story.

Jordan was still standing there and amazingly hadn't slapped Dwight round his ugly mug. Not only had he propositioned another girl in front of her, but he knew I was a tabloid journalist. The guy was even more of a simpleton than he looked.

So much for sisterly solidarity. Playing with one of her rats'-tail hair extensions, my new best friend chipped in, 'Ooh, did you hear that? Come on. Come with us to the boat. Don't leave me on my own.'

'Oh no, I'd better not. I'm fine thank you,' I told them, as if I was turning down the offer of a slice of cake at a vicar's tea party.

Dwight shrugged his shoulders and looked pityingly at me as if I'd just turned down *the* most sensational sexual encounter of my life. I wanted to bolt out of there, but I pretended to be nonplussed by the situation. Deep down I was disgusted. How on earth could Jordan bear to get into bed with this man every night?

Dwight located his mate – who was every bit the minger I had expected him to be – and we all left the club.

'Are you sure you don't want to come?' Jordan asked as she got into a car. Dwight hung back, and we watched as he started trying to persuade a blonde girl to join them. Jordan looked distinctly unimpressed.

'Please come with us. I think he wants to have sex with her,' she implored.

'No, really, I best be going,' I said, moving away. I waved goodbye and hailed a taxi. As I got in, I heard Jordan shout out at me as her car screeched past.

'It's my birthday tomorrow, so promise me you'll hang out. I want a mad one. Come on!'

It wasn't going to be the last I saw of Jordan, then.

I sat in the back seat of the taxi as it whisked me through the empty, quiet streets of Monte Carlo to my hotel, still reeling from the shock of what had taken place. Had all this really just happened? Back in my room and before I could even think about passing out, I rustled around in my handbag for my soft-covered red notebook and scribbled down everything that had gone on. I read back the words on the page. Piers, Richard and Kevin had wanted me to do an entire column from the Laureus World Sports Awards, and I certainly had enough to fill the page. And it even involved a sports star.

I chucked my clothes on to the floor, got into my pyjamas and crawled into bed, my head still spinning with the prospect of what would have happened if I had taken Dwight up on his offer.

★

I woke up at 9am, an hour ahead of London. Feeling super-keen I rang up Richard's direct line, knowing he'd be at work early. Since he'd become head of news he came into the office even earlier than he did before.

'Hi, Richard, how are you? It's Jess here,' I said brightly down the phone, trying not to sound as if I'd just woken up and was hungover.

'Ah, Callan. How's it going in Monte Carlo? You drawn a sober breath there yet? Got any scoops for your Uncle Dicky? Your Daley Thompson piece went in today.'

'Well, actually, you'll never guess what happened last night,' I told him.

'Oh, fucking hell, what sordidness have you been up to?' he laughed.

'I didn't do anything, I promise! I turned them down,' I replied.

'What? Turned who down? Tell me!' he said, sounding serious all of a sudden.

'Well, I ended up hanging out with Jordan and Dwight Yorke last night. She told me how he shags around and treats her with such little respect. He really is an absolute disgrace. Then she kissed that actor Eriq La Salle from *ER*, and got felt up by F1 boss Eddie Jordan in the back of a car on the way to Jimmy'z nightclub. And then Dwight asked me to join him and a mate for a threesome on a yacht. Anyway, of course I said no. But I thought it would make a funny lead in the column. I've got more than enough to fill up the entire column tomorrow,' I explained, hardly stopping for breath.

There was a silence.

'Hello?' I asked, thinking we'd been cut off.

'Dwight fucking Yorke asked you to have an orgy with him and a mate on a yacht in Monte Carlo? Fuck me, Callan. Piers will fucking love this. He's been a bit down on the showbusiness department recently and has wanted one of you lot to come up with a juicy story. Right. Get writing. Every cough and spit, as usual. File it over to me as soon as you can. I'll tell Piers at conference at 11am and call you back.'

And with that he hung up.

Shit. I hadn't really expected that. I knew that Richard would think it was an amusing tale for the column, but it sounded like he had other, bigger plans for the story. And now I had to type it all out, and quick. I caught a glimpse of myself in the mirror. I was still in my pyjamas and hadn't even attempted to put in my contact lenses yet. I was so glad no one from the office could see me now; I was hardly the epitome of a glam gossip columnist. I jumped into the shower, dressed, grabbed my notebook and got into the lift.

Embarrassingly, I must have been the only journalist at the event not to have a laptop with me. The *Mirror* laptops tended to be quite old and slow, but now I really regretted not having borrowed one. I had to get to the media centre straight away, bash the story out and email it over. There was no time to read it to a copytaker. It was only a five-minute walk, but I ran all the way as I didn't want to waste any more time.

'So, how was last night? I saw you hanging around with Dwight Yorke and Jordan. I take it you've got a hot scoop. You know the rules. Don't forget to mention Laureus in the piece, please.' Toby was manning the media centre, looking marginally less frazzled than he had the night before. Maybe it was because the stroppy photographers were still in bed.

'Er, yeah, it was a bit of a mad one. I've got to file it all over now. Is there a spare computer?' I asked him.

'Sure.' He led me to the media room, where there were several sports reporters silently tapping at computers. They really were a different breed from showbiz hacks, who seemed unable to keep quiet, especially when writing. 'A few of the other showbiz reporters saw you hanging out with Jordan and Dwight at the party and then at Jimmy'z, and are desperately trying to find out what story you've got. They know they'll be in for a bollocking from their showbiz editors if you've got a good one,' whispered Toby before he winked at me and walked off.

Bollocks. I hadn't even thought about the rest of the gang. I hadn't seen or spoken to any of them since the early part of yesterday evening. As much as they were wondering what story I had about Dwight and Jordan, I also began to worry that they might have all joined forces to get a story and not tell me. This was something that happened frequently when all the showbiz lot were covering the same event. If you were seen not playing the game, landing your own scoop and quite rightly refusing to let the others in on it, then they would sometimes gang up and share whatever stories they had with one another, deliberately freezing you out. Either way, everyone would end up getting a kicking from their bosses, as even if you were the one with the exclusive you would have missed out on a story that the other papers had.

I knew I had to do my own thing. Piers had always drummed it into us that hanging out with the rest of the press pack was lazy journalism. You had to work on your own and hunt your own exclusives down. That was the only way to operate if you wanted to make a name for yourself, he decreed. But I didn't like the idea of completely isolating myself from the others. Besides, I genuinely liked most of them.

On the other hand, I didn't want to screw up this great opportunity. If they wanted to bitch about me over their breakfast together on the poolside terrace of the Grand Hotel, then fine.

I started to type up every detail from the night before. Amazingly, given the vast amounts of champagne and white wine I'd consumed, I remembered everything. I had been warned by my dad – who'd spent years combining heavy drinking with reporting on parties for the various gossip columns he had worked on – that I had to remain sharp at all times, even if I was sloshed. I didn't want to end up some washed-up, bloated boozer with severe memory loss. So I began to train myself to stay in control. I soon realized that I behaved differently when I was drunk at a party I was covering for the column than when I was pissed and out with mates. When I was partying with pals, I tended to forget entire conversations. At awards ceremonies or premieres I often felt drunk – and I knew I certainly looked it whenever I drank red wine, staining my lips and teeth – but the day after I could recall everything that had happened. I guess when you know you have to stay focused, no matter how many cocktails you find yourself putting away, you do just that.

I sat staring at the computer screen and cringed at the part where I had written about Dwight Yorke asking if I liked black men. I hated to think what my mother would make of the whole saga. She was a no-nonsense New York-born news editor of the London bureau of NBC News, and covered serious news stories. I wasn't sure how much she'd approve of her daughter writing about footballers making bad passes, and not in the sporting sense.

My mobile rang.

''Ello. Is that Jessica? This is Dwight Yorke here. Do you fancy a threesome?' It was a man putting on a crap West Indian accent.

It had to be Richard back in the office, it was totally the type of thing he'd do.

'Ha bloody ha. Piss off, you unfunny twat,' I laughed.

'Morning. It's Piers here!' he said.

Oops.

'Oh, hi Piers. Sorry about that. I thought you were someone else.' Bollocks. I had just called the *Mirror* editor a twat.

'Absolutely love the story. This is just the sort of thing I want from 3am. We're splashing on it and giving you a double-page spread, so don't leave out one single detail. It's the awards ceremony tonight, isn't it?'

'Yes, Piers.'

'Well, make sure you get in with her. We're going to do Day Two of 3am girl Jessica Callan's extraordinary encounter with Jordan.'

'Actually it's her birthday today, so she asked me to hang out with her tonight after the ceremony,' I said.

'Fantastic, even better. Make sure you get more of the same, please. I'll pass you on to Dicky.'

Richard came on the phone. 'As you can hear, the editor loves it. We're drawing up two pages on it, so I want plenty of colour. What she was wearing, what you were all drinking, the time schedule of everything that happened. All of it. Email it to me. Piers wants to see it as soon as you send it over. Did you do pictures?' He was talking at warped speed.

'Yes. Richard Young took photos of me and Jordan at the party,' I replied, feeling a little dazed.

'Great. I'll tell the picture desk and they can get on to him. Come on, Callan. Get on with it. Call me when you've pinged it over,' he instructed, and hung up before I could answer him.

This story had really become a lot bigger than I had imagined. I went back to my story and finished off the evening's shenanigans. I also wrote up small stories I had picked up that night, such as socialite Tamara Beckwith's complaint that she had been mistaken for Jordan.

'As if! I'm smuggling grapes, for God's sake!' she had barked at anyone who was in her general vicinity in the VIP area.

I also wrote picture captions to go with the photos I had done with David Ginola, Michael Douglas and Catherine Zeta-Jones. I ended up taking the piss out of Michael's deafness and Catherine's strange new vocal chords.

I rang up Richard to tell him I had emailed everything over and was going to go back to the hotel to get ready for the awards ceremony, which was starting in a few hours' time. Walking back to the hotel, I thought my legs were going to buckle under me. I hadn't eaten or drunk anything all day, was suffering from a delayed hangover and had that exhausted feeling after a prolonged adrenaline surge has passed. I had a few hours to kill, so I got back to my hotel room and tried to have a nap. It was impossible because my mobile kept ringing. It was either the sub-editors at the office with queries about my article, Toby with details about the awards ceremony that night at a place called the Grimaldi Forum, or the other showbiz journalists trying to find out what story I had.

'Look, you know I can't tell you what it is. But it's highly unlikely you would have got the story. That's not an insult by the way. You'll see tomorrow when it's in the paper. But let's just say it helped that I'm a girl,' I explained to one reporter.

After failing to have any sort of power kip, I got changed for the awards ceremony. This time I made an effort: I put on a long, flowing black skirt slashed up to mid-thigh, a strappy black top and high heels. I was exhausted, and had no idea how I was going to get through another long night of drinking. But I just had to no matter what.

An hour later I arrived at the Grimaldi Forum. This time there were triple the number of photographers outside and more teams of security men. Everyone was even more dressed up than they had been the night before.

Toby had left me a press pass in the hotel lobby, so I flashed it at the doormen and waited inside where the rest of the reporters were standing around, watching to see who was arriving.

I didn't have a ticket to see the actual ceremony, but I wasn't bothered as there was a sports reporter from the *Mirror* there who would be covering the winners of the night specifically for the sports pages. My brief was to stick with Jordan again.

And there she was. Amidst the popping of hundreds of flash-bulbs, I saw the birthday girl. She hadn't got to grips with the stylish black-tie dress code at all. She was wearing pink satin hip-ster trousers, which were so low cut there didn't seem to be any room for knickers, and a cropped pink satin jacket with nothing underneath. She had matching bright pink lipstick on and was clinging to Dwight's arm. The tuxedo-clad soccer star was too busy beaming for the snappers to pay her any attention.

'Hi! Happy birthday!' I beamed at her when they had finished posing.

'Oh, hi! Thanks. We've got to sit through the ceremony now, but come and find me at the after-show party,' she said, winking at me.

I joined the other reporters at a bar nearby, where we could fill our time usefully while the ceremony was taking place. They all looked about as hungover, tired and stressed as I felt, and were hitting the booze. No one questioned me again about Jordan. I guess they didn't want to appear as if they were panicking about it. But the question was very much there, hanging in the air. Even the guys I got on with very well were acting differently, and were slightly offhand. I felt very uncomfortable. The only way to deal with it was to join everyone else with a glass of wine.

I was also worried about what would happen when the first edition of the paper came out in England. It would be on sale at various train stations from about 11pm onwards. The other newspapers would get copies of the *Mirror* too. What if one of the journalists out here got wind of my article and told Jordan that night what I had written about her? Jordan was much sweeter and more girlie than I had imagined, but I could sense that she could really turn on someone. I just knew she wouldn't take kindly to what she'd see as a treacherous act.

In my defence, I had been very careful in my description of her. Bearing in mind what had happened with Mel C, I had deliberately presented her in the most flattering light by writing about what a cad Dwight was. But I had the feeling that Jordan would not be best pleased with my regurgitations of every comment she had made to me about Dwight.

Finally the ceremony was over, so I made my way to the after-show party. I spotted Jordan and Dwight standing on their own, drink in hand and ignoring each other. She wasn't exactly hard to locate in that bright pink outfit.

'Hey there, how was the ceremony?' I asked.

She cheered up instantly. Oh no, I thought, please don't think I'm your best friend! How was I going to get through the night without feeling like the biggest two-faced cow in the world?

'Hiya! Oh, it was so boring. Will you come with me back to my hotel? I want to change outfits before we head out. We can meet Dwight and the other boys at the Sass Café,' she chirped.

I had two pages to fill. I looked her straight in the eye. 'Course I'll come with you,' I replied.

Once more Dwight just looked relieved that Jordan was off his back.

We got into one of the chauffeur-driven cars outside and were whisked back to Jordan and Dwight's hotel room. She let us into the suite and I braced myself for the worst. I didn't know what to expect and was worried it would look like some sort of S&M torture chamber. Instead I was struck by the amount of cuddly toys that were lying about, and the countless bottles of lotions and potions for her face and body. Well, at least I think they belonged to her. You never could tell with these meterosexual footballers.

'Sorry about the mess. Right, now, where's that catsuit?' she mused, picking up various items of skimpy clothes strewn about the room.

Catsuit? Oh, dear God. After scurrying around through several suitcases – she was only in Monte Carlo for two nights but had enough costume changes for a two-week holiday – she located the skintight costume.

'Here it is. Will you help zip me up? You do realize that every time I go to the toilet, you're going to have to come with me and squeeze me back into this? I can't do it on my own!' she laughed.

How had I become Jordan's personal dresser? She removed her underwear, while I took a sudden interest in one of the pink teddy bears.

'Dwight will love this. If I dance in this, my nipples will pop out!' She forced her skinny limbs into the silver catsuit while I continued to look at her teddy bears. ''Ere. Can you help me?'

Oh, sweet Jesus, I thought to myself. I turned to face her. There, in front of me, was a naked Jordan trying to force the zip of her catsuit past her crotch area.

'Um, why don't you get the zip as far up your body as you can before I try? I don't want to catch your flesh in it or anything,' I stammered.

The last thing I wanted to do was catch her pride and joys in a zipper. I really hoped the *Mirror* was insured if I punctured one of her implants.

'Oh, all right. I'll hold the sides as close together as I can and you zip it carefully round my boobs,' she explained.

Somehow she circumnavigated her nether regions, and then she tried to contain her breasts in the catsuit while I zipped her from her tummy button upwards as carefully as I would have zipped up a newborn baby in a Babygro.

'There we go. Let's hope I don't need to go to the loo for a while!' she giggled.

I stood there sweating badly. After she had applied another layer of make-up, we finally left the hotel and got another car to the Sass Café.

The café was a tiny bar with a few tables and enough room for a singer and a small band. It was packed with people in black tie who had come straight from the awards ceremony.

I followed Jordan to a table where Dwight was sitting with his Manchester United teammate Ryan Giggs and two other male pals.

'So, you're a 3am girl, are you?' Giggs enquired.

'Yes, I am,' I answered, trying to look as innocent as possible.

'Excellent. Which one are you then? Are you a good girl or a bad girl?'

'Oh, very good,' I assured him.

This was getting very weird again. I really hoped that I wasn't about to be propositioned again. Mind you, Ryan Giggs was a hundred times better looking than Dwight Yorke.

'In that case, come and sit down while they sort the champagne,' he said, and pulled a chair out for me.

Jordan had sat down next to Dwight and was busy necking drinks and rearranging her breasts in her catsuit. I had two glasses of champagne and sat there with increasing dread that any minute Jordan's or Dwight's mobiles would ring and they'd be told that I had done the dirty on them in the newspaper. I felt sick all over again, and this champagne wasn't helping. I still hadn't eaten that day, and I had thought hair of the dog might do the trick.

'Excuse me, I'll be back in a minute,' I said, and ran in the direction of the loo.

I burst into the ladies, locked myself in a cubicle and started to vomit.

Brilliant, I thought to myself, you've now peaked a little too early and the night has just begun. Once I had stopped retching I closed the toilet seat lid and sat on it. I put my clammy head in my sweaty hands. I felt appalling. I had survived on less sleep and much more alcohol before. Maybe my body couldn't take it any more. Not eating hadn't helped me, though. And the churning in my stomach was also due to my being terrified of being caught out and getting a smack in the face from Jordan.

Speak of the devil.

'Oi, where are you? I need to pee. Can you help me out of this?' squealed Jordan.

'Sure. Come in.' I flushed the loo and a pissed Jordan tottered in.

There we were, squeezed into the same toilet cubicle. She managed to wriggle out of the catsuit and had a pee while I looked determinedly the other way. I then found myself grappling with her boobs while trying to carefully zip them back into her outfit. This was definitely someone's idea of a fantasy, but it sure wasn't mine.

We walked back to the table and I turned down another glass of champagne. I would have been sick all over Jordan's outfit if I had taken so much as one sip.

'Let's go to Jimmy'z club. It's my birthday!' she suddenly shouted.

The others agreed. It had just gone midnight. When would this night end?

We jumped into another car and went the short distance to Jimmy'z. As I got out of the people carrier outside the club, my skirt flew open and I quickly held it down so no one could see my knickers.

'You're wearing red pants, aren't you?' leered Ryan. 'Dwight and I saw them.'

Oh, this was going to be hours of fun, I thought to myself.

We walked into Jimmy'z, which was even more packed than the night before. We were instantly steered to a table by the dance floor. Girls started flocking over. Footballers, no matter how ugly, certainly seemed to attract the ladies.

Rachel Hunter, who was shimmying away nearby in a full-length pink and black frock, began to dirty dance with Dwight. I didn't dare look at Jordan. I didn't have to.

'Can you believe Dwight is dancing like that in front of me? In front of his girlfriend! What a c***!' she screeched in my ear.

I fully expected Jordan to fly at Ms Hunter, and prepared myself to see the pair of them rolling around the dirty floor, tearing each other's hair out. Instead, the glamour girl sat watching the duo's suggestive dance routine, her eyes filling with tears.

'I think he's trying to pull her. He has so little respect for me. I can't believe he's behaving like this on my birthday.' She looked at me, wiping a tear away. 'He never shows me any affection. What's wrong with me? Why can't he be nice to me? Look at him. He's eyeing up girls and doesn't care about me. All I want is to be loved.'

I was so ashamed to be sitting there in that noisy, vile club filled with playboys, footballers and wannabe kiss-and-tell girls, trying to comfort Jordan. I felt awful that she didn't know yet that in tomorrow's copy of the *Mirror* I had gone into excruciating detail about her dysfunctional relationship with Dwight.

She asked me to accompany her to the ladies' and to be on zip duty again. As she squatted over the loo, she filled me in on what had happened the previous night with Dwight, his mate and the blonde girl Dwight had replaced me with.

'I ended up going back to the hotel. Dwight went on the yacht with that blonde girl. And you know what? He didn't come back until 11.30 in the morning. He didn't even have any sort of explanation or excuse. One day I'll just leave him. Then he'll regret it.'

There was no point explaining to her that I was sure he wouldn't care less if she dumped him or not. I was convinced her friends and family had probably told her countless times that he was a total shit to her. But she'd have to get there on her own.

We made our way back to the table, where Ryan Giggs was giving a piggyback to his ex-girlfriend, society girl Caroline Stanbury. His current girlfriend would have been thrilled if she'd been there, I thought to myself. Meanwhile, Jordan had a plan.

'I'm going to dance and see if Dwight notices me.'

She stood up and did some sexy moves.

'Is he looking?' she asked. To me she looked like a child performing a dance routine for her parents. Her boyfriend was still far too busy gyrating up against Rachel Hunter to notice anyone else.

I spent the next two hours reassuring Jordan that male clubbers there were indeed checking out her boobs. She seemed to need constant attention, but all she really wanted was a show of affection from Dwight. It was all so sad.

Come 5am I found myself on my hands and knees helping the then Chelsea soccer star Marcel Desailly look for his expensive watch, which he had dropped on the floor.

'So are you 'er sister?' he asked, pointing at Jordan.

It really was time to go. Besides, I had enough material to write a piece about Jordan's tragic birthday night out. 'Look, I'm knackered and I've got a flight back home in a few hours. I'm going to go,' I said to Jordan. 'I hope you had a good birthday. Will you be OK?'

'It's fine. I'll have a laugh no matter what. But do you want to know something? It's true what they say – all men are total bastards!' she giggled. She gave me her mobile number and told me to ring her the following week. I had a feeling she wouldn't be quite so friendly towards me if I ever dared call her.

It was getting light outside and I felt even more dreadful than I had earlier on in the night. Still, back in my hotel room I resolutely set my alarm for three hours later. I was going to have to write up the story of my second night on Planet Jordan before getting my plane back to Luton. I'd have to get through it no matter what.

The alarm went off after what seemed like a twenty-minute snooze. My eyes felt like someone had rubbed gravel into them.

I ran around my hotel room, picking up my crumpled clothes and chucking everything in my suitcase. After I'd packed I sat down on the bed and wrote down Dwight and Rachel Hunter's dance routine, Ryan Giggs's slimy chat-up lines and my experiences as Jordan's personal dresser. I rang Richard from the car on the way to Nice airport and told him about my evening. 'I've got a flight in two hours, so I'll file it from the airport,' I told him.

'No problem. Your story looks great in the paper today. Big picture of you and Jordan on the front page, and you've got two pages inside,' said Richard.

By the time I got to the airport I was frantic with worry that I'd bump into Jordan and Dwight. There was no doubting that they'd have heard about the article by now. I was sure Jordan would have no hesitation in making a scene.

I checked on to my flight and hid in a corner of the departures lounge, reading my story over my mobile to a copytaker. By the time I had finished I had ten minutes left before boarding, so I wandered to the gate, reassuring myself that Dwight and Jordan were unlikely to be on my EasyJet flight to Luton.

'That's her. That's the girl I was talking to at the party. She never said she was a journalist!' a man's voice barked in my direction.

I froze. It was Daley Thompson, dressed in yet another scruffy tracksuit and T-shirt. He was with someone who looked like his agent. And they both looked furious with me. I had completely forgotten about Daley and the story he had inadvertently given to me about dumping his girlfriend. I couldn't bear the thought of a confrontation with an apoplectic Olympic athlete in a crowded airport when I was this hungover, tired and already far too busy hiding from other probably livid celebrities. So I wimpishly blanked him, racing into the nearest ladies' loos. I hid in a cubicle for ten minutes, not daring to come out.

I finally got on to the plane and shut my eyes, relieved beyond all belief that I had managed to get out of Monte Carlo alive and unscathed.

No matter how glamorous the location I was sent to, I now realized that being a 3am girl was much harder work than I had ever imagined. As Piers was often to remind me, it really was the greatest job in the world. But it wasn't about swanning around at parties, all dressed up and swigging free champagne. Not for a minute did I feel like a guest at any of these parties. I was slogging away harder than ever before and felt like I wanted to sleep for a week.

There was a new development, though. I was now being recognized by celebs as a gossip columnist. This meant no more eavesdropping on stars in loos and in dark corners of clubs and parties. I was now learning on my feet about immersing myself in the story. What would happen next? Surely famous people would be too wary to talk to me in case I stitched them up in the way I had turned Jordan over? I wasn't friends with these people and nor did

I want to be, but if they refused to talk to me, how would I get any stories?

I'd just have to toughen up. I had to remind myself that Jordan had known exactly who I was, and if she was daft enough to reveal her innermost thoughts and paranoias to a gossip columnist, then she only had herself to blame. Besides, I reassured myself, I had been as kind about Jordan as I could in the articles. It was Dwight who I had made to look like the fool he was.

I landed at Luton and gasped when I saw the front page of the *Mirror* at a news-stand. Half of the splash was a picture of Jordan and I hugging. Alongside was a photo of Dwight Yorke and the headline 'Exclusive – What Dwight Yorke asked 3am's Jessica in front of his girlfriend Jordan: Do you fancy a threesome? Full hilarious encounter pages 12 & 13.'

I bought a copy and read it on the train as I headed home. Eva had rung me up from work that morning to tell me I had made the front page with my story. But actually seeing it in print was another thing. I felt a mixture of pride at having a front-page story and total humiliation at the tone of the piece. My mother rang me on my mobile to tell me she had bought ten copies to send my cousins in America.

'Are you sure that's a good idea? It's not like I've rumbled some big political scandal. I was asked to have a threesome!' I whispered down the phone on the train.

'Oh, don't be silly. It's great. You look lovely in the photo,' she said.

'Er, thanks. I think,' I replied.

I made my way back to my flat, where I got straight into bed.

The next day at work, I pushed away any remaining thoughts of guilt and was thrilled at that day's paper – my story was on the front page again, as well as the whole of page three. This was what it was all about.

'Well done on the Jordan and Dwight Yorke business,' said Piers when he strode down to our department after morning conference.

'Thank you, Piers,' I replied.

'I've had lots of phone calls about the threesome story from people, and I've been reassuring all of them that you did indeed join in. Don't try and claim otherwise. We all know you didn't make your excuses and leave,' he boomed with that foghorn voice, so that everyone in the office could hear. Naturally they all readily believed him. Just my luck.

Polly, Jay Kay and me

7. Racy Behaviour

'Don't you dare decide you're going to an event without talking to me first. You just thought you'd take the other pass without saying a word, did you? How would you like it if I'd done that to you?' We were on the Tube going to the *Tomb Raider* premiere in Leicester Square, and Eva was having words with Polly on the Northern Line.

The three of us had been invited to the British Grand Prix Ball that was taking place later that July, but there were only two VIP tickets for the actual race at Silverstone. I had spent a long time hitting the phones and had finally sorted out tickets with the PRs for two of the race sponsors, but they only had one spare pass each. I had taken one of them as I had put in a lot of work tracking the bloody things down. Polly then told me she wanted the second one as she knew a female racing telly presenter who'd be there with her PR and who was always a good source of stories.

I had told Eva that Polly had decreed she should have the second ticket. Eva wasn't that bothered about spending her Sunday at the car race – it meant spending Saturday night in the Holiday Inn in Milton Keynes, for a start – but she did object to the way Polly had failed to tell her about bagging the remaining ticket.

So Eva had decided to confront Polly about it that evening.

Despite Polly's reputation for having a bad temper, her bark was in fact far worse than her bite. Eva on the other hand could be very intimidating with her steely glare and frosty manner, and on this particular occasion she was scaring me shitless. I was glad I wasn't in Polly's shoes.

'Did you just think you could take the spare ticket and not mention it to me?' demanded Eva loudly in the packed tube carriage.

I was determined to stay out of this one. But it was difficult to pretend nothing was going on, as the train was packed and we were practically on top of each other. I still tried to look the other way.

'Look, Eva, I really don't want to fight about this. Please can we not argue?' pleaded Polly. 'I didn't know you wanted to go so much. I'm only going because Amanda and Ghislain will be there. But you can have it. I'm really sorry.'

Eva refused to answer her and we spent the rest of the journey in silence. To be honest, these kinds of spats were few and far between, and thankfully this one had blown over by the end of that night.

'I'm not really pissed off,' Eva whispered to me at the cinema. 'I just wanted her to know that it's not all right to go flouncing off with tickets without discussing it first. I did shut her up, didn't I?'

She sure had. Polly was always very careful with Eva from that point onwards.

Ten days later the three of us were getting ready in our hotel rooms in Stratford-upon-Avon. It was a Friday night and we had an hour to go before getting on a coach to take us to the grounds of Stowe School in Buckinghamshire – my old school – where the Grand Prix Ball was taking place.

'I just don't know what to wear. I hate everything,' I moaned to Eva, who was trying to help me sift through the pile of party clothes I had brought with me.

'I told you to limit yourself to one outfit. That way you'd have no choice but to wear it. You've got too much stuff here.' She shook her head at me.

Eva was looking stunning in a purple silk halter-neck dress. After going through a rapid change of four dresses, I finally plumped for my old favourite: a black strapless dress from Kookai. 'Ooh, what about these? Shall I wear them?' I held up a pair of cream stiletto heels from Gina that I had yet to wear. They were incredibly high. Perfect for wearing to a black-tie ball in a marquee.

'Oh, yeah. They're great. Can you walk in them though?' asked Eva.

I tottered around the room. 'Er, probably not for long, but I'll just pop them in my handbag later, like you do,' I replied. Eva always wore stunning but towering stilettos, and tended to take her shoes off halfway through the night at parties.

'Why don't you just wear something more comfortable then?' she asked.

'No way. I bought these recently and they are begging to be worn. Even if I cripple myself.'

'Great idea, mate. Just bring a big enough handbag.'

We finally left my hotel room and met Polly in the lobby. She was wearing a low-cut Catherine Walker black satin dress, which made her boobs burst out. I didn't blame her for having them on show. They were always a talking point for male celebrities, who could never keep their eyes off them.

Forty-five minutes later we pulled up at the grounds of Stowe.

'You went to school here? Are you kidding?' asked Eva incredulously.

It was a ridiculous place to allow schoolkids to run amok. A boy's boarding school with girls in the sixth form, Stowe was a former stately home set in 750 acres of landscaped gardens run by the National Trust. I had attended from 1991 to 1993 and had got my first taste of selling stories to the tabloids during that time. Looking back, I'm not overly proud of what I did. I was already so keen to become a tabloid reporter I regularly flogged tales about my classmates' activities to the papers.

I knew that the tabloids loved stories about posh kids behaving badly, so when two sixteen-year-olds in my year were caught romping in bed with each other, were subsequently expelled, and the entire sixth form protested by refusing to sing hymns in chapel that Sunday, I was eager to get the story into print.

I rang my father up – he was a writer on the *Daily Express* at that time – who passed the story on to an old friend of his at the *Sun*. The reporter rang up the school to get a statement from them. They confirmed the story and it ended up on page three. The headline, 'Psalms Like it Hot', ran alongside that day's topless model, with the school's Latin motto printed below it.

I kept my betrayal quiet. Unfortunately there was a boy in my year whose father was a journalist on the *Evening Standard*. Poor George got the blame, even though everyone knew my father was also a journalist. I guess I looked more innocent.

Arriving at the school grounds this time, there were of course no sixth-formers running around, just hundreds of guests in black tie drinking champagne on the south front lawn, where a gigantic marquee had been erected, overlooking the lakes and ancient temples in the gardens. We'd barely had time to get ourselves a drink when we were suddenly deafened by the sound of helicopters landing, heralding the arrival of the Grand Prix stars.

'Oh, look, it's Eddie Irvine. Isn't he tiny?' I hollered to Polly.

He was barely my height. I was amazed yet again by the number of celebrities who were vertically challenged. Were they *all* short arses?

We gathered around him to pose for a picture for the column and laughed as he explained how he would have loved to dance with us but wasn't really allowed to party two nights before the British Grand Prix.

'Hi, girls. Can I get some words from you about the Grand Prix for the show?' Beverley Turner, a presenter for ITV's Formula One coverage, was standing nearby with a TV crew, waving a microphone at us.

I was taken aback. Were we so well known that people wanted to interview us on terrestrial TV? I wasn't sure what to say. Polly had no such qualms. 'Why not?' she replied, walking confidently towards Beverley.

Eva and I followed behind her. As we waited for Beverley and the crew to start filming, I felt increasingly panic-stricken as I knew next to nothing about Formula One and didn't want to be filmed standing there like a dumbstruck idiot. So I thought the best policy was to answer Beverley's first question before Eva and Polly, and to say whatever came into my head first.

'So, girls, what do you think of the Grand Prix drivers?' Beverley asked us as the cameras started rolling.

I jumped in. 'Well, I'm just shocked by how short they all are.

If I'd have known, I would have come to the ball on my knees!'

There was a short stunned silence. Bollocks, why had I said that? I should have modelled myself on Eva's silent technique when it came to TV: less was definitely more. My inane comment ended up being screened on ITV as part of their 2001 British Grand Prix coverage that Sunday.

I put the interview behind me and decided to focus on what I did best – reporting on celebs behaving badly. I'd been told Jordan was going to be there, and was looking forward to seeing her again for some more scandalous stories. I'd got over my feelings of guilt and paranoia. She had of course read my two-part series about my experiences in Monte Carlo and predictably had fallen out with me, pretending she couldn't hear me when I called her a week later, and slagging me off to other journalists. Surely there would be fireworks if she saw me.

Several hours later we were in the thick of the raucous ball in the marquee. There were more than 500 people inside the mammoth construction, whose black ceiling was decorated with thousands of tiny lights to look like the night sky. Champagne, wine and any spirit you could have wished for were on tap, and 1970s disco legends Sister Sledge were providing the entertainment.

Unfortunately my favourite busty model had failed to show up. She was to have been seated at our table, but we were informed by Eddie Jordan at 10pm that her frock had failed to materialize at her hotel and she therefore couldn't make it.

It was all a bit dull without her. Former *Coronation Street* star Tracy Shaw was there, but the party-loving actress was on her best behaviour with her new husband by her side all night. Instead of whooping it up and making the most of the bar, as she used to do at these types of events, she instead regaled us with tales of how fantastic married life was. So much for any scandals we could write about in the column.

Polly, Eva and I decided the best course of action was to get into the spirit of things instead. We'd noticed that there were a few journalists from the Sunday papers there, and as it was a Friday we knew they would run any stories from the ball in their own columns before we could do so on the Monday. Any scandal we'd write about would be old news. So we had our photos taken with Tracy Shaw and Eddie Irvine, obtained quotes from them, and decided to enjoy ourselves.

A few hours after the dancing had started we'd really got stuck into the party. We'd met up with some friends of Polly's and were all dancing together. One of the blokes, Mark, drunkenly explained to me his instantly forgettable job in the City and then almost fell over on the dance floor. He was completely legless, but I was instantly smitten with him. We danced together. I sensibly refused to let him try to kiss me in the marquee as I felt it wasn't the done thing to be necking like a teen when I was meant to be working.

Everyone decided to call it a night at 2am. A coach was taking guests back to the hotel in Stratford, and Mark and I sat together, but when we got to our hotel I said goodnight to him. I let myself into my room. I was tired and looking forward to going to sleep. Mark hadn't booked a room and I assumed he would crash in the room of one of his mates. I got into my pyjamas and was about to nod off when I heard a knock on the door.

City Boy was swaying in my doorway. 'I can't find any of my mates. Can I sleep in here?' he announced, and before I had time to reply, he'd barged into my room and dived on to my bed.

I got in under the covers next to him. It didn't take long before a hand reached out, made contact with my arm and moved around to my front. 'Oi! What do you think you're doing?' I said sternly. But I'd hardly got the words out when I heard him begin to snore, and I subsequently passed out myself. We were both dead to the world.

I woke up to the trill of my phone ringing.

'All right, mate. How are you? I can't believe you didn't pull that bloke last night. You two were all over each other!' It was Eva.

At the same time I felt someone beside me, and saw to my amazement that Mark was in my bed. I had completely forgotten that he'd invited himself in. 'Er, I'll call you back,' I whispered groggily into the phone. I gave Mark a nudge. He looked as startled as I had felt when I realized we were in the same bed.

'Oh, hi. Good morning. Erm, so sorry about last night. Thanks for letting me stay. Can I use your bathroom?' he stuttered, making a dash for the loo.

He came out a minute later, got dressed, mumbled a goodbye and ran out of the room.

'Well, that went well. Another man, another failure to secure a phone number,' I thought to myself. I was getting good at this.

I dialled Eva's number.

'That guy was in your bed? So what the hell happened?' she asked.

'Nothing! He banged on the door late last night, barged in and passed out. He couldn't wait to do a runner when I woke him up just now.' I sighed.

'Oh well. I'm sure there'll be many more exciting guys at the Grand Prix tomorrow,' she said, trying to reassure me. 'Good luck. I'm off to get my train back to London. See ya!'

I packed my stuff and met Polly in the hotel lobby so we could check out and get to Milton Keynes, where we were staying the night.

I filled her in on my late-night guest.

'Jessica! I hope you're not going to see him again. I think he may have a girlfriend,' she scolded me.

'Oh God, really? I had no idea. Funnily enough he didn't get round to mentioning her. And why are you so shocked? Since when did you turn into Sister Straight-Laced? Nothing bloody happened anyway.'

That evening in Milton Keynes we sensibly opted for a quiet night in. We were both concerned that while we'd had a great time at the Grand Prix Ball, we were lacking in a lead story for Monday's column. We didn't know for sure which celebs would show up at the next day's races, but it was a daytime event and one that wasn't famous for stars behaving badly. I lay in my bed that night, trying not to panic too much. I didn't relish the abuse

Kevin would unleash on us if we came up with a crummy lead story. I prayed that someone would misbehave the next day.

'Blimey! Who'd have thought there'd be such a huge traffic jam of cars trying to get into Silverstone,' I exclaimed.

Polly gave me a withering look. The roads around Silverstone were backed up with racing fans eager to get the best spots around the track. I'd never seen anything like it before. I wasn't exactly the biggest racing fan in the world, but even I could appreciate the sense of excitement and anticipation in the air on this gloriously sunny day in mid-July.

After an hour of waiting in the queue, our taxi dropped us off and Polly and I searched for the gate we had been told to head for. We had guest passes allowing us to roam around in the VIP area. Youngy was away, so we were teaming up with one of the sports department's photographers. I filled him in on the sort of action shots we required for the column.

The race started, and Polly and I sat in one of the corporate bars to watch it on a screen. We were bang in the middle of the racetrack and all we could hear was the droning of the engines as the drivers looped round and round the track.

So far the only faces we'd recognized were the Duchess of York, who had already left in a helicopter, and Amanda Holden, who had told us she wanted to follow us for a new TV role. 'I'm playing a journalist who is involved in a honey trap and ruins someone's career. Not that you girls do anything like that, of course. I just thought that you would be great, as I need to play someone tough and hard-nosed and I would love to come and visit you at the *Mirror* and watch you at parties,' she said to Polly and I.

I couldn't work out whether she was being incredibly friendly to us or outrageously sarcastic.

'What are we going to do? There's literally no one here. How on earth can we spin Amanda Holden wanting to be a 3am girl into a lead story,' I asked Polly.

'We've got to find something quickly. I'm sure everyone will leave immediately after the race to try to beat the traffic.' Polly frowned.

We walked around the paddock area where the VIP corporate-sponsored bars were crammed with guests. But none of them were the sort of stars we'd write about in 3am. We did another circuit, on the hunt for someone up to no good. The race had just ended, and Mika Hakkinen had come in first. We had half an hour, if that, in which to fill that big blank space in the next day's column.

'Oh, I say. You two are far too buxom to be *Mirror* journalists.'

Polly and I stopped dead in our tracks.

'There is a God,' whispered Polly to me. Swaying on the path in front of us was an utterly inebriated Jay Kay.

We had met the singer a few times before. We knew he wasn't a big fan of the press, and especially not of photographers. After a few drinks and a bit of banter from the paparazzi, he had been known to lash out and find himself in the centre of tussles. Attempts to take on entire troops of snappers aside, he was a frisky fellow who had always bemoaned his lack of sex life since his split from Denise Van Outen.

He'd clearly had a few drinks during the afternoon. Unfortunately he had a group of friends and bodyguard-lookalikes round him, no doubt to keep him out of trouble. We'd have a few minutes, if that, to talk to him before he was whisked off out of harm's way.

Jay was in high spirits, that was for sure. Peering down our tops (at my non-existent cleavage and Polly's ample bosom), he grabbed us for a group hug, planting slightly damp smackers on our cheeks.

'So, what are your plans for the rest of the afternoon?' Polly asked, flirting with him.

'Get shagged,' he growled, hip thrusting in our direction. 'Why don't we have a glass of wine and go back for a tensome at mine? I can handle anything.' He'd obviously been watching *Austin Powers* for some tips with the ladies. 'Does the roar of the engines make you two feel frisky?' he leered, grabbing our hands. He made Polly hold up his right foot so he could retie his shoelaces. 'I want my kids to be like Jenson Button. I'll have 'em strapped to me in a car as soon as they're born,' he said, sounding serious for once. And then he was back to flirting outrageously. 'Look at those bodyguards. Aren't they hunky, girls? Do you want me to fix you up with them?' He couldn't stand still for a second. Before we could answer him a group of statuesque promotional models for a mobile phone company strutted past us. Clearly we weren't attractive enough to retain Jay's attention and he was off, trailing the leggy blondes before we had a chance to say goodbye.

There were some stars we could always depend on to behave in a mischievous manner. Jay Kay never disappointed over the years, and despite getting into grapples with members of the media, he was always happy to see us. He was never short of rollicking offers, which we never took him up on.

August came and went. It was always the quietest month of the year for us showbiz journalists, and we took indecently long lunches most days. But then 9/11 happened, and the whole world witnessed the life-changing events that were the terrorist plane attacks on America.

I had been in a bar in Canary Wharf that lunchtime with some former colleagues from the *Daily Telegraph*. Someone's mobile went, and a TV was switched on. We watched the live footage of the second plane ploughing into the South Tower of the World Trade Center in total shock. We then said goodbye to each other and raced back to our respective offices.

At the *Mirror* it was mayhem. News reporters and feature writers had been dispatched to attempt to board flights to America. All the phones were ringing off their hooks and news-desk bosses were barking orders at the anxious-faced writers still in the office, hunched over their computer screens. A team of production staff and reporters had been sent off to the nearby London City airport to jet to Glasgow, where the Scottish edition of the *Mirror* was based. That way, if Canary Wharf had to be evacuated, the newspaper could still be put together. Every TV set at the *Mirror* had been switched over to Sky News. The situation was changing every second, but the executives were firm and decisive with their orders. Piers had been off sick after a back operation, but made it into the office that day, determined to oversee the production of the paper.

Our little corner of the office was not included in the frenzy of adrenaline that was surging through the paper. We crowded around one of the televisions instead to watch the grim scenes unfold.

'Oh, shit. People are jumping out of windows,' groaned James.

We felt out of place in the office. Quite rightly the 3am pages had been cancelled the next day as every page in the paper was being devoted to the coverage of the most catastrophic terrorist attacks the world had ever seen.

Privately, I was very worried about my younger brother, Jamie, who was living in New York and working for CNN's financial news section. He worked down by the Twin Towers a couple of times a month and I prayed he hadn't been there that morning. It was impossible to get through to anyone in New York on the phone, so I rang my parents in London and we all reassured each other that Jamie was fine and was unlikely to have been near the World Trade Center. But as I put the phone down, I didn't feel reassured at all. We just didn't know for sure if Jamie was OK or what else would happen in New York that day.

A few hours later, after we had all witnessed the live, shocking and unexpected coverage of the towers collapsing, my phone started to ring. I heard my mother's breathless voice. 'What are you still doing at your desk? They're evacuating Canary Wharf. It's another target,' she urged.

'We haven't been told to go anywhere. I'm not leaving. I'll look like a total wimp. I don't want to go. There might be something I can help with,' I replied. There was no chance I'd want to leave the office at a time like this.

'Are you kidding me?' she asked.

'No, I'm bloody not. If your office were a target, you wouldn't leave, would you? It's your job to stay and help deliver the news, so that's what I'm doing.'

She didn't reply for a while. I knew she agreed with me. She was a journalist and knew what it was like. 'How are you going to get home? There are rumours they're going to shut the Tube down.'

'Oh, I don't know. I'll get a boat home. Who knows? Let me know if Jamie rings.' I hung up just as an announcement was made in the office that the American banks in our tower were being evacuated, as were many companies in Canary Wharf. The newspapers were staying. The secretaries in the office were told they were allowed to leave. No one else wanted to go. I didn't even dwell on the obvious thought that being based in Britain's highest office block, and one that was such a glaringly prominent landmark, right next to the London City airport flight path, made us all vulnerable.

My mother called again to say that Jamie was fine. Deadline came and went and we were instructed to go home.

'I think the column will be back in the paper the day after tomorrow,' said Kevin.

Chronicling celebrity tittle-tattle at a time like that had never seemed so pointless to me. Surely no one would care about who was snogging whom, who had thrown a strop trying to blag their way into a club and who was drunk and disorderly. I was deeply envious of the news reporters and feature writers who were writing about a historic – albeit horrifying – event.

After eventually getting home on an eerily silent Tube, I tried to go to sleep to the alarming sound of police helicopters sweeping over west London. It was going to be really difficult to write the column tomorrow and to pretend that it was business as usual. But if Piers wanted it then who was I to argue?

Nothing of note happened the rest of the week anyway. Premieres and launch parties were cancelled as it was deemed an inappropriate time for celebrities to saunter down the red carpet and pout for the cameras. We couldn't help but feel it was because no stars wanted to be seen having fun, drinking champagne and going on the pull at such an awful time. The organizers of such events also knew that the newspapers would be focusing on the aftermath of 9/11 instead of plastering their front pages with photos of celebrity bashes.

Piers rewrote his strategy for the paper. It had got an amazing reception following its coverage of the terrorist attacks, and he now really wanted to focus on serious news stories. He felt the readers had embraced the taste for those kinds of articles rather than just showbiz goss. Celebrities were being removed from the front page of the paper. For now.

A few weeks later showbiz land was back to normal, and Eva and I attended the premiere of the film *Mike Bassett: England Manager*, starring Ricky Tomlinson. Everyone wanted some light relief, and the screening in Leicester Square attracted some cheeky behaviour from the stars of the film. Keith Allen stole the show on the red carpet when he turned up in a rip-off of Liz Hurley's famous Versace safety-pin dress, complete with fake boobs.

The after-show party was at the Café de Paris. Apart from Keith, Ricky and a couple of Atomic Kitten girls, the bash was lacking in stars.

'What are we going to do? This has been the only decent party for a while and there's no one of much interest here,' I groaned to Eva. 'Mind you, Piers is still a little anti-showbiz at the moment anyway. Do you think he'll give a toss that Keith Allen is here in a dress? I doubt it.'

It was hard to judge the mood at work. I hoped Piers wasn't regretting the idea of 3am. Did we still have a place in his new serious paper? There was no point in dwelling on what lay ahead for us. We just had to get on with our job and do the best we could.

We stood at the bar, bored and desperately waiting for something to happen. It didn't take too long for us to perk up, as just then in strolled the Tottenham star and former England player Teddy Sheringham.

I'd never been a football fan. I did recognize him and vaguely recalled that he had played for Manchester United and had recently broken up with his fiancée. He'd also snogged my old pal Jordan during a break from his long-term girlfriend. But other than that I knew very little.

He walked up to the bar and I peered at him. He was all dimples, naughty grin and flirty eyes. He was gorgeous! I nudged Eva like a besotted schoolgirl. 'Oh my God! How cute is he? Who does he play for again?' I whispered to her.

'Are you having a laugh? You're such a numpty. That's Teddy Sheringham. He plays for Tottenham. Do you really have no clue?' She stared at me uncomprehendingly.

'Yes, I know who he is,' I hissed back. 'And I was pretty sure he's with Tottenham. I just wanted to double-check before I made a total prat of myself. Mind you, sometimes these footballers need a reality check now and again. It'll probably do him good if I ask him which team he's on.'

I had never come face to face with a good-looking footballer before, apart from David Beckham. I'd met the ex-England captain at the launch party for Police sunglasses in January. The bash was in a drafty warehouse in London, and he'd agreed to meet Eva, Polly and I. Any pretences we had of being cool around the footballer went straight out of the window when we met him. He was an hour late for the event, but when we were finally beckoned to the VIP area we were in a very forgiving mood.

Wearing a William Hunt black-and-white pinstripe suit and white polo neck, Becks was every bit as gorgeous in the flesh. He was also incredibly flirty. He stood there grinning at us, a cheeky, sparkly glint in his eyes, as we squabbled about who would stand next to him for the picture. It was every girl for herself. Polly and I forced our way either side of him, leaving Eva to stand next to me.

'Hi, girls, it's nice to meet you at last. I'm sorry I haven't been around when you've seen Victoria. I expect it's because I'm always up north,' he said with a smile.

OK, so his voice was strangely high-pitched, but with a face and body like that, who needed him to talk?

'Wow! Look at that watch!' I exclaimed, and reached out to grab his chunky platinum-and-diamond Cartier timepiece.

Eva sniggered. She knew what I was up to. Anything to touch his flesh.

'It's so heavy! How do you manage to keep it on your wrist all day long? It must weigh a ton!' I exclaimed. By now I was clutching on to his firm wrist, and not letting go. Becks giggled shyly and pretended that the watch was so heavy his arm was being pulled to the ground. We all laughed. I was still hanging on to his wrist for dear life.

'OK, thank you, girls. Time to go!' said Alan, his PR.

'Oh! But we haven't even started yet!' I exclaimed.

But Beckham – who was still grinning at us with those come-hither eyes – was on a strict time rota and was being moved on to the next reporter. She was from the *Daily Star* and was even more over-excited than me, fanning her beetroot-flushed face with the Police sunglasses press release. The tough, ball-breaking women of the tabloids had all crumbled in his presence without him saying more than three sentences to us. Pathetic.

I sidled over to say hello to Teddy Sheringham to see if I could get any gossip out of him. He wasn't a regular on the London party and premiere scene, and I had never seen him in Chinawhite or the Met Bar, both stomping grounds for the kiss 'n' tell brigade who made their fortunes from scoring with soccer stars. I assumed it wouldn't be long before he found himself in some sort of scandal that night with one of the many identikit busty, fake-tanned, faux blondes.

'Hi. Who are you?' he asked.

'Jessica.' I decided to leave out the bit about being a gossip columnist. I'd thought there was a possibility he might have recognized me from my near-threesome story, as it had come out when Dwight Yorke and Teddy were both still playing with Man U. But he didn't seem to have a clue that I was a hack, so I wasn't going to ruin his night by telling him I could potentially print everything he told me. 'Sorry for being extremely dense, but I know you're a footballer, I just don't know who you play for. I'm not really up on my sports,' I said innocently. I wasn't exactly lying. Until I had asked Eva, I had no idea which team he played for.

'It's refreshing to hear,' he said with a laugh. 'Let me get you a drink. So what do you do?'

At this point, I sometimes came clean with celebrities about what I did. There was always someone at a party who recognized me, Eva or Polly, so if I had lied, I knew I could easily be caught out. But this time I was reluctant. I found I had a pathetic crush on Teddy. He had such an incredibly disarming smile and lovely eyes, and I knew I was going bright crimson.

I glanced over to where Eva was standing. She was with his friend, who was blatantly trying to chat her up. Amazingly her ice queen act was thawing and she was giggling away. Making sure she couldn't hear me – as she'd have certainly choked on her Jack Daniel's and coke – I said to Teddy, 'I work for an American TV company based in London.'

Where on earth had that come from? I stood there with my alcohol-flushed cheeks glowing and a slightly leering smile spreading across my face, praying he wouldn't tell me that he knew I was a journalist and how sad I was for pretending otherwise because I clearly fancied him. But he just smiled. So I continued to witter on.

Half an hour later we were still chatting away by the bar. The party was emptying out, and Eva was still being hit on by Teddy's mate. It was time for me to fill her in on the situation.

'Will you excuse me?' I said.

I grabbed Eva by the shoulder. 'Come with me,' I hissed at her.

She followed me to the ladies. 'What on earth is going on there?' she asked, wide-eyed with curiosity.

I jumped up and down. 'I know I'm being a total sad arse, but I really, really fancy him. Fuck. A footballer. What's wrong with me? Have I learnt nothing from all those stories we run about what little weasels they all are?' I asked her.

'It's mad that he's chatting you up when he knows you're a 3am girl. How brave of him!'

I looked down, unable to look her in the eye. 'Er, not quite. I told him I work for a TV station.'

Eva opened her mouth to start reprimanding me.

'Don't start. Please,' I begged.

Eva started laughing. 'You what? You freak! What the hell did you do that for? Oh, God. You're not going to try and pull him.

Callan! Don't you dare go there! You're at a premiere. What are you going to do? Drag him out to the dance floor and hoover up his tonsils in full view of everyone? Oh no, I've got it. You're going to go back to his mock Tudor mansion in the middle of buttfuck nowhere and get papped by the snappers outside. Great idea, mate!'

She wasn't helping me come up with a plan of action, to say the least. I didn't respond.

'Oh, for God's sake. You're serious, aren't you? How the hell are you going to pull him?' She put her hands on her hips. 'Please be careful. I know Piers wants us to get involved with celebs for the column, but he doesn't want us to take it too far. He was only teasing when he scolded me for not going off with Robert De Niro after that BAFTA party when he chatted me up. He'd be horrified if you did anything with Teddy Sheringham. And anyway he's a Spurs player. Piers is an Arsenal fanatic, remember?'

'Yeah, I know that. How could I forget? All I'm doing is having a harmless flirt. I'm not an imbecile. I'm not going to latch on to Teddy like a randy Jack Russell and try to dry-hump his leg in public!' I laughed.

But I knew Eva had a point. What on earth was I thinking? I knew that Teddy was flirting with me. And he kept offering to go to the bar to top me up with drinks. He was definitely keen too. But there was no way I should consider dragging him to a dark corner of the Café de Paris and start misbehaving. No, that was far too unprofessional. I berated myself for even considering it.

Eva and I walked back down to the bar where Teddy and his mate were waiting for us.

'Can I have a word?' Teddy whispered in my ear.

'Sure.'

He led me by the hand to a dark corner of the club, gently took my head in his hands, smiled naughtily and softly kissed me on the lips.

Oops.

'Er, I don't think this is the best idea,' I said, pulling away from him, but only after a good five minutes of snogging the face off him. 'I really don't want the whole club to see me. I'm not that type of girl, you know.' Shit. Had I really just said that? What a cheesy line. Teddy didn't seem to care and moved his face close to me again, zooming in on my lips. 'No, no, really. Please don't. I'm not into public displays like this,' I said, desperately trying not to fall for his charms again.

It was a bit too late for that. Besides, he was a sensational kisser. But my worry that a camera flash would go off in my face surfaced in my mind. I pulled back from him again. 'Right. No. I'm being deadly serious now. I can't do this. Will you stop it?' I asked him.

'Fine. Let's go somewhere else then,' he said with a shrug.

'OK. I live in west London. Let's go there,' I chipped in immediately. So much for my 'I'm not that sort of girl' claim. I wasn't planning on sleeping with him. That would be far too much of a cliché. I just wanted to get away from the prying eyes of the other journalists at the party. Yes, journalists have huge double standards: while my job was to expose the private lives of everyone else, there was no way I wanted my own antics known about.

'Er, Eva. I'm going to go now,' I announced to her.

She eyed me up and down suspiciously. 'OK. I'll share a cab with you. I'll drop you off,' she replied.

We usually shared taxis from parties and I'd jump out at my flat near Gloucester Road Tube station while she continued to Battersea.

'Fit Footballer Boy is coming back with me,' I whispered to her, while Teddy was busy chatting to his buddy.

'What? What the hell are you doing?' she asked me, horrified.

'I've just snogged him in the corner and I'm scared stiff that someone has seen. I'd rather get out of here. Don't worry, I'll get him to leave separately so he doesn't get photographed leaving with me,' I said.

Eva tried to stifle a giggle. 'I am going to tear you to shreds about this tomorrow. And the next day. And for ever more. Do you know what you're actually doing? You're taking a footballer home with you! Mate! Don't tell me we're not going to write about this in 3am!'

'No bloody chance. You can't tell anyone!' I instructed her, as Teddy walked over to us.

'Hi,' he said.

'Hi,' I responded.

'Hi,' he repeated.

Eva coughed.

'Right, so, um, Eva's going to drop me off at mine and you're more than welcome to pop along too. But best you meet us around the corner as I'm sure you don't want the paparazzi chasing you from this place, do you? We'll take the first road on the right and meet you there. Byee!' I beamed and headed for the stairs.

'You've got that one all worked out, haven't you, Footballer's Wife Girl?' screamed Eva as she chased after me. 'Ooh! You lurve Teddy Sheringham! Hee hee!'

'Oh, do shut it. I happen to know there's a road nearby that is very quiet where we can meet him. If we do get stalked by the snappers, you're with us too so it'll look like we're off for a jolly little threesome. And I won't be correcting anyone either!' I retorted triumphantly.

We got our coats from the cloakroom and walked out of the club, nodding hello to the paparazzi boys we knew who were waiting outside, cameras poised. I would sometimes help these guys out by telling them which celebs were still inside clubs and parties, and they in return would sell me stories they'd picked up off the doormen of the clubs they regularly waited outside. But on this occasion I wasn't feeling quite so helpful.

'There's no one left of any interest. I'd call it a night if I were you lot. We're off now as it's all a bit dreary in there,' I told them.

Eva and I walked slowly round the corner.

'Are you sure you know what you're doing?' Eva asked me, looking concerned.

'Yes, course I do. It's all a bit of a laugh. I'm not going to do anything too reckless,' I replied. But the sharp September night air had sobered me up slightly, and I began to wonder again whether Eva had a point. Before I could say anything, Teddy appeared from around the corner.

'Hi,' he said with a grin.

Any concerns I had about bringing not only a total stranger but also a famous footballer back to my flat disappeared instantly and lust took over. 'Right, let's go. We'll never get a proper taxi at this time of night in the West End, so let's get a dodgy minicab,' I announced.

We soon found a shifty-looking bloke with a beaten-up Ford Mondeo lurking nearby, and after haggling a price we all got into the back. Teddy sat between Eva and me. The illegal cabbie recognized Teddy, and the pair started to talk football. It all suddenly felt a bit too surreal, and I started to giggle. I looked out of the window to stop myself from exploding into full-blown hysterics. I could sense that Eva had the giggles too. We really were pathetic. It was just like that time we were trying not to laugh in the ladies' loo at the Tom Cruise premiere. Luckily Teddy ignored us and carried on talking to the driver.

I started panicking about being caught out again, and got the taxi driver to drop us halfway down my road, just in case he decided to ring up a newspaper and alert them to Teddy's latest pull.

'Bye. See you tomorrow,' I said quickly to Eva, and slammed the door before she could catch my eye, look at me disapprovingly and make me laugh. I didn't even have time to think about whether I had lied to Teddy, and said that Eva worked with me on my imaginary TV station too.

I opened the front door to my block of flats and tried to remember whether my flatmate, Nicola, had said she was around this week or abroad on business. I was pretty sure she was away. But then again, I couldn't be 100 per cent sure. Bugger. This could be embarrassing.

Our flat was on the top floor, so I led the way up our three huge staircases. I usually panted my way up – I no longer had time to go to the gym since joining 3am – but on this occasion I kept stopping and pretending to look for mystery objects in my bag so I could subtly catch my breath.

'Nearly there!' I exclaimed as we finally approached the flat. I leant against the door for support as I fiddled with my keys in the lock. What the hell was I doing? It was 2am and the reality of the situation was beginning to hit home. I suddenly prayed that Nicola would be in.

The door was double-locked. The flat was empty.

We walked in. I marched straight over to the small living room and turned on the main light, desperate to look like I wasn't going for the atmospheric lighting approach to get him in the mood.

'Do you want a drink?' I asked before he could pull me towards him on the sofa, where he had already made himself comfortable.

'Sure,' he said with a grin.

That sexy smile was beginning to unnerve me.

I darted into the kitchen. Nicola had installed optics in there, so we had vodka, gin, whisky and rum literally on tap. While I was looking for a bottle of tonic I was hit by a worrying thought. I had a habit of chucking the contents of the various bags I used for work on the floor by the bookshelf in our living room. The pile consisted mostly of tissues, old biros, used notebooks and also – oh dear – my business cards with the *Mirror*'s logo printed all over them.

Shit. What if Teddy saw? Deeply unimpressed wouldn't even begin to sum it up. He'd probably think I had cameras hidden in my flat and that I was planning on stitching him up. I had created a web of lies because I was too embarrassed to say I worked for 3am in case he ran a mile from me. What had seemed like a good idea was in reality spiralling out of control. Things had suddenly taken a turn for the serious. Why hadn't I just left it at the snog in the club?

I was about to race back into the living room to casually throw some cushions on to my pile of mess on the floor when Teddy appeared in the kitchen.

'I'm just trying to find some ice,' I said, laughing nervously, opening the freezer door and rummaging around.

He didn't say a word but came towards me and started to kiss me again. Oh sod it, I thought. He can't possibly rumble me if he's busy snogging the face off me. I'll just have to keep him in the kitchen. There was no way I was going to let him into my bedroom anyway as it was the size of a broom cupboard and I knew for sure there was a pile of business cards next to the bed.

Just then, he put his hand up my skirt, and I totally panicked. The thought struck me again that I had a total stranger in my flat. I was well aware that some footballers had bad reputations, and although Teddy had been nothing but pleasant and totally unsleazy, I suddenly felt very uncomfortable having him there, particularly as I'd had to lie to him as well. It was time to come clean and see what his reaction would be.

'Um, I've got something to tell you,' I said after removing his hand and pulling away from him. 'Firstly, I've got my period.'

He looked instantly appalled.

'And secondly I need to tell you what I really do for a living.'

He looked utterly freaked out. I suddenly realized how that must have sounded. He probably thought I was about to confess to being a prostitute.

'Oh shit, that sounds terrible. It's nothing bad. Well, you may not be too thrilled. Oops. That makes me sound awful,' I gabbled nervously.

He had now backed away from me by a few inches and was no longer grinning at me sexily. In fact, he wasn't smiling at all, and actually looked like he wanted to be sick. Oh, great.

'Um, well, I'm a journalist. But I'm not going to write about you. I just didn't think you would have wanted to kiss a reporter,' I said, trying to explain.

'Who do you work for?' he quietly asked. He was not looking amused by my confession.

'The *Mirror,*' I replied.

'Oh, God. You're not one of those three girls are you?' He backed away further and moved towards the kitchen door.

'Er, well, yes, I do work with two other girls. The column is called 3am. But I'm not going to put this in the paper,' I tried to reassure him.

He'd heard enough. 'Right, I'd better be going,' he said to me over his shoulder as he bolted out of my kitchen and headed towards the front door of the flat.

What was he doing? He had recoiled from me in horror as if I had just stripped off my skin to reveal I was actually a flesh-eating alien. Surely he didn't have to leave this second?

'Don't you want me to call you a taxi?' I asked as I followed him.

'No. I'll get one in the street,' he shouted back, trying desperately to open my front door before I could get to him. I was running towards him now in my haste to explain myself. What on earth did he think I was going to do? Force him to stay and take compromising pictures?

The door swung open after he'd grappled with the latch, and I trailed after him as he legged it out and raced down the stairs, even jumping down the last few.

'Are you sure you don't want me to call the local cab firm? It's no bother!' I shouted over my banisters. But he was in no mood to even answer in his rush to get away from me. Anyone would have thought I had just owned up to having taught Hannibal Lecter everything he knew about the best way to serve up a human.

I heard the front door to my block of flats slam shut. I walked back into my flat and headed for my bedroom. I sat on the bed and started laughing.

Eva was going to love this. It was bad enough snogging a footballer in the corner of a party when I was supposed to be working, but then chasing after him as he desperately tried to get away from me was even more embarrassing. My first celebrity kiss, and he had run away from me. What a catch I was.

My alarm went off at 8am and my first thought was how relieved I felt that I had confessed all to Teddy. I couldn't imagine anything worse than waking up hungover next to him, and with hazy recollections of our night together.

I arrived at work at 10am and was surprised to see Eva already at her desk. She usually had time-keeping problems, which would earn her a bollocking from Kevin. But today she had made an extra-special effort to come in on time.

'So? How are you today?' she asked, cool as a cucumber. She

wanted to torture me nice and slowly in front of everyone else in the department.

'Fine, thank you, Eva. How are you?' I replied, trying to sound casual but ending up sounding strained and overpolite.

'Oh, really? So you got any stories from last night? For the column?' Eva's eyebrows were raised so high, they looked painted on. She was determined to wind me up. Thankfully, no one else seemed to notice that we were both acting oddly with each other.

'Oh, you were there, mate. You know how boring it was.' I sighed as I logged on to my email.

A few seconds later I had a message from Eva in my Inbox. 'So what the hell happened? Tell me all. Don't be so cagey.'

'Stop trying to embarrass me! You know it won't be long before someone picks up on your bizarre line of questioning. And I'm not going to email you what happened,' I wrote back to her.

I watched Eva as she read my email. She then got up from her chair, walked past me with a look of mock innocence and headed for the ladies' loo. Everyone in the department was still too busy checking their emails and voicemail messages and going through their notebooks to notice that Eva and I were being weird. I got up and followed her to the loo.

'So, come on then! What happened, Footballer's Wife wannabe?' Eva was standing by the sinks in the ladies, ready for gossip.

'Shh! Eva, shut up! Someone's going to hear!' I urged as I checked all the cubicles to ensure we were alone.

'Oh, stop being so paranoid. There's no one in here. Did you shag him?' she asked, getting straight to the point.

'No, I bloody didn't. He got as far as putting his hand up my skirt and I freaked out and told him I was a journalist. Then it was his turn to freak out,' I whispered, still anxious that someone could hear us.

'What?' she asked, laughing at me.

I told her what had happened once we'd arrived at my flat.

'Oh, mate, that's brilliant. I bet he couldn't wait to get away from you! Why did you tell him you were a journalist?'

'Because I didn't want to sleep with him and thought it was the right thing to do. Oh, I don't bloody know. I thought it was better coming from me than if he saw a 3am business card on the floor. I mean, shit, I'm not that bad, am I? He actually bolted from my flat. I even chased after him as he made for the front door, to ask him if he wanted to wait while I booked him a cab. He must think I'm some sort of stalker,' I moaned.

Eva shook her head. 'Forget him. You'll never see him again, so what do you care?' she replied.

But I did care. It hadn't done wonders for my ego. In the space of three months two men had snogged me and then couldn't wait to run away from me. It was so hard to meet decent blokes in this job. They were all married, slimy, gay or commitment-phobes. I was beginning to think that my love life was doomed while I was a 3am girl.

Eva looked at the expression on my face and snapped her fingers. 'Oh, stop it. Who wants a boyfriend anyway? We haven't got the time as it is. And there's no one out there at the moment worth chasing, so just have fun,' Eva instructed me, as we headed out of the loo and back to our desks.

'But maybe stay away from footballers in future,' she added.

Me, Bryony and Eva

8. More Bust-ups and Break-ups

I had overstepped the line: I had taken a celebrity home with me. OK, so he couldn't wait to escape once I had unveiled my true identity, and our little adventure had come to an abrupt end. But I had been truly unprofessional. No one at work knew about my humiliating indiscretion apart from Eva, and thankfully she hadn't breathed a word to anyone. However, I wasn't allowed to put the sorry incident behind me and move on. My best friends outside the journalism world took every opportunity they had to rip me to shreds about my celebrity fling.

A few weeks later Sheringham scored at the England versus Greece match.

'Teddy scores – and not for the first time' read a text I was sent by one of my mates, a TV lawyer called Sarah.

She didn't help matters by biking over a package to me at work one day soon after the Teddy incident. On the front of the padded envelope she had scrawled the message 'Do not open this without Eva next to you'.

I wasn't stupid enough to obey her instructions, which were no doubt planned to shame me further. Instead, I hid the envelope on my lap at my desk while I subtly tried to open it without anyone seeing. As we would each be sent at least two deliveries a day of CDs to review, press releases and strange gifts from PRs, no one took much notice.

Eva, however, had been sent an email from Sarah instructing her to hover by my desk when a package arrived for me that day. I didn't notice her pretending to fiddle with bits of paper nearby. A book slid out of the padded envelope on to my lap. I turned it over. It was a biography of Teddy Sheringham. On the front cover Sarah had drawn a bubble coming out of his mouth and had written inside it: 'A journo? A bloody journo? Get me a cab quick!'

'What's that, Jess? A book for us to write about in the column?' Eva asked, loudly enough for Polly to turn around in her chair to see what I was looking at.

'Er, no, nothing interesting like that. It's just a book I ordered for a friend of mine,' I stammered quickly, giving Eva a death stare.

'Ooh, let's have a look. Who's it about?' she asked, determined to wind me up even more. It was working. I really didn't want Polly or anyone else to notice I was getting so flustered.

'Oh, no one that you'd like to read about,' I replied, stuffing the book back into the envelope.

'But I might find it interesting. Let's have a look,' Eva said, trying to snatch it from me. I was still sitting at my desk and Eva was now standing over me. We tussled over the package like sisters fighting over an unopened Christmas present. 'Why are you acting so strangely, Jessica? I just want to have a look at the book,' Eva said, laughing.

'Give it back. You won't like it,' I said through gritted teeth.

She managed to wrestle it out of my hands.

'Honestly you two, what are you doing?' tutted an exasperated Polly.

'Nothing. Eva's being a nosy cow about something very dreary,' I replied.

Polly turned back to her computer, her eyes already glazed over with boredom at our schoolgirl behaviour.

'Oh, Jessica. A book on Teddy Sheringham. What have you got this for? I didn't have you down as a football fan,' Eva said theatrically while waving the book in front of my face. 'Didn't you meet him last week at that premiere?'

'Oh, shut up,' I snapped under my breath, getting up from my chair and snatching the book back.

'Ooh. Touchy girl!' she sang back, laughing while she walked back to her desk. 'No need to be like that. I'm just a bit bored and wanted to see what you were reading.'

And so it went on. At any available opportunity, Eva would make references to my new interest in football.

It didn't help matters when Eva and I went to a party at the Atlantic Bar in Piccadilly a few weeks later and ran into the actor Ade, star of *Snatch* and *Casino Royale*. We had chatted to him at the party for *Mike Bassett: England Manager* before I'd met Sheringham later that night.

'So, Jessica. I hear you're a Tottenham fan these days,' Ade said with a straight face. I knew he and Teddy were mates as they had arrived together at the bash at the Café de Paris.

'What are you talking about?' I asked nonchalantly.

'You know exactly what I'm saying.' He laughed.

'No, no idea. I don't follow any football team.'

Why didn't I just shut up instead of making it worse, I thought to myself.

'Oh, really. That's not what I hear. Or what I saw. You looked like you were really enjoying yourself in that corner at the party,' said Ade.

I didn't have time to think of a great excuse. Instead, I pointed to the door of the club. 'Look who's just arrived!' I exclaimed, and ran off.

Clearly it wasn't the most intelligent response, but Ade had caught me off guard. I had no idea that anyone had spied me kissing Teddy at the party. I had panicked madly at the time that another gossip columnist had seen us, but I had no idea a celebrity had witnessed the act. Shit. This was the last thing I needed. Especially since they were friends and Teddy *must* have filled Ade in on the whole tragic tale.

I spent the next few weeks worrying about the story leaking out and ending up in a media gossip column. I may have enjoyed baiting celebs about their love lives in our paper, but the possibility of information about my own life coming out made me feel sick with fear. I was fully aware of the double standards I was living by. But that was gossip columnists for you. I felt genuine shock and outrage whenever I heard rumblings about myself on the journalists' grapevine. 'Don't they have anything better to talk about?' was a phrase Eva, Polly and I – and other gossip columnists – would frequently utter when stories came back to us. I realized how ludicrous I sounded when I complained about others gossiping about me, but I really was that oversensitive.

Luckily distraction came in the unlikely forms of Chris Moyles and Gordon Ramsay.

Since Moyles had bitched about our looks when we had first launched the column, we had ignored his taunts, which were fairly regular. He seemed to take an active, personal dislike to us. I'd no idea why.

'I opened the column and just thought it was crap. There was a story about Ronnie Wood's daughter and Mel B's sister and you think, "if you can't get any decent celebrities then don't bother",' he once claimed in an interview with *Heat* magazine.

That autumn Moyles upped the ante and told his listeners to ring us up with spoof items for our surveillance section. We collectively decided the time was right to start laying into him, having ignored him for the past year. So we printed his email and direct line at Radio 1 in the column and invited our readers to tell him what they thought about his show.

The next day we tuned into his afternoon show and heard him encourage his listeners to ring the phone number we printed in the column every day to share their innermost feelings about us. The phone extension we used for readers' stories was a useful source of material. But Moyles's Radio 1 listeners soon brought the phone line crashing down. We had to take it off the hook as it was ringing constantly with people hollering obscenities at us.

Kevin was particularly appalled. 'That fat slob is now messing with the day-to-day business of getting the column out. Fuck knows what stories we've missed out on since we've had to take the 3am hotline phone off the hook. Right, he's fucking in for it now,' he sneered.

It had been a year or so since our last proper celebrity spat with the Spice Girls, so we all relished the chance to take on Moyles, who appeared to be a very angry man indeed.

We retaliated by printing the direct line of Moyles's boss, Andy Parfitt, the controller of Radio 1, so that 3am readers could tell him what they thought of the DJ. Moyles continued to read out our phone number on air the next day.

'Right. Now let's teach him what happens when he continues to be an arse,' Kevin announced to us the next day at work. 'I want someone to get me Lard Boy's home phone number.'

With the help of an agency I used to track down information on people, I soon got hold of Moyles's home number and emailed it to Kevin. He couldn't sit still in his seat, he was so excited by the prospect of what we were about to do to the self-styled saviour of Radio 1.

'What have you got in mind, Kev?' asked Eva.

'Right. I'm going to dictate it to you. We'll keep it short. But fuck me, he'll have a fucking heart attack when he reads this in tomorrow's column,' he cackled.

I didn't have any sympathy for Moyles, who apparently had received a massive bollocking from Andy Parfitt. He had even been forced to announce on air that the escalating feud was over. But knowing Kevin, the argument was about to take a turn for the even more evil.

'"It's over," said lard bucket DJ Chris Moyles yesterday as he attempted to end his feud with 3am. Well, tubby, it ain't over till the fat boy weeps. If you couldn't get through to his boss Andy Parfitt yesterday, why not try Chris at home on 0207 XXX XXXX. Still laughing, fatso?' Kevin dictated to Eva, who sat typing it up at her computer.

'Bloody hell.' Eva laughed nervously. 'Are you sure about this?'

'Course I'm sure. Don't say you feel sorry for the fat twat,' Kevin exclaimed. 'He deserves everything he fucking gets. Let's see if he's sorry now. I think you'll find he won't be mentioning you lot on air again.'

'Shit. He's going to lose the plot. What do you think he'll do back to us?' I said to Eva and Polly.

We sat at our desks in silence. Polly started laughing.

'Oh, it is funny though. Just imagine the look on his face when he starts to get lunatics screaming down the phone at him and then realizes what we've done. I think Kevin's right. I think he'll stop after that,' she said. 'There's no way he'll continue to bait us after this. The last thing he wants is a hate campaign, especially as he's already had a bollocking from his boss.'

Polly was right. The worst he could do was read our home numbers out on air. I didn't even have a landline at my flat. And my mobile was a company phone, so I didn't really care if he read that out.

We ran the article the next day. Later Kevin rang up the head of press at Radio 1 to pass on another message to the DJ. As Kevin had predicted, Moylesy had been inundated at home with calls from our readers taking the piss out of him. He'd taken the phone off the hook and had arranged for his number to be changed. 'You just tell Moyles that we'll stop if he stops,' Kevin snapped down the phone to the Radio 1 PR. 'But if he says one more thing about the girls, then we'll print his parents' home phone number. See what he says about that.'

'Kev! Isn't that a bit OTT?' I exclaimed when he triumphantly hung the phone up.

'No, it bloody isn't! He loves his mum and dad and the last thing he'll want is for them to be harassed. He won't dare mention you guys ever again. He's just being a bully and this is the only way to deal with his sort.'

The message was relayed to Moyles, who went apoplectic. It filtered back to us that he was furious we were planning to bring his parents into our ridiculous fight. We weren't though. It was just an empty threat, and we had no intention of actually going that far.

I was worried we had let things get out of hand by responding to Moyles's bullying in kind. And anyway, it all seemed a bit self-indulgent. Did our readers actually care?

Piers had always encouraged us to wage campaigns against celebrities if they were misbehaving, but we did have to be careful about who we targeted. In 2001 Gordon Ramsay may have been a darling of the restaurant world, but the irascible chef was not yet the potty-mouthed international TV star that he is today.

He was about to open his phenomenal restaurant at Claridges. Someone had told us that he had been spotted at the West End club Attica getting smoochy with a mystery blonde, so we ran a story about the craggy-faced chef.

Our story did not go down well with our editor at all. The day we ran the story, a furious Piers strode down the office to our desks. 'For fuck's sake, girls, what is this story you've run today?' he huffed at us.

We all looked up from our desks, shocked and taken aback by his reaction.

'What do you mean? It's about Gordon Ramsay snogging some bird in Attica,' replied Eva.

'Yes, I know what it bloody says. But what are you up to? Gordon's a mate of mine. He's not best pleased about this. It's not true at all. OK?' Without waiting for our response, Piers turned back to his office and marched off. Everyone sitting nearby tried not to stare too hard at us.

I felt well and truly stung by his outburst. 'Bloody hell. That's charming, isn't it? Just because Gordon Ramsay says it's not true doesn't mean we got it wrong. Course he'd say that. Anyway, how are we meant to know he's a mate of Piers? We're going to have to write up a list of his friends so we don't run anything on them,' I said to Eva and Polly.

I turned back to my computer and typed Gordon Ramsay's name into the cuttings library, which had every article published by a British newspaper since 1987. It was a reference tool we used every day. 'Oh, shit. No wonder he's blown a gasket. Ramsay's wife is pregnant. She must have gone mad at him when she saw our story.' I turned my computer screen round so Polly could see the article.

'Ahh. Right. Well, no wonder. He doesn't seem the cheating type anyway,' said Polly.

A few weeks later a PR informed me that Ramsay had banned me from attending his book launch at the Groucho Club later that week, even though I'd received an invitation. I thought this was ridiculous, particularly since Ramsay had publicly declared our story was untrue.

Strangely, during a radio interview to publicize the cookbook a couple of days after my conversation with his PR, he announced he was dedicating his new recipe for Bakewell tarts to us. He explained that the 3am pudding was just like Polly, Eva and I: 'sweet and gooey on the inside and hard on the outside'. We were wildly flattered but also a little perplexed: was that good or bad? Were we still enemies or were we friends?

A few days later I received a call from Ramsay's aides to inform me the ban had been lifted and I could attend his party. Kevin ordered me to go and make amends. I worried Gordon would still be furious, regardless of the new truce. I wandered over to Eva's desk to have a moan. 'This could well turn out to be a total horror show,' I said.

'Yeah, well, good luck! And remember, we have to suck up to him now that we know he's on Piers's Christmas card list,' Eva reminded me.

'Great! So he could assault me with a tray of foie gras canapés and I would still have to write nice things about him.'

Both Polly and Eva refused to come with me to the party, so I left the office alone, slightly fearful about what Gordon Ramsay had in mind to get back at me. Stomping towards Canary Wharf Tube station, I dreaded my punishment. It was so unfair. It hadn't even been my story in the first place. But who wanted to hear that? If I even tried to explain to a grouchy Gordon that the snogging story had nothing to do with me, he'd probably want to introduce my face to a vol-au-vent.

I boarded the packed train for the journey into Soho in a grump. I was pissed off that Eva and Polly wouldn't come with me. I definitely would have shown them support by going with them, had they needed me. Before I'd left the office Kevin had instructed me to have a photo taken with the culinary wizard and write a glowing piece about him as amends for our article. What if he refused? What if his heavily pregnant wife was there? She'd want to sling soufflés at me and all sorts. I didn't blame her. Bugger. Why was I the one having to face him alone?

After yet another painfully torturous Tube journey squashed up against stroppy commuters, I finally arrived at Piccadilly Circus. I took my time, walking slowly to Dean Street and the Groucho Club.

The party was in a private room. There was still a chance I didn't have to go: tabloid journalists weren't allowed into the club, and I was hoping I'd be turned away. Unfortunately the member of staff on the door found my name on the list, ticked it off and invited me upstairs to the party. Bollocks. There was no turning back now.

I entered the room. It was littered with copies of Gordon's new book, appropriately titled *Just Desserts*. I grabbed the nearest glass of champagne and lurked in a crowded corner, hoping I wouldn't be seen by Gordon or any of his team. Of course, I knew I couldn't hide from him all evening. I'd just have to get on with it.

I headed for the ladies' loo so I could regain my composure. I pushed the door open only to find Gordon's pregnant wife, Tana, washing her hands at the sink.

She glanced up and then gave me a look that utterly crushed me. It wasn't a look that said she wanted to put my head down the loo and flush it, more one that demanded to know how I could ever suggest her beloved man would do the dirty on her. She looked like she wanted to cry. I felt ashamed and turned away as she dried her hands.

I walked into a cubicle and locked the door, feeling like an utter wimp. I cursed myself for not saying anything to her, and felt like a total coward. Mind you, I didn't have the first clue about what to say and besides, I didn't want to upset a pregnant woman and have her weeping in the loo because of me.

I heard her leave and planned my own exit route. There was no way I was going to stay at the party now. Sod the photograph. I had upset Gordon's wife, who by now had no doubt told him I was there. I left the toilet and sneakily made my way towards the exit.

'Oh, look! It's a Bakewell tart!' Ramsay hollered, pointing at me.

I turned around, wishing the earth would swallow me up.

'Come here. Let's do a photo together to say all's forgiven,' he boomed, beckoning me to go over to him.

I prayed it wasn't a ruse and that he didn't have a towering trifle hidden somewhere to throw into my face. But he couldn't have been friendlier. So much for the caustic chef act.

'I'd love you girls to come to the launch of my new venture at Claridges,' he said, squeezing me around the waist as we posed for a photograph.

'Thanks. Yes, we'd love to come!' I replied, happy that he hadn't sworn at me in front of everyone in the room.

I headed straight for the door and left. Well, there was no point hanging around in case he had another change of heart.

We were never rude about Gordon again.

The autumn came to an end, but not without an important announcement in our department. Eva and I had noticed something was up with Polly around that time. She was more secretive than usual and wasn't spending as much time with us at parties. In fact, we hadn't hung out with her at the same party for quite some time.

One night in November after we'd finished the column and were hanging around our desks, waiting for the sub-editors to lay the column out so that we could proofread it, I overheard Polly ask Kevin if he could go for a quick drink with her. They packed their bags, grabbed their coats and off they went.

'What do you reckon that's all about?' I asked Eva. I got up from my chair and moved to Kevin's desk, which was opposite Eva, so we could talk a little more subtly about what was going on.

'She's been acting strangely lately. She's definitely up to something. Oh Christ, you don't think she's about to quit?' I said.

Eva stared at me wide-eyed. 'Do you think so?' she exclaimed. 'That would explain a lot. She's been keeping herself to herself even more than usual and has been very quiet in the office. Something's definitely about to happen around here. I'm sure Kevin will fill us in.'

Neither of us said anything else. I volunteered to stay behind and proofread the column so that Eva could have an early night.

It was 8pm and the office was almost empty. A few night-shift news reporters tapped away at stories at the newsroom desks, and four feature writers sat in silence behind their computers, finishing off articles. Everyone from the showbiz department had called it a day too and had either gone home or stopped off at one of the smoky and buzzing Canary Wharf bars to bitch about the bosses and moan about their wages.

Waiting for the subs to finish up, I picked up a scrapbook that we called 'The Book'. It had been lying there among sachets of soy sauce, indigestion tablets and taxi receipts, near Kevin's desk. Consisting mainly of photos taken at office parties or out on the job, it was put together by our department, and flicking through it always turned me into a giggling wreck. If I ever felt a bit down or wanted a quick five-minute distraction from a difficult story, I often turned to 'The Book'.

The photos were stuck in with cheeky, or in most cases downright coarse, captions scrawled underneath. Richard Wallace still liked to pop down occasionally to our end of the office to write something obscene about one of us alongside some terrible photo. For some reason he'd written countless comments about me looking like a lady boy. I never did understand Richard's obsession with this. I'd got off lightly though. Others were ripped to pieces about their mothers, fancying their dogs, denial of overuse of hair dye, being 'lezzer whores' and being fat and ugly. Of course, there were also many jokes about drugs and strange sexual practices.

I hadn't looked at 'The Book' for a while, and this time I was struck by the fact that I'd only been at 3am for sixteen months. It felt like I had been there for so much longer. I could not have been happier than I was at that very moment. I was in my dream job and was working with an extraordinary bunch of people. Tabloid journalists are stereotyped as being tough, tenacious and savagely ruthless. While we all had our moments, I felt our department consisted of entertaining and thoroughly captivating characters who loved to misbehave.

I turned to the photographs of the department's Christmas party from the previous year. It had been a disgraceful off-the-record affair. It was my first at the *Mirror*, and I had been warned the day before that what went on in the private room of restaurants across London at Christmas time remained private. And after the shameful conduct of December 2000, I soon realized why. I'd come to understand that the other reporters at the *Mirror* always expected the worst from our department, but if they had witnessed what we'd got up to at the Neal Street Italian, where the owner, Italian chef Antonio Carluccio, gatecrashed our party and proceeded to tell us a graphic joke about blowjobs, which he illustrated by dribbling milk down his chin, even they would have been appalled. There were no sexual indiscretions though. Thankfully there never were in our department. There were only a few boys in our team and they all had partners. They weren't our types anyway.

I sat at Kevin's desk, reading all the disgusting jokes we had written about each other, wondering if Polly was at that very moment handing in her notice to Kevin. I couldn't imagine ever wanting to leave.

Neither Kevin nor Polly came back to the office that night, and I didn't get a call from either of them. Eva didn't hear anything either.

The next day on my way to work I just knew that an announcement was about to be made. In the office Polly and Kevin were behaving strangely with Eva and I, not looking either of us in the eye and typing furiously into their computers. I had never seen Kevin so quiet in the office before. They were obviously emailing each other.

I was apprehensive. Eva and I hadn't heard so much as a whisper about Polly planning to leave. It was pretty much impossible to plot any sort of move within the world of newspapers without everyone finding out and gossiping about it before an announcement had been made. Perhaps we were all going to get sacked? Since day one of 3am, journalists at other papers had started circulating rumours that Piers was bored of us already and that we were about to be given the heave-ho. I always did my best to ignore the bitchy tittle-tattle about us, but this time I was finding it hard not to feel a tad nervous.

'Guys, can I talk to you for a second?' asked Polly.

It was 11am and Kevin had just left his desk to go to morning conference in Piers's office.

'Sure. What's up?' I asked, peering round my computer and trying to sound casual.

'Well, I'm leaving 3am. I've been offered the job of running the gossip column on the *Sunday Mirror*. Piers knows about it and is fine with me leaving. I've got to stay here until we find a replacement though,' she told us.

Eva was the first to react. 'Shit. Nice one, Pol. That's brilliant news. When did all that happen?'

'Yeah, congratulations. How on earth did you keep that quiet for so long?' I chipped in.

It was no secret that Tina Weaver, the editor of the *Sunday Mirror*, was after a new gossip columnist. The current one, Ian Hyland, wanted to move to another area of the paper, and he'd been asking all the gossip columnists if we wanted to apply for the job. I didn't want to leave the *Mirror*. I loved being part of the 3am team and building the 3am brand. We had only been here for sixteen months, and we had already surpassed Piers's expectations of us. We had spawned imitators on other newspapers who had copied our cheeky and saucy tone and the idea of an all-female gossip team.

But Polly felt the time was right to front her own column. 'Well, Tina approached me a few weeks ago, we had a few meetings and she offered me the job. It's going to be really strange only writing one column a week instead of six!' she exclaimed.

'So what did Kevin say?' asked Eva.

'He understood that I wanted to write my own column and says we need to start thinking of a replacement right now. So who do you reckon would be up to it?'

I couldn't believe how quickly things were moving. Polly had only just broken the news to us that she was leaving, and two seconds later she was asking who we should give her job to. She was clearly in a hurry to find someone, anyone, so she could leave and get going on her own column.

I desperately wanted to talk to Eva so we could go over what had just happened, and think about who we could possibly recruit.

'Um, I have no idea who we could get. Whoever it is has to be able to cope with the late nights, have good contacts, have the confidence to talk to famous people and know how to get a story,' I replied.

'Yeah. It's a lot harder than anyone thinks, that's for sure,' Eva said. 'Oh God, I've just had a terrible thought.' She sighed, putting her head in her hands. 'You know how much Piers loved that *Pop Idol* show on telly? Well, you don't think he'll make us do a search for the new 3am girl by holding auditions, do you? How horrific. That's just the sort of thing he'd think was funny. Oh shit.'

We all laughed. Little did we know that Piers actually would bring up the idea of a *Pop Idol*-style audition process for Polly's 3am replacement. Luckily it was quickly suppressed.

A few weeks later we were wading through letters and emails from people wanting to be Polly's replacement. Eva had mentioned a girl she knew who worked on the *Daily Telegraph*, Bryony Gordon. She hadn't been there when I had worked on the paper, but I had heard of her and although she was very young (at twenty-one she was six years younger than Eva and I) she was a showbiz reporter and we'd been told she was keen and lively.

Eva and I arranged to meet her for a drink and talked the job through with her. Most of the job applications we'd received had gone straight into the bin. These were the letters littered with spelling mistakes or written by applicants who had no experience in journalism but who liked 'to go to parties, drink champagne and meet famous people'.

Bryony was just what we were looking for: tall, blonde, busty and very pretty. This, of course, was an added bonus: she also had a great knowledge of the showbiz industry and a long list of contacts. However, it had been gently hinted to us by the powers that be that we shouldn't hire a dog. If we had a buxom long-haired blonde working for us, then male celebs would be more willing to spill the beans than if we had a ropey-looking reporter. It really was that basic. I felt slightly like a madam, hiring a new girl for the escort agency. Of course we didn't tell Bryony this. We didn't want to scare her off the job before she had started.

'I think she'll be great. She looks the part, glams up really well and she knows most of the PRs we have to deal with,' I said to Eva.

We arranged for her to meet Kevin. Once he gave the thumbs up, he told Piers, who then interviewed her. Within a week the deal was done. Polly was given her leaving date, Bryony had handed in her notice at the *Telegraph* and our new trio would start in December.

It was strangely unsettling to see Polly go. I was so used to the three of us working together in the office, hunting for stories at parties, propping one another up after too many cocktails and teasing each other about our disastrous dates. It felt like the end of an era. I really hoped Bryony would gel with us.

We organized a leaving party for Polly at Brown's restaurant in Canary Wharf.

'Well, that's it. No more Polly,' I said to Eva at the party while we watched her opening the Tiffany jewellery we had bought her as a leaving present. 'I'm going to miss her. Polly's one hell of an operator. I learnt a lot from her. She was fun to work with, wasn't she?' I asked Eva.

'Yeah, she was. Let's hope Bryony knows she's got some pretty big stilettos to fill.' Eva smiled.

I shook my head. 'God, first Richard goes, now Polly. You'd better not be next!' I prodded Eva's arm.

'Course I'm not! I'm not going anywhere. Well, for now,' she replied.

We launched Bryony in 3am at the beginning of December and she was immediately chucked in the deep end. It was the crazy pre-Christmas season and we were invited to one big celeb bash after another. The first *Lord of the Rings* premiere, the British

Comedy Awards and the premiere of Robbie Williams' documentary, *Nobody Someday*, all took place within two weeks of each other.

Robbie Williams' screening took place in the unlikely setting of the Warner Village cinema in Shepherd's Bush. We knew that Robbie hated the press, and that was putting it mildly. He particularly disliked the British tabloid contingent. We were never allowed near him, he wanted nothing to do with us and refused point blank to do interviews with our sort.

Even if he'd had glowing write-ups and reviews, he still thought of the press as the lowest life form on the planet and definitely wouldn't have pissed on us had we been on fire. So we were looking forward to trying to tackle him at his premiere and at the after-show party in a studio in Shepherd's Bush.

We weren't surprised when Robbie blanked us and the rest of the print press when he arrived at the cinema. As for us, we couldn't face watching his dreary documentary about his last tour, which seemed to be yet another self-aggrandizing exercise in self-loathing. We headed to a nearby bar to fill in the time before heading over to the party. It seemed like such a futile exercise.

'He's going to ignore everyone, stay for about five minutes as he hates parties and doesn't drink any more and then leave. There are no other celebs here tonight either. What a pointless waste of time,' I whined to Eva and Bryony.

'Yes, but we have to go. You know the one time we don't is when he'll do something,' replied Eva.

It was hugely irritating that one of Britain's biggest stars refused to talk to the tabloid press. He'd allow the broadsheet papers to interview him, but would he ever allow the likes of *Heat* magazine or the *Mirror* near him? No. It might have been mainly tabloid readers who bought his albums, but he didn't want to reveal anything about his quest for love and his battle with his demons in our publications. And yet we were expected to be humbled and grateful when his PR granted us permission to print his new album cover or a still from his latest video. He wanted publicity then. But only highly controlled publicity. It would have been easier for everyone concerned if he just took an ad out in the papers instead.

We arrived at the party and joined the other bored showbiz journalists. They were all as fed up as we were about having to give publicity to someone who we reckoned thought we were bigger scumbags than Myra Hindley. Some of the other hacks were planning to follow him around the party to wind him up and make him nervous. I didn't want to join in as I thought that was the sort of behaviour he expected from us anyway. He would then feel that he was right to detest us. Not that my act of defiance would curry me any favours with the singer. He'd still think I was a piece of dirt.

'Oh, here he is. Check out the size of his entourage,' Eva exclaimed.

Robbie was looking incredibly uncomfortable. He refused to meet anyone's eye and visibly shrank when he saw the assorted media milling around, waiting and watching his every move. He was surrounded by a pack of humourless lard buckets who would never be able to chase any deranged stalkers, but might kill them if they sat on them. Robbie's best mate Jonathan Wilkes was also in tow, on hand to keep the former Take That star entertained and help deflect the press. At least Wilkes talked to us.

'This is going to be a fun-filled night!' I said to Bryony. 'Let's watch Robbie Williams watching us. It's just one big stand-off. All he's got to do is be a bit of a man about it, get the reporters to stand together, and say hi and talk a bit about the film. It's as simple as that. But he can't even do that. We'd all back off for the rest of the night. He doesn't want to be here either. Why can't he just play the game?'

We stared at Robbie, who was skulking in a darkened corner, protected by his man mountains.

And then suddenly he was off. He was walking in a determined manner, and he was heading straight for Eva, Bryony and me. Before I even had time to open my mouth and say hello, the sweaty singer launched in.

'What goes on behind your eyes?' he demanded.

'Er, what?' was all I managed to reply. I could see that the other showbiz reporters were staring at us. They were unable to hear what he was saying and thought we were getting a great chat out of him. Each and every one of them had the look of fear that reporters got when they thought they were missing out on a scoop. If only they'd known . . .

Robbie continued criticizing our lack of a moral code while we just stood there taking it. We were too dumbstruck to think of any sort of comeback. You'd think we had just ripped out the beating hearts of a pack of puppies and eaten them, the way he was carrying on.

He was dragged away by Wilkes and an equally horrified-looking aide to his corner of the room, where he could survey from afar what until that moment had been the world's most miserably boring showbiz party.

'Er, what the hell was that all about?' asked a calm-sounding Bryony, as quietly as she could so the other reporters couldn't overhear her.

'I've no idea. I know he's the most miserable man in pop, but I didn't realize he was also the most foul-tempered,' I said to her, while Eva was too appalled to say anything.

We hadn't slagged Robbie off in the column. In fact, we hadn't written about him for ages. Maybe that was the problem. He hated being written about in the tabloids, but it seemed he hated being ignored just as much.

But Robbie hadn't finished and actually came back to us for more. 'Are your mothers proud?' he demanded.

I'd had enough of this. 'Yes, my mum's very proud. Is yours?' I fired back. I couldn't help myself.

Robbie ignored my question and stomped off like a tetchy teenager, after giving us all an appalled eyeballing. And with that, Britain's biggest pop star left his own party.

'You lucky cows! Robbie Williams never talks to journalists. And he came straight over to you lot. Twice! I'd have wet meself if he talked to me. I bet you've got a really good story out of him,' said Niki Waldegrave, a showbiz reporter who worked on Polly's column on the *Sunday Mirror.* The Yorkshire-born blonde was practically panting with jealousy.

'He's special all right. Oh yeah, that's some scoop we've got on our hands,' I said with a laugh.

At least we had plenty to say about Robbie Williams in our column. Vindictive, us? We were just doing our jobs.

Elton John and me

9. Sugar Daddies and Secret Agents

Robbie Williams clearly loathed the 3am girls and everything we represented. I'd been in the job seventeen months and was, by now, used to feeling like I was the most detested human being in the room at premieres or parties. I'd even managed to stop feeling fazed by the reactions of people outside the showbiz industry when I told them what I did for a living. I was constantly cancelling friends at the last minute, but on the odd occasions I did make it to dinners with mates, I often had to defend my job to snooty sorts – friends of friends – who looked down their noses at me.

'You work for a tabloid? Oh, God. Why would you want to do that?' a chinless estate agent asked me one such night in December.

I just gritted my teeth and ignored him. I didn't want to waste any of my energy defending my life to such a man.

Those whose jobs were more useful to society, like teachers or charity workers, were often patronizing and appalled in equal measure by my existence, and to my face too. But it went with the territory, so I soon got used to it and didn't let it affect me. If it made people feel better to insult my career and me out loud in front of my friends, then that was their problem. They were usually the types to ask for insider gossip on their favourite celeb ten minutes later anyway.

Bryony, however, wasn't prepared to put up with this kind of crap. She was a very sweet girl, perhaps too good-natured for the ruthless, fast-paced world of tabloid gossip. After two months on 3am, she decided it was not her sort of thing and elected to leave. I could see why she found it a struggle. You either loved this life and everything that went with it, good and bad, or you had to bail out. Bryony had a boyfriend too, and unlike Eva and me she couldn't put every single iota of energy into the job.

The annual *Mirror* columnists' Christmas lunch at a private room in the Mirabelle that December didn't help matters. Piers traditionally made a rude speech about those who penned columns for the paper, whether they were staff writers or celebrity columnists. The latter regularly included Carol Vorderman, Barry McGuigan and Sir Alan Sugar. Jonathan Ross – who for a time was the paper's film reviewer – stopped showing up, thankfully for the sake of the paper's Christmas budget, especially after he took advantage of the cigar box being offered round the room one year and pocketed an indecently large selection of Cuba's finest.

Piers didn't disappoint that day with his sarcastic and coarse jibes as he insulted everyone in the room. We all took it in good humour apart from poor Bryony, who looked aghast when Piers made a joke about her not having yet learnt to flash her cleavage at celebs in the way that Eva and I did. The other guests all fell about laughing over their stodgy Christmas puddings and brandy butter, but Bryony turned scarlet and looked like she wanted to run out of the room. I don't think the editor of the *Daily Telegraph* had ever dared refer to her breasts.

So we waved goodbye to her. She penned a farewell article in the column: 'We go to star-studded parties and Jessica and Eva swan up to these famous people and chat to them as if it were nothing. I suppose I simply can't get used to that being a normal part of my life. I think I should make way for someone more suited to the party lifestyle.'

The reality of working on 3am was that it wasn't one champagne-soaked glamorous moment after another. It was a hard slog, especially when it came to filling the column with stories and quotes from celebs who could barely stomach the idea of posing next to us, let alone talk to us. We were journalists, no matter how glittery our outfits or how high the heels we tottered about in, and we had to write attention-grabbing pieces about these events. We also had to accept that we'd be loathed by many people.

But not everyone disliked us. At the start of the year an article in one of the broadsheets had published the results of a questionnaire with media students. They had been asked about their role models in the print world. The broadsheet papers were outraged that instead of voting for campaigning investigative heroes, the 3am girls had been elected as the journalists most students aspired to be.

Naturally, we weren't allowed to let this go to our heads for even one second. The boys in our department laughed and jeered.

'Wonder if those drugged-up student kids know that all you do is get pissed and fall about with your norks out?' one of them asked.

The hunt started up again for yet another member of our 3am team. One who would dig her sharpened heels in and get tough.

In the meantime there were more parties and ceremonies to cover. It was the month of February, which this year consisted of one self-congratulatory boozy shindig after another.

One day I was busy typing away at a short piece about the two events Eva and I had attended the night before. The first was about the Brit Awards. Bryan McFadden had been sent back to his hotel room in disgrace by his record company after challenging the entire crew of So Solid to a fight with the rally call of 'Come on, then! I can take you all on!'

The second was about our friend Jay Kay. At the BMG record company post-Brits bash at Home House, he hadn't disappointed and had tried to brawl with photographers once more. He then attached himself to Eva and I, saying, 'You look kinky. I like that! Let's get closer to the fireplace to check out my log.' Yet again we declined his invitation.

As I was rereading my copy, my phone rang. It was a writer called Nancy from *Vanity Fair* magazine. The prestigious American glossy had heard about 3am and wanted to follow us around at parties, observe us in action and write an article about us. If we were happy with the idea, Nancy would fly over from New York the next day.

'Do you think they'll try to stitch us up?' I asked Eva, a little worried.

We had been approached countless times by TV production companies who had wanted to make fly-on-the-wall documentaries about us and the everyday life of a 3am girl. We had turned every single one of the offers down flat. It didn't take a genius to work out that pretty much everyone who agreed to take part in such shows would be made to look like a total tool. But *Vanity Fair* was a different offer altogether, so we agreed to Nancy writing a feature on us.

'Bloody hope they don't do us over!' laughed Eva.

It was just one article and we would decide at which parties we would let Nancy follow us. How bad could it be?

'We'll just have to make sure we don't make twats of ourselves,' I said.

Eva rustled around in one of her desk drawers and located her leather-backed diary. 'There are so many parties going on this month we should really go for it and invite Nancy to the biggest ones,' she said, flicking through the pages. 'We've got invitations to that ludicrous event that Jude Bore and Sadie Frost are throwing for their PETA campaign. Their PR said we're the only press going. Jude's a pretty big name in America, so let's take her to that.'

Looking in my own diary, I noticed that the BAFTA film awards were coming up, and that Russell Crowe was to be guest of honour at the opening of a new Emporio Armani shop. There was no way in hell we'd ever be invited to such a fancy event as the Armani party. The organizers would be more than happy if photographs of the spindly socialites dodging the canapés at the party appeared in 3am – Youngy was invited, of course – but they'd rather pass out than allow our sort actually into the event.

'We could try and gatecrash that Armani party?' I suggested to Eva.

She frowned at me. 'Can you imagine if we didn't get in – which I'm sure we won't be able to? *Vanity Fair* would witness us making total dicks of ourselves.'

'Good point. Well, it's the same night as Jude and Sadie's swanky, cocktail-fuelled cruelty-to-animals do, so we could play it by ear. I think we should give it a go. You never know!' I replied.

Eva looked unconvinced.

A few nights later we took Nancy to Sadie Frost's anti-fur video launch party at the Aveda spa in Holborn. She and her husband Jude Law were the only celebs at the sedate affair.

'This is not the sort of vibe I'd been expecting,' I whispered to Eva. 'I'd assumed it was going to be a really wild affair with all sorts of saucy shenanigans going on. What was I thinking? Of course they wouldn't invite us to *that* sort of party.' I suddenly noticed Nancy looking like she was questioning a sullen-looking Jude. 'Oh, shit. What do you think Nancy's quizzing Jude about?'

Just then Nancy and Jude looked over at Eva and me. They were definitely talking about us. 'I'm thinking he's not telling her how much he admires our work,' I commented to Eva.

Eva rubbed her hands. 'Right. Time to wind him up and ask him for a photo. He's got to or Sadie will chew his head off seeing as we now write nice things about her,' she said.

Naturally Jude wasn't pleased to see us, and even less so to stand between us for a picture, but his PR was ever so persuasive with him. After wrapping our arms lovingly around his stiff and uptight concave body for the photo, we decided it was time to leave and move on to the next party of the night.

With no invites to the A-list Armani bash on New Bond Street we put into practice that tried-and-tested technique of simply walking past the sullen-faced clipboard commandants, pretending we had a God-given right to actually be there. We just sucked our cheeks in, put on patronizing expressions and tried to look as haughty as possible. It seemed the more stuck-up you appeared to be at a fashion party, the more likely it was you'd be welcomed in. Amazingly, it worked. No one asked us if we had invites or checked that our names were on the guest list.

Russell Crowe – who inexplicably was the star guest of the night – was late and looked like a hungry rhino as he stampeded his way through the shop with his bodyguards in tow.

'What is *he* doing with security?' I gasped to Eva. 'What is it with these beefy, hard-arse actors needing to have bodyguards? Russell and Vinnie Jones really need to have a word with themselves.'

Although the Armani aides had had no idea who we were when we waltzed in uninvited, Russell's guys recognized us.

'Now he doesn't want any of *that*!' one of his bodyguards said, pointing to Eva and I as we followed him around the store.

So that's why he has security, I thought to myself – to bat us scary showbiz reporters away from him.

Five minutes after he'd arrived he was already heading for the door, but we really wanted a photo of him with us for the column.

'Good luck at the BAFTAs!' I shouted to get his attention as Eva and I jumped either side of him while Youngy took pictures.

'Yeah, thanks,' growled Russell.

We found out he was going to the after-show party at Hakkasan, a swanky restaurant off Tottenham Court Road. We decided to pursue him, taking Nancy with us.

'This is going to be a teensy bit tougher to blag our way into,' I whispered to Eva as yet another black-clad, morose yet gorgeous party organizer stood his ground outside the restaurant. We didn't have much time to come up with an extraordinary plan to gain entry into the party. 'Sod it. Let's just tell them we work for *Vanity Fair*,' I suggested, out of earshot of Nancy.

'Why not? It's not an outright lie. The party will get a plug in the article. And it's *Vanity Fair*. Who doesn't want to get a mention in the magazine?' replied Eva.

We asked Nancy to wait and marched up to the organizer.

'Hi, we're from *Vanity Fair*. We're on the list,' Eva said, with that steely look in her eyes.

The clipboard-wielding PR gave us both the once-over and examined his list. With great flourish, he turned the top page over. 'You don't appear to be on our list,' he sniffed.

'Well, we were invited. If you want to be the one responsible for stopping us from coming in and writing about the party then fine by us. But you'll have a lot of explaining to do to Mr Armani, who begged our boss to cover the party in the next edition of the magazine,' I lied, getting into my role as a stuck-up fashion writer mega-cow.

The camp door bitch flared his nostrils at us, attempted to put on a smile and through gritted teeth said, 'Of course. Go in.'

We grabbed Nancy and darted in before he tried to ring the Armani PR to check our story.

'That was unbelievable. We must do that again,' I giggled to Eva as we walked down the precarious staircase into the dark, windowless restaurant.

After half an hour of watching Mick Hucknall crash and burn with some six-foot glossy-haired brunettes, we were thrilled to see Russell and his other half, Danielle Spencer, arrive and sit down on a sofa. He knocked back a few drinks, smoked a fag and looked miserable.

He did perk up, however, when Sting showed up. We watched as the two men walked off together to the kitchen. Two young women then appeared and strolled in to join the men. Any attempts we could have made to pretend we were waitresses who had left their tray of canapés in the kitchen were scuppered when we noticed a bodyguard patrolling the door. Twenty minutes later the laughing foursome came back out of the kitchen together. We never did find out what had amused them so much.

A few days after that Eva and I put on our most dazzling outfits and went to the BAFTAs. The annual British luvvie-fest was usually a very staid affair. But luckily that year the organizers had had the bright idea to wash the red carpet outside the Odeon Leicester Square with shampoo only hours before the ceremony took place. They hadn't counted on the British weather doing its usual thing of pissing down with rain.

Unfortunately for the celebs – who included Nicole Kidman, Kate Winslet, Russell Crowe, Sting, Warren Beatty and Dustin Hoffman – who were all decked out in formal evening wear, there was so much white foam that they had to skid down the carpet in front of thousands of fans, assembled photographers and TV crews.

'Someone help me! I've got white stuff all over my shoes! Help!' shrieked Kate Winslet.

'I thought she was meant to be so normal and down to earth. Kate Winslet in a huff because she has a bit of ick on her borrowed shoes – who'd have thought it?' I said to Eva as Ms Winslet was attended to by various strangers, all mopping away at her high heels.

After the ceremony everyone headed for a three-course dinner at the Dorchester. Eva and I decided the time was right to accost the stars and persuade them to pose for photos. Photographers were usually banned by the organizers from covering the dinner, so Eva and I had to depend on our trusty throwaway cameras, which we had smuggled into our handbags.

To our delight, Warren Beatty happily obliged, as did Sting, who invited Eva and I to sit on his lap for the picture, commented on Eva's firm thighs and mock-innocently enquired why we had waited for his wife Trudie Styler to leave their table before we had approached him.

But for me Dustin Hoffman was the true star of the night.

'Excuse me, Dustin, do you mind if we have a picture with you?' I asked the diminutive and scruffy actor. His salt-and-pepper hair was sticking up and his black tie was skew-whiff. He did not look like your average Hollywood superstar.

'No problem!' he squawked back at us.

I handed our camera to a male film reviewer from another paper who said he didn't mind acting as our unofficial photographer for a bit.

Dustin pulled Eva and I towards him, gripping us a little too tightly under our breasts. 'So, what about this white foam on the carpet tonight?' he growled in our ears. 'It was like being back in the '70s. I didn't know whether to get on my knees and start snorting the stuff up!' He carried on chatting to us. 'I've brought my daughter Jenna with me tonight. But all these guys keep hitting on her. It's a nightmare. Look, there's one now! I've got to get rid of him!'

And with that the Oscar winner scurried off in the direction of the hot young Brit actor Oliver Milburn.

The next day was the annual NME Awards. The ceremony that February had attracted The Strokes, Radiohead and So Solid Crew. But the highlight of the afternoon for us was meeting Ricky Gervais. The star of *The Office* usually stayed away from showbiz parties but had accepted the invitation to this one as he was being honoured for his character David Brent.

Along with the rest of the nation, Eva and I were massive fans of the show, but we were sorely disappointed by his reaction to meeting us.

'I'm sorry, I don't do this kind of thing,' he kept repeating to Eva and me when we introduced ourselves as reporters for the *Mirror*. We were hardly asking him for the finer details of his love-making abilities.

'Oh, come on, Ricky! Don't be like that,' Eva replied, her eyes boring through him with her death stare.

'No, really, girls. I really don't do this,' he stammered nervously.

'Do what? All we're doing is saying hello,' I pointed out.

By now Eva and I had backed him into a corner of the cavernous venue in Shoreditch, with our photographer Richard Young standing nearby.

'We're not going to bite. How about a quick photo and then we promise to leave you alone for ever!' she cajoled.

He eventually caved in, but only because we were embarrassing him with our loud pleading.

'I really don't want to do this,' he said to us through gritted teeth.

As Richard fiddled with his camera, Eva and I jumped into position on either side of Ricky and tried to put our arms around him, like we usually did with stars. But he was having none of it.

'No, no! Please don't do that!' he screamed. 'I'll do a picture but no touching.'

We ran a very odd photo the following day of Ricky grimacing for the camera and gripping his own arms so that his flesh came nowhere near ours.

Nancy left the next day and we kept our fingers crossed her article about us would be favourable. As a consequence of her visit, Piers decided to jet us over to Los Angeles to mix it up with the Hollywood types at the Oscars, which were taking place in a fortnight's time. We had never covered the awards before, as it was deemed a waste of money to send reporters there when it was impossible to get access to any of the celebrities.

But after our *Vanity Fair* interview, Piers thought we ought to give it a go. *Vanity Fair* hosted *the* post-Oscar party in LA. It was where the A-list hung out after the ceremony and where the winners would make an appearance with their statuettes held aloft before hot-footing it to Sir Elton John's rival – and less stuffy – bash.

Eva and I knew we didn't have a chance of being allowed into the ultra-exclusive party, but Piers was having none of it. 'You lot are going to be in the next month's issue of the magazine – course they'll let you into the party,' he retorted.

I pulled a face at Eva and as soon as Piers had walked off I scurried round to her desk. 'There's no chance they'll let us in. It's the most notoriously difficult party in the history of parties to get into. Forget it,' I said to her.

'You're telling me. We've got to give it a go though,' she replied.

We spent the following week tracking down phone numbers and emails of the magazine's party organizers. The *Vanity Fair* annual party – held at Morton's restaurant – had been planned months before: VIPs had already RSVP'd and no latecomers were to be even vaguely considered – especially not a couple of gossip columnists attempting to blag their way in at the last minute. We couldn't even get through to the PA of the PR.

'What are we going to do?' I wailed to Eva that Thursday afternoon after yet another *Vanity Fair* minion had refused to take a message and asked us to send another email that would be ignored. Sir Elton John's Aids Foundation event at Moomba restaurant was also a non-starter: we were told the British press were not allowed in. We were going off to LA the next day. Our flights were booked, our hotel rooms paid for. But we still had no parties to attend. We would just have to wing it.

The next morning Eva and I met at Heathrow airport for our eleven-hour flight to Los Angeles. We spent hours on the plane racking our brains for a plan.

'What are we going to do if we don't get in anywhere?' I asked Eva.

'We can't even think like that. It's just not an option. Piers and Kevin don't want to hear us saying we couldn't sort it out. When we land let's give Youngy a call, see if he's heard anything about anyone, and if he can't help, we'll go to the Beverly Hills Hotel and see if any stars are around,' Eva replied grimly.

I grimaced. I had hoped we'd get closer to the stars and parties than resorting to hanging about in a hotel lobby. Youngy was one of the very few photographers allowed into the *Vanity Fair* party. We had already begged, pleaded, whinged and whined to him several times over the past few days.

'Hey, girls, you know I would try to help you if I could. But it's just impossible,' he'd told me over the phone.

We couldn't accept that as the final answer though.

After landing Eva and I collected our bags and hailed a taxi to our hotel, the Beverley Hilton. I got into my room and barely had time to chuck my suitcase on to the floor when my phone rang.

'Shall we just go for it and pay a visit to the bar at the Beverly Hills Hotel and see who's there?' Eva was obviously feeling just as tense as I was. We could either sit in our hotel rooms and mope and panic about what we were going to do or we could force ourselves to get out there and start pounding the streets, so to speak.

'Yeah, you're right. We'd better see what we can find. Meet you downstairs in twenty minutes,' I replied.

The Beverly Hills Hotel, on Sunset Boulevard, was nicknamed 'the Pink Palace' due to the rose hue of the place. The super-plush five-star hotel was set in twelve acres of tropical gardens and was a home from home to many superstars. With any luck some of them would be staying there at that moment.

'Shit, look who it is!' I exclaimed to Eva as our taxi pulled up outside.

A number of doormen stood outside, while uniformed valet parking men dashed about and bodyguards barked into their walkie-talkies. But among the madness I had spotted a famous face, or a famous butt to be precise. It was Jennifer Lopez and her husband, Cris Judd. They strolled into the hotel without anyone doing a double take.

'Oh, excellent. Do you think there's a party going on inside?' I excitedly asked Eva while she paid the cab.

'Well, if there is, we're getting in there.'

We dashed into the hotel and tried to find J-Lo and her hubby. They had completely disappeared. We couldn't find them anywhere.

We did find Youngy with some of his LA mates in the Polo lounge bar.

'Hi, guys. How are you? Good flight?' he asked.

'We're pretty buggered to be honest. We haven't got any invites and Piers is expecting us to swan about at A-list parties. What are we going to do?' I sighed as we took our seats at a table.

'Sorry to hear that. Well, you have left it rather late, you know.' He laughed.

Eva shut her eyes. 'Yes, Richard, we know. Piers only just decreed that we were to come out here. So *Vanity Fair* is out. What else can we do? Any ideas?' she asked.

'Well, you know Elton John and David Furnish are staying here? They always stay at the bungalows out in the hotel grounds,' he suggested.

'Ooh, we could knock on their door and beg for help!' I exclaimed.

It sounded like the start of a great plan.

'Well, I'm not sure about that. Elton's security, and not to mention the security here at the hotel, may not take too kindly to that idea,' said Richard.

But Eva and I decided it was worth a try. All we had to do the following day was a photo shoot for the paper. We were to pose for pictures by the Hollywood Hills in a limo and on Rodeo Drive pretending we were something out of *Pretty Woman*.

The next morning Eva and I hailed another taxi outside our hotel and made the return journey to the Beverly Hills Hotel. We walked into the lobby and sat down in a quiet corner to come up with an emergency plan of action.

'OK, so I'm not sure asking the front desk if we can be put through to Elton John's bungalow is the best idea. They'll think we're loony fans or something. And besides, I'm sure he's booked under some ridiculous pseudonym like Betty Swallows, like celebs do when they stay at hotels and don't want to be tracked down,' I said. 'So let's write a begging letter instead.'

'Cool. In fact, let's write it to Elton's boyfriend, David. If we get him on side then he'll hopefully be able to persuade Elton to let us come to the party,' Eva suggested.

'You'd better write it. I've got the handwriting of a seven-year-old. I'll get you some notepaper.' I jumped up from my chair, walked up to the front desk of the hotel and asked for some headed notepaper and an envelope. The man behind the desk obliged and I handed them to Eva, who was triumphantly holding up one of her business cards that she'd found in her handbag.

'I can attach this to the letter, so it looks vaguely professional,' she said, and started scribbling on the piece of paper.

'Let's say that we've been sent over here at the last minute, that we've always wanted to come to Elton and David's Oscars party, which is arguably the best party of Oscar night, and that we'll donate money to Elton's Aids charity,' I suggested.

'Yeah, good one. It's the least we should offer to do,' she replied, putting the finishing touches to our begging note. She popped her business card into the envelope and handed it over to the concierge, asking him to deliver it to Mr Furnish. We returned to our hotel, where our limo was waiting for us.

'How cringey is this,' I moaned.

A small crowd of people had gathered by the blacked-out stretch limo, which bore the number plate Too Hip. The rubber-neckers were obviously expecting some Hollywood starlet to totter out of the hotel to be whisked away to one of the numerous pre-Oscar events that were taking place that weekend. Instead they got Eva and me.

Waiting by the car was an American photographer that the *Mirror* picture desk had booked to take pictures of us in the limo. The idea was to look as if we were being chauffeured in style to a showbiz party. The irony . . .

'This is pretty cool. Shall we get going? I thought we could go up to the Hollywood Hills so I could get you guys with the

Hollywood sign in the background,' enthused John, the American snapper.

Eva and I both groaned.

'This is beyond cheesy. We can't even vaguely get out of this, can we?' I grumbled.

'No way. We have no choice in the matter. Richard, Kevin and Piers want us to be pictured doing the LA thing at Oscar time. This will be the closest we're going to get. Hanging out of a hired limo with the Hollywood sign in the background,' Eva said with a sigh.

We scrambled into the back of the ludicrously OTT car with the photographer. John had brought along a bottle of cheap fizzy white wine and two champagne glasses so we'd look as if we were on the sauce in the snaps, and we had packed glam dresses and high heels so that we would really look as if we were on our way to an Oscar party.

Navigating the tank-sized limo up the windy roads near the Hollywood sign took longer than we had anticipated.

'This is a bloody nightmare,' I said to Eva as we bounced around in the back seat over the bumps in the road. 'And we still have no plan of action about the parties. What the hell are we going to do?' I added, gripping on to the armrest.

'Who knows. We're a bit screwed, aren't we? Gatecrashing a party here in LA should be interesting on Oscar night with all the other losers attempting the same thing,' she replied, clutching her stomach and trying to fight car sickness as the limo driver lurched around a bend in the road. We'd have done better with a London bus driver at the wheel.

We double-checked our seatbelts were fastened and held our tummies as the limo climbed up the winding roads. We finally pulled over just as I thought I was going to be sick. We then proceeded to crouch down in the back of the limo while we changed into our black dresses.

'I don't think I've ever felt so unglamorous in my entire life,' I laughed as I wriggled out of my jeans. 'My friends all think I'm the luckiest girl in the world to be coming out to LA on Oscar weekend, driven around in a limo and hunting down celebs. What on earth could be glam about this?'

'Yeah, I know what you mean. If only they knew it's the middle of the day and we're trying to look as if we're off to a party full of celebs. A party we can't get into. Not one!'

I chucked my jeans, top, socks and trainers on to the floor and stepped barefoot out of the limo, clutching my Gina heels. I shivered. So much for the blazing Californian sunshine.

'OK, ladies, if you could both punch the air with one arm so you look like you're actually having a great time here,' instructed John, who seemed determined to wipe the grimaces off our miserable faces.

We tried to look upbeat.

'Come on, guys! You're dressed up, you're looking hot, and you're on your way to a wild party full of Hollywood A-listers. Leonardo DiCaprio and Brad Pitt are waiting for you with champagne on ice!' he continued, in the hope that his idea of a great night out would cheer us up.

This made me even more depressed. John finally lost his cool.

'For fuck's sake, Jessica, smile!'

'I'm going to push him off the hill,' I muttered to Eva through gritted teeth as I tried to muster an excited look on my face.

Once John had taken enough pics, we headed back to our hotel, where we would do a few more shots leaning on the car with palm trees in the background.

'I think I've lost the will to live,' Eva said with a sigh. 'We've been sent all the way out here at huge expense and we're going to come home in disgrace. Can you imagine the bollocking we're going to get?'

We both looked out of the limo windows at the soulless, empty boulevards of LA. For a party city it seemed totally devoid of any personality. I spotted only a few people walking around the streets and they looked like tourists. Considering LA was the beating heart of the billion-dollar movie industry, it wasn't the most glamorous of places. Everyone we had seen so far looked identical, with their plastic pouts and heavily Botoxed, expressionless faces.

And they all looked so serious. Or maybe that was just their facelifts.

Without their teams of stylists, hairdressers, colourists, make-up artists, manicurists, facialists, fake-tan appliers and not forgetting the plastic surgeons, what the hell did these Hollywood types actually look like? Would they even know how to get dressed, let alone put on some lipstick by themselves? No wonder they were hardly ever photographed popping out to the shops wearing a scabby tracksuit and no slap. They must have looked a right fright without the stage-managed beauty and fashion miracle workers.

Just as I was slipping off into a daydream about what the likes of Cameron Diaz, Nicole Kidman and Gwyneth Paltrow looked like first thing in the morning with a hangover, Eva's mobile trilled into life. She scrabbled around in her handbag trying to find it.

'Hello?' she asked. 'Oh. Hi. How are you?' She looked wide-eyed with shock and thumped my left knee with her fist.

'Ouch! What?' I asked her.

She mouthed something incomprehensible at me.

'What?' I asked again.

She put a finger to her lips. 'Yes, we'd love to come! Thank you so much. We'll put in the plug no problem, and as we said in the note, it goes without saying that we'll give a donation to your charity. Thank you so much. Bye!' she said, putting on her most polite voice.

She turned her mobile off. 'Oh, fuck!' she exclaimed. 'That was Elton John. On my mobile!' She stared at her phone, looking dazed, and fell back into her seat.

'You're kidding! What did he say?' I asked.

She sat staring ahead.

'Eva? Hello? Come back to me.'

'Shit. He was so nice. I always thought he was meant to be a moody shit. But what a lovely guy. He said he and David are both huge fans of 3am and of course we can come to the party. They loved our note and he said he thought it was really sweet. He's giving my mobile number to his PR guy out here so we can collect our tickets for tomorrow night.'

Now it was my turn to look dazed and lose the power of speech. Talk about landing the greatest fairy godmother a gossip columnist could wish for.

'I think I love him,' I finally muttered. 'A lot.'

We spent the rest of the journey to our hotel gabbling at each other in a highly excited state about what had just happened. Elton made a point of not allowing any journalists into his Oscar party, so we couldn't begin to imagine what went on behind closed doors at the glitzy bash.

We finally pulled up at the hotel.

'OK, guys. Just pretend you've had the biggest night of your lives and you've drunk gallons of vintage champagne,' hollered John as he reeled off pictures of Eva and me pretending to be passed out in the back of the limo, with our heads resting against each other's. It would be quite some time until we'd be able to enjoy a rest like that.

The next morning I woke up thinking of nothing else but the fact that Sir Elton John had come to our rescue. For a multimillionaire megastar who was usually portrayed as a stroppy, cantankerous old git who was out of touch with reality, he had responded so kindly to our letter. I wished we had used that tactic of bypassing the tough-talking ranks of PRs and publicists before.

Eva and I spent most of Sunday writing up our story about Sir Elton waving his wand and letting us come to his party. I had called Kevin and Richard that day to tell them what had happened.

'Shitting hell. What a fucking legend he is. Remember to fill out a form for the accounts department when you're back so we can whack him a hefty donation. I'll sign it off for you,' Richard enthused down the phone. 'Write it up as if you already had invites to every party in town but that you were opting to go to Elton's as he's such a fucking great superstar and your old friend. Go, go, go.'

We picked up our invites for Elton's Oscar party later that day. We were instructed to bring our passports with us to prove who we were when we arrived at the party. I had never heard of such strict security measures before. Our names would be ticked off the list at the door once we showed our ID and handed in our invites. And then we'd have to go through the metal detectors.

The meticulous rules and regulations to gain entry to the party merely made me more excited about going. Who knew what would be taking place behind the closely guarded doors to the VIP party? I couldn't wait to find out.

The party didn't kick off until 10pm, so at 5pm we sat on my bed in our dressing gowns to watch the Academy Awards. So much for being in Los Angeles to cover the Oscars. The *Mirror* had shelled out more than £4,000 on air tickets, hotels and expenses for us to watch it on the telly.

We ordered burgers and chips on room service while we watched the Oscar marathon on TV, munching our way through enormous portions as we listened to Halle Berry's tearful and stirring Oscar acceptance speech. It was definitely going to be the talking point of the night.

We finally got dressed at 8.30pm. I had never taken so long to get ready. I was more used to a quick change into a frock in the ladies' loo at work.

'Shall we go? It's 9.30. Bugger. I didn't even think about the traffic. Do you think we should have ordered a taxi earlier? Can you imagine if we can't get there?' I anxiously asked Eva.

'That's a point. Well, we haven't got much choice now. Let's go,' she replied.

Halle Berry was very much at the forefront of our minds. We knew the *Mirror* would go mad for her because her mother was English. I suspected Richard would ask us to try to track her down. We knew that Halle was in the middle of making the new James Bond film in Spain and had only flown in for the night. Apparently she was jetting off first thing the next day. Unless the office wanted us to blag our way on to her private jet to Spain, we didn't have much chance of interviewing her. We would just have to hope she showed up at Elton's party.

Ten minutes later we were outside Moomba. There was already a queue of fifty people waiting for the doors to open.

'I guess this is the Z-list guest list then,' I remarked to Eva as we shivered in our little black strapless dresses.

We had both failed to consult each other on what we were wearing. When Eva had knocked on my hotel room door to get me, we had both looked each other up and down and burst out laughing at our near-identical dresses. However, mine was mid-calf and slashed to the thigh while Eva's was above the knee.

'Oh, sod it. I can't be bothered to get changed,' Eva had said.

'Yeah, me neither. We really need to sort out our wardrobes, though. Everyone I meet thinks the *Mirror* have lavished huge budgets on us so we can wear lots of cool outfits. If only they knew the truth. If Piers says to us one more time that we should try to persuade designers to lend us party clothes so we look drop-dead glam when we're at parties, I'm going to cry.'

'You can really see Alexander McQueen allowing us to run amok in his store so he can get a plug in the column, can't you?' agreed Eva.

'At least we've got those 20 per cent discount cards from Warehouse, though. It's a start! If only we had the time to actually use them.'

We looked around at the other guests in the queue waiting to get into the party. Even though Elton had personally rung us up to invite us, there was a definite pecking order. His A-list pals who weren't invited to the Oscars had shelled out thousands to be guests at the dinner and auction he hosted during the ceremony. Everyone else had to wait to party until the end of the awards.

Behind me in the queue was a tall, spindly blonde who was covered in goose pimples. She was throwing a huge strop at the young bloke she was with.

'This is a joke. I want to go in now. I'm freezing,' she pouted.

It was Paris Hilton. In those days she didn't get to skip the guest list queue.

Half an hour later we shuffled our way to the front of the queue and handed over our invites and passports. Once our names had been double-checked and ticked off the guest list by one of the ten clipboard-wielding party organizers who were sat behind the desk outside the entrance, we had to undergo the handbag search and then pass through the metal detectors. I guess you just couldn't trust these Hollywood celebrities.

We came across an awning where at least forty TV crews were crammed into a press area just outside the actual entrance to Moomba. They were waving their microphones at Elton John. He looked fabulous, decked out in a black Versace suit complete with black sequins sewn on to the lapels.

We wanted to have our obligatory photo taken straight away. As we weren't allowed to bring a photographer into the party, Eva and I had borrowed one of Youngy's small digital cameras so that any snaps of us with celebs could be downloaded and sent to the *Mirror* from his laptop. We just didn't have anyone to actually take the pictures. On top of that there were big, beefy security men circling him, so even if we wanted to beg him for a photo when he had finished talking to the TV interviewers, he'd be whisked away immediately.

'We're going to have to move bloody fast,' Eva muttered as they barked at us to move into the party and not stand in the way.

And then we saw David Furnish waving frantically at us. 'Hey, how are you? We're so glad you made it! Let me get you a glass of champagne,' he shouted. He beckoned over a waiter who was hovering nearby, and thrust two glasses of champagne into our hands.

At that precise moment Elton was being interviewed live on BBC One's Breakfast News. The tuxedo-clad reporter was midway through his live link with Elton (it was now 6.20am in the UK) when Furnish shouted out, 'Hey, Elton, the 3am girls are here!' Elton spun around, leaving the speechless BBC man gripping on to his microphone and staring at the back of Elton's head.

'Hi, girls. I'm so glad you're here,' he exclaimed, and then planted a kiss on both of our cheeks while we nervously clutched our glasses of champagne.

'Sir Elton, Sir Elton, you *are* on BBC Breakfast News live, so when you've finished your kisses,' implored the BBC interviewer.

Elton turned back to the camera to finish his sentence about how much money had been raised that night for his Aids Foundation.

Eva and I remained rooted to the spot in shock.

'Er, did I imagine that or did Elton John just break off a live interview with BBC Breakfast News to say hello and kiss us?' I whispered to Eva out of the corner of my mouth.

'How did that just happen?' replied Eva, who was grasping her champagne glass so tightly I was convinced it was going to shatter into the palm of her hand.

David apologized profusely. 'Sorry Elton can't chat to you properly yet, he's got to finish talking to the TV people,' he explained.

'No, that's fine. Don't worry about it at all! Is it OK if we get a photo with him though?' I asked, coming to my senses.

'Sure, that's no problem. I'll take it for you,' he said sweetly.

Elton had finished his interview and David beckoned him over. 'The girls want to do a photo,' he said.

'Of course. It's so good to see you. We love the column,' Elton said as Eva handed David the digital camera.

We all grinned for David.

'I'm afraid it's strictly Diet Coke for me,' the teetotal singer told us. 'But don't worry, we're going to blow those old farts from *Vanity Fair* out of the water. I'm so glad you're here. It's nice to have a few Brits around. Enjoy yourselves.'

And with that Elton and David disappeared back into the party.

Eva and I walked into the main room, still a little stunned.

'That was a bit surreal. To say the least,' I finally said.

My mobile phone rang in my handbag. It was a text from Daniel, a PR contact.

'Oh, bloody hell. I've just had a text from Daniel at Avalon. It says, "Am watching BBC One and just seen you elbow the interviewer out of the way to get Elton. You are totally shameless". I think the entire nation has just seen us exchanging air kisses with Elton John,' I gasped.

'What? Let me have a look at that,' said Eva, grabbing my mobile out of my hand. She read the text message. 'Oh, shit. That is ridiculous.' She laughed, covering her mouth with her hand.

We did a circuit of the party, still giggling about our impromptu telly moment where we'd clearly looked like a pair of showbiz luvvies. The party was in full swing. I couldn't help but notice that many of the American guests were some of the most atrocious dancers I had ever seen. It was a vast venue with six bars, all serving free champagne and vodka. By all accounts it was a great party. But where were the celebs?

'I take it that's the VIP area,' Eva said, pointing to a closed black door that was heavily guarded by a team of Hagrid-sized bodyguards.

Our first attempt to swan in resulted in our being body-blocked by one of the Man Mountains.

'Sorry, ma'am. This is the VIP area. If you do not have the correct wristband I am going to have to ask you to move away,' one of them grunted at Eva.

She rooted about in her handbag, pretending to look for her imaginary VIP pass. 'It's in here somewhere,' she assured him as she dug around in her bag.

He looked at her with unsmiling eyes. It wouldn't have surprised me if he'd been a human X-ray machine who instantly knew her handbag contained nothing of the sort.

'I think I left it in the loo. I know Elton's PR, who is inside there. He can vouch for us. Can you get him for us?' she asked, playing for time.

'I'm sorry, lady. You're going to have to move away,' he snarled.

There was no sweet-talking this hulking git, who had seemingly undergone a sense of humour bypass as well as overdosed on growth hormones.

Eva and I discreetly backed away from the door.

'We can't even make a dash for it,' said Eva. 'They're all guarding the door as if the crown jewels were in there. I overhead someone say Bob Dylan, Sting and Paul McCartney are inside the VIP area. I reckon we wait by the door outside to see who else arrives, and tag along after them and try to get in that way, by pretending we're part of their crew.'

We waited. I was feeling quite anxious, concerned we'd have

no stories for the paper. I lit a cigarette. I didn't consider myself to be a full-time puffer, but at times of stress I reached for the Marlboro Lights and smoked like a beagle.

'Mate, I don't think you're allowed to smoke here. The whole of LA is a cigarette-unfriendly city,' said Eva, waving away the smoke from my fag.

'Oh, sod it. They can chuck me out. I'm gagging for a smoke,' I replied.

'Don't be like that. It's not worth being asked to leave because you're gasping for a fag.' She sighed.

A tall, camp American leaned over. 'Excuse me, do you have a spare cigarette?'

'Sure,' I said, giving him one out of my packet and lighting it for him.

'Oh, thank you so much. I've been dying for one for hours. But no one smokes around here,' he said.

Ten minutes later I had handed out eight cigarettes to desperate Americans. So much for their healthy way of life. They were all waiting for one person to light up before they all gave in too. Uptight LA was improving by the minute.

Eva nudged me. 'Someone important is arriving,' she said, grabbing my arm.

Camera flashes were going off at the entrance, and there were shouts coming from the snappers and TV crews outside. We pushed our way through the crowd. The night's big Oscar winners, Halle Berry and Denzel Washington, were standing together, waving their gold awards at the crowds, who were applauding and whooping with delight at the pair.

'We've got to get them,' gasped Eva.

Elbows out at the ready, we ploughed into the crowd that had formed around the toasts of the town. But a team of Herculean henchmen had other ideas. With one sweep of their arms, two bodyguards swatted Eva and I to one side when we were only a few feet from Halle and Denzel.

'Don't touch me!' yelled Eva at one of the grim-faced giants.

He turned around and gave Eva a glare that I interpreted as a warning he'd tear her arms off and bash her over the head with the soggy ends if she gave it another go. What was it with these LA security men? This was meant to be a private party. They were acting as if every female guest was a potential celebrity serial killer.

Before we could make another attempt, Halle and Denzel had been magicked away into the VIP area.

'Where the hell have they gone? How did they disappear?' Eva asked, spinning around and wearing a slightly crazed expression on her face. 'We've got to get to Halle. You so know Piers will have decided she's the woman of the moment. And we were within a few feet of her before being practically attacked by those dribbling idiots.'

I put my hand on her shoulder. 'Calm down! I'm sure she'll leave at some point. Let's just wait by the VIP door for her,' I said.

'But there are clearly two doors. How else did she and Denzel disappear like that out of our sight?'

We spent the next hour and a half waiting outside the main door to the VIP area again, watching the comings and goings. Sir Ian McKellen waltzed by, happily stopped for a chat and posed for a photo with us. Boris Becker, Benicio Del Toro, Jon Bon Jovi, Joan Collins and Heidi Klum all came and went, but there was still no sign of Halle.

Kevin had already rung Eva and I on our mobiles to ask what stories we had for the paper. It was 9.30am in London. We told him about what had happened with Elton and BBC Breakfast News.

'You're kidding me! That's what we want more of. You two trampling TV crews beaming live to the studio so you can pretend to the whole of Great Britain that you're chummy with superstars,' he chuckled. 'I'll tell the picture desk to call up the BBC and get a copy of the segment biked over on a tape so they can take grabs of your big moment snogging Elton.'

It was 1.30am by now. Our flight back to London was in less than fifteen hours. Sleep hadn't even occurred to me.

'I reckon Halle has done a runner and escaped through some

top-secret underground tunnel. She has literally vanished into thin air,' moaned Eva.

The party was winding down. Even British socialite Tamara Beckwith had called it a night. I walked outside to the press area, where the last of the photographers and TV crews were packing away their stuff.

'Have you guys seen Halle Berry leave yet?' I asked one of the cameramen.

'Oh, yeah. She went a while ago,' he replied.

I grimaced. How bloody frustrating!

Eva and I decided to give the *Vanity Fair* party a go. It was just up the road. We knew it was meant to end at 2am, but we thought it was worth going to, just in case Halle had gone there. We collected our goodie bags on the way out. Well, it would have been rude not to. As we struggled to walk up the road in our high heels, we rustled around in them to see what we had. Marc Jacobs and Versace perfume, pens, make-up, candles and CDs; it was all lovely stuff.

'Presents for the others at work!' I exclaimed.

'Sod that. I'm keeping the lot,' laughed Eva.

We eventually reached Morton's, our feet aching, but apart from a few stragglers the party seemed well and truly over. We spotted Youngy standing in the doorway of the restaurant.

'Hey, Richard! We've got a picture with Elton John for you. Here,' said Eva, handing him back his camera.

'Thanks, well done.'

'Anyone still in there? Halle Berry?' I asked hopefully.

'Nah. Everyone's gone for the night,' he replied.

'It's not the done thing to be seen as the last to leave over here, is it?' I said.

'Kevin says we've got to track down Halle Berry for a photo,' Eva told him. 'Do you have any idea where she might be staying?'

'You could try the Four Seasons Hotel. Along with every other journalist in town!' He laughed.

Eva and I groaned.

'She'll have gone to sleep if she is even there anyway. Let's go back to the hotel. We've got to write everything up for the column and file it now,' I said.

This time we took our high heels off and walked down the street looking for a cab. On the way back to our hotel we sat in gloomy silence. There was no time to think about sleep as we had two pages of stories to write up before we could hit our beds. By the time we'd emailed Kevin from the computers in the hotel's business centre, it was 4.30am. Kevin had instructed us to get some kip before trying to locate Halle Berry. Piers, as we had predicted, had anointed her the star of the night. Eva and I returned to our hotel rooms for four hours' sleep before starting our hunt for the elusive Oscar winner.

Eva called me on the phone in the morning. 'You ready then? Let's just get a taxi straight to the Four Seasons Hotel. I've packed my case. We might as well check out now as we haven't got long until our flight.'

She sounded as shattered as I did. We had been in LA for three nights, still hadn't combated our jet lag and were flying back to Heathrow later that day. For now, we had to track down Halle Berry, along with the rest of the world's media.

Two hours later, after several circuits of the Four Seasons Hotel, we had to admit defeat.

'Well, she either left first thing this morning or she's still upstairs in bed with a hangover of epic proportions,' I said with a sigh.

Our flight back to London was looming, so we decided to head straight for the airport. In the cab, Eva dialled the office on her mobile and had a short chat with Kevin. I stared out of the window like a zombie, not listening to their conversation and trying hard not to close my eyes and fall asleep.

'Well, they're certainly keen on Halle Berry all right,' she said after she had hung up.

'What do you mean? She's clearly not here any more. She must have already jetted back to Spain for the Bond film,' I pointed out.

'Exactly. And that's where Piers and Kevin want us to go. To Cadiz, where Halle and Pierce Brosnan are shooting *Die Another Day*. We've got to get our flight back to London today, spend time trying to persuade the PRs for the movie to let us interview Halle, and get out to Spain. We have to find her. Full stop.'

I was suddenly very awake. 'To Cadiz? Pierce Brosnan? Ooh, I've always had a major crush on him!'

'What? Ewwww. Yuck. He's so old!' shrieked Eva.

'Underneath that jet-black hair is a major silver fox. An amazingly suave one,' I replied confidently.

Eva wrinkled her nose at me. She didn't look too convinced.

The following week, after spending days trying unsuccessfully to get a meeting with Halle Berry through her PRs, we found ourselves shivering in Cadiz. The Bond movie makers were using the Spanish city as a substitute for Cuba, which was in principle a great idea, apart from the bleak, chilly weather.

We had managed to obtain permission to attend a press conference there with the stars of the film. It was meant to be for Spanish journalists only, but probably because of our daily phone calls, Geoff, one of the PRs, had sent us invitations. I called him just after I'd checked in.

'You're not allowed to ask any questions. This is for the Spanish press only. Don't ask me again if you can get an interview with Pierce or Halle as it's never going to happen,' Geoff told me. It had taken me five days to get this far with him. 'You know it's not my choice. I know all you want is a photo with Halle Berry, but it's not up to me. You can sit quietly at the press conference, but that's it. It's more than any other British journalist is getting!' he declared.

It wasn't good enough for us.

'We've got to use that *Vanity Fair* article as some sort of leverage,' I said to Eva once I'd hung up the phone.

'Yeah. You'd think it would help,' she replied.

The article in the American magazine had just run, and we'd been astonished to see how much space had been devoted to Eva and me. There was a full five-page feature complete with photos of us. Even Piers was surprised. We'd devoured every word of the piece just before arriving in Spain, laughing at Jude Law's dismissal of us ('I don't read the *Mirror*') and feeling relieved that Nancy didn't give us a hard time for claiming to be writers for *Vanity Fair* magazine in order to get into the Armani after-show party.

The *Mirror* ran a page three piece on our appearance in the magazine, taking the piss out of us, of course. Kevin added at the end of the article, 'Last night Eva and Jessica refused to comment about their latest triumph. A spokesman said: "The girls don't want to talk about it. They're furious. They were promised the cover." '

The article had no effect on Geoff. Feeling desperate, I tried him again several times on the phone, begging, flirting, sobbing, throwing a wobbly or giggling, basically using every technique I could muster to persuade him to allow Eva and I access to Halle Berry. But I didn't get anywhere. Resigned, we made our way to the press conference in the centre of Cadiz.

'Now, girls. I've been told to look after you two troublemakers, so just take a seat over there. And no, Jessica, don't go waving that camera about. You're not going to get close enough for a picture,' tutted Geoff.

The grey-haired middle-aged man led Eva and I to two chairs at the back of the crowded room. It was pointless. We'd never be able to catch Halle's attention. Geoff's act of 'kindness' in reserving Eva and I these seats was clearly a ploy to keep us well away from the stars. What did he think we were going to do, I thought to myself, storm the stage, get Halle in a headlock and scream at her, 'Pose with us for a picture, you elusive bint'?

Pierce and Halle were eventually ushered into the room. They smiled and waved at the Spanish press, who greeted their arrival with cheers and applause.

'Where do they think they are? A football game?' I asked Eva. 'They're meant to be cynical hacks, not dewy-eyed fans.'

I had clearly forgotten about how I had almost licked David Beckham's arm the year before. I did, however, enjoy watching Pierce Brosnan. He was every bit as gorgeous as I'd hoped. But we still weren't getting anywhere with this mission to interview Halle.

We sat through the painfully turgid press conference for the next twenty minutes. One of the highlights was when one Spanish journalist asked Halle Berry, 'Have you tried the fish here?'

'I think I'm going to cry. They ban us from asking questions but they let someone ask her if she's tucked into a bit of cod for dinner,' I whimpered as I rocked back and forth in my chair in frustration. 'All we want to do is congratulate her on her Oscar and pose for a picture. I'd say that's a lot less painful for her than having to sit through bizarre questions from this lot. If anyone asks her what her favourite colour is, I'm leaving.'

Five minutes later the press conference was over. I was in a thoroughly bad mood. We must have looked utterly downtrodden.

'I told you it was pointless for the *Mirror* to send you all this way,' said Geoff. 'You're not going to get near her. But at least I got you into the press conference.'

'Oh, yes, thank you awfully, Geoff. At least we have a story about Halle Berry feeling peckish for some local sea urchin. Shall we beg Piers to hold the front page?' I asked tersely.

Geoff ignored me and turned his back on us.

'Thanks, Geoff. I know it's been difficult for you to help us out and that if it was up to you, you'd have let us meet her,' said Eva, trying to butter him up.

'Yes, well, it's hard you know. They're in the middle of filming. Give me a ring tomorrow morning.'

We left the press conference and headed for a bar near our hotel, where we met John Ferguson, a *Mirror* photographer who had been sent out to meet us in Spain to take the Halle Berry photo.

'So, we off to meet her at her hotel then?' John asked, laughing, as we sat down with him.

'Yeah, right. Because they're all so eager to help us,' sighed Eva.

'Well, we haven't got much time left. Our flight leaves from Gibraltar tomorrow afternoon. Piers and Kevin will be seriously pissed off with you two if you don't manage to sort it out,' he said.

'Thanks, Fergie. You don't bloody say,' I replied, sinking a glass of red wine.

The next morning I turned on my mobile and prepared myself for a bollocking from Kevin. I was surprised to hear a message from Geoff asking me to ring him back as soon as possible. Usually I was the one who left him messages, and plenty of them at that.

I dialled his number.

'Hi, Geoff, it's Jessica, returning your call,' I said.

'Hi. Yes, well, don't say I don't help you out. Pierce Brosnan has heard that you two are in town and wants you to come up to the set today. They're filming some great helicopter scenes by the fort. I'm not sure if Halle will be there or not. You better get your skates on. You've got to be there in an hour,' he said excitedly.

I stared at my phone for the next ten seconds with my mouth hanging open. Sod it if Halle wasn't there, we were going to meet *the* James Bond, I thought to myself.

I snapped out of my daydream and dialled Eva's number. 'OHMYGOD!' I screamed down the phone. 'GUESSWHAT GUESSWHATGUESSWHAT?'

'What the hell are you talking about? Stop shouting,' she snapped. It was clearly her turn to be in a bad mood.

'Ohmygod. Ohmygod,' I panted.

'What is it, you weirdo? Stop huffing and puffing like a pervert,' Eva replied.

'OK, OK. Sorry. So Geoff just rang. He must have seen how despondent and pathetic we looked yesterday and realized how we're going to be publicly flogged at work for totally failing out here, as he's just rung to say Pierce bloody gorgeous Brosnan has invited you and I on to the set. In an hour!' I screeched.

'Seriously? No way! What about Halle? Will she be there too?'

'Oh Halle, schmalley. Whatever. It's all about Pierce. Geoff doesn't know if she'll be on set today or not. But as if Piers will be angry with us for meeting up with Pierce Brosnan on a live James Bond movie set! Who'd be pissed off with us for that?' I asked.

'Hmmm. Well, he doesn't do it for me at *all*. But I take your point. He is James Bond after all,' replied an utterly underwhelmed Eva.

'Let's check out now. You ring Fergie and tell him to meet us in the hotel lobby in ten minutes so we can check out and get to this fort. I'll ring Kevin and tell him what the score is,' I said.

I tucked my phone between my chin and my left shoulder, dialling Kevin's number and dashing around my room packing my small case. After we'd finished with Pierce – and I had no idea how much time we'd get to spend with him – we would have to head straight for the airport in Gibraltar.

What the hell was I going to wear for the heart-throb, I wondered, as Kevin's number rang. I really was acting like a pathetic fan. Even more than those Spanish journalists who had rushed up to the stage after the press conference to beg Pierce and Halle for their autographs. Eva and I had pulled faces and cringed at their actions. British journalists would never dare to embarrass themselves by behaving in such a manner, we had said, laughing. Yet here I was panicking about which revealing top best showed off my boobs for my interview with Mr Brosnan.

Kevin answered the phone.

'Hi, Kev, it's Jessica. We've finally worn the PRs down enough and Pierce Brosnan has intervened and asked for Eva and I to meet him on the set in an hour. They don't know if Halle will be there,' I said.

'Fantastic! Pierce's stepson has just been caught doing drugs, so ask him about that,' he replied.

'Sure. Will do. I'll ring you afterwards.' I put the phone down.

Bugger. I could really see Pierce taking a shine to me if I asked him about his stepson's class A drug problems. I'd probably be removed from the set. Nice one, I thought to myself. There go my delusional fantasies of landing Pierce Brosnan.

Eva, John and I checked out of the hotel, threw our cases into the boot of John's hire car and drove off.

'I hope he's not running late as we're going to be cutting this quite fine. We're not that close to Gibraltar. And I've got to return the car to the hire place,' said John as he navigated his way through the streets.

'We haven't even got to the set yet! If we miss the plane, we miss the plane. All you photographers moan so much! Where is this bloody fort anyway?' I asked anxiously.

'Ignore her. She's just in a state of high excitement as she wants to mate with Pierce Brosnan,' Eva said to John.

'He's a bit bloody old, isn't he?' he asked, pulling a confused face.

'He's older than you, yes. But he is so much more of a sex god than you will ever hope to be, Fergie,' I answered. I wasn't going to let anyone criticize the man of my dreams.

After half an hour of trying to find a parking space near the fort, and making five frantic calls to Geoff to tell him we were on our way, we raced to the set with me leading the way. 'Hi, Geoff, we're here,' I panted down the phone.

'Right. I'll come and get you. Stay where you are.'

The metal door to the set next to the fort seemed eerily quiet and strangely empty. Two security guards looked completely unbothered by our presence. What was going on?

'Hi there. Follow me!' instructed Geoff, who popped up at the other side of the gate.

The security men let us through.

'Right, it's a bit quiet as they're not actually filming the helicopter scene until later. Halle's not filming today. Oh, and I'm sorry, but Pierce is running a bit late as he's having his back looked at,' Geoff continued brightly as he led us to the catering area.

'What? How late? He hasn't changed his mind, has he?' I asked.

'Probably about an hour. But you can have a nice cup of tea and explore the set while you're waiting.'

'We've got a plane to get. From Gibraltar,' said John. He was sounding very tense.

'Well, I'm sorry, but Pierce is busy. He does want to meet the girls, though,' Geoff replied.

'That's fine. We'll wait for as long as it takes. If we miss the plane, we miss it,' I said.

'Well, I don't want to miss it,' replied John.

Eva simply rolled her eyes and said nothing.

We poured ourselves cups of steaming tea in the catering area.

It was a cold and blustery day, and I was grateful for having something to keep me warm. My flimsy top wasn't really doing the trick, so I had borrowed Fergie's jacket.

We waited, John anxiously striding up and down the set. Geoff came back to us.

'Right, girls. Pierce has had his massage. He's on his way up now,' he said.

It had just started to chuck down with rain. We stood under Geoff's umbrella as I flicked my hair every way possible until Eva told me to stop getting my split ends in her eyes.

'Here he is!' said Geoff, as a strapping Pierce Brosnan made his way over to us.

'Oh . . . my . . . God,' I gasped.

He strode towards us with a great big grin spread across his face. I hadn't been able to see him properly at the conference and was delighted to discover that he was much taller than I had imagined. After meeting Brad Pitt and Tom Cruise, I had expected all actors to be weeny. But Pierce far outweighed my expectations. He was broad like a rugby player and well over six foot.

He was wearing faded blue jeans. Admittedly, they were slightly too high up on his waist, and he had tucked a dark blue denim shirt into them (what was it with the head-to-toe denim look?) and was wearing a large leather jacket. His shirt was unbuttoned to show a chest and neckful of salt-and-pepper hair. Despite the middle-aged wardrobe, which was creepy in the extreme, he had buckets of sex appeal. And once he opened his mouth and started to talk to us in that Irish lilt and with just a hint of an American accent, I could have sworn Eva joined me in going weak at the knees.

'Hi, girls. I am so glad to meet you! I've been reading about you in *Vanity Fair*. You're so famous!' he said after kissing us both.

'Hi! Thank you for having us,' was all I could come out with.

'I keep reading about you girls. You seem to be having so much fun. Congratulations on your success. Who's your publicist? If you haven't already got one, now's the time to hire somebody. Trust me!'

All I could do was grin like a lunatic and flick my hair some more.

'Do you mind if I take a picture of you with the girls? We've got a flight to catch,' said Fergie.

I glared at him. Why end our meeting now? He was ruining any chances I might have of being invited back to Pierce's trailer.

'Of course. Come on, girls. And don't for a second think you are going to pose for photographs wearing jackets and cardigans,' he purred.

I was a giggling wreck as Pierce then proceeded to help us pull our layers off. We ended up standing either side of him in our jeans and skimpy tops. Eva may have insisted she didn't have the hots for him, but she'd still worn a slinky little low-cut number.

'I'm going to have to warm you two up! You're shivering, you poor things!' he said as he rubbed his soft hands up and down our arms.

I tittered so much, I snorted with laughter and the ensuing photo that ran in the next day's column showed me cuddled up next to a pouting Pierce with not so much a smile on my face as a huge guffaw.

'So how's filming going here?' I finally asked after recovering from having my goose pimples caressed by Bond.

'Oh, great. We asked the lady mayor of Cadiz if she wanted a cameo role in the film. But she said no. That's the first time I've been turned down by a woman, which is a shame. Bond has a reputation with the ladies to keep up, you know,' he said, and grinned.

'Is she mad!' I barked, sounding a bit hysterical by now.

'So, how's Halle Berry? How brilliant that she's just won that Oscar!' Eva interrupted before I could embarrass myself any more.

'Oh, amazing. Just wait till you see the bedroom scenes. I started out on top. The next minute she was on top. It's a great thing – Halle is such a convincing actress,' he enthused.

I suddenly remembered Kevin telling me to question Pierce on his stepson's recent drug problems. It was time for me to stop simpering.

'I just wanted to say we are so sorry to hear about your stepson,' I said, putting on my most sympathetic face. I desperately hoped he wasn't going to blast me for bringing up such a personal matter. It was the end of our brief meeting with him, so it was the best time to ask him such a difficult question. That way, if he did storm off, we already had our picture and some quotes in the bag.

'Thank you so much for asking how he's doing. That's very thoughtful of you. Drugs are the scourge of our time, you know. We'll get through this. Well, lovely to meet you. Safe trip back and see you at the premiere!' he said.

We watched him stride off towards his trailer, with his leather jacket billowing out behind him in the wind.

'Come on, Eva. You so would. He is just, just, just, ahhh. Amazing. He *is* James Bond.' I sighed.

'Did you check out his hairy chest, which was totally on show? Ewww.' She wrinkled her nose.

'I would have climbed right into his shirt given half the chance,' I replied, ignoring Eva's horrified look. 'How nice is he? He was even nice when I asked about his hellraising stepson. Anyone else would have told us they don't talk about their private life. What a superstar he is.' I sighed again.

I rang Kevin from my mobile and told him, without sounding too much like a drooling fanatic, about our meeting with Pierce and how he had talked about his son.

'Great. File it now. We're going to put Pierce's photo at the top of the column between you and Eva,' said Kevin.

'Excellent. Can we keep it there all the time?' I asked.

'Piss off, Callan, you sad arse. No. Don't forget you and Eva have to find a new 3am girl when you're back.'

Eva and I ran back to John's car. As we waited for John to plug his camera into his laptop to upload the photos, I reminded Eva of our hunt for a new girl. 'We've had so many letters and emails, and no one's up to the job at all. If we don't hurry up, I hate to think who Kevin and Piers will pick. Knowing our luck they'll get a glamour model with big boobs. We're going to end up doing all the work with someone like that. I don't think Piers was joking when he said the other day he wants us to get a blonde girl so it balances out our photos on the top of the column. If that's his only criterion, then we're buggered.'

John plugged his mobile into the laptop so he could send the photos to the *Mirror*'s picture desk.

'Nah, mate. It won't be that bad. Piers wouldn't really do something like that. We can't rush it, or we'll end up with someone who realizes they don't want this life after all,' Eva replied.

'Who wouldn't enjoy this? We've just had our cardigans ripped off by Pierce Brosnan!' I sighed once more.

John banged the steering wheel in frustration. 'Shit! This is taking longer than I thought. This computer is so bloody slow. You guys are going to have to buckle up. I'm going to have to put my foot down the entire way to the airport.'

Eva took control. 'Look, hand me your laptop and tell me what to do. You drive, Fergie. Don't go too fast. It's still pissing with rain and the roads are going to be very slippery,' she said, getting into the front passenger seat.

She put her seatbelt on and positioned John's computer on her lap, with his mobile still attached to it. John started the engine and we shot off down the road and out of the city.

'Please don't go too fast,' scolded Eva. 'I don't want to die.'

'Well, if I'm going to go, it may as well be on the day I've nestled into Pierce Brosnan's armpit,' I swooned.

'Shut up, Callan, don't encourage him. Fergie, slow down!' she shouted.

John ignored us both and we spent the next hour and a half skidding around in the rain. I wrote up our interview with Pierce Brosnan and read it over my mobile to a copytaker, trying hard not to be sick down the back of John's head. It was the most torturous car ride I had ever endured.

We finally made it into Gibraltar with ten minutes before check-in closed.

'We haven't got time to drop the car off at the hire place,' shouted Fergie as he zoomed into an underground car park. 'Fuck it. We're leaving it here.'

We scrambled for the doors of the car and grabbed our cases out of the boot.

'Fergie, you can't dump the car here,' said Eva.

'Watch me,' he said, laughing, as he left the keys in the ignition. 'I'll get someone in the picture department at the office to ring up the hire place and tell them where the car is.'

He jotted down the level of the car park he'd left the vehicle on, and we pegged it out of there, towards the departures terminal.

After being the final passengers to check in, we boarded the plane and collapsed into our seats. We'd made it, and we were still alive. And I'd met the first Hollywood actor who did not disappoint in the flesh. I had spent the day snuggling up to the utterly enchanting Pierce Brosnan on the set of a James Bond film. Talk about the best job in the world.

Me and Mick Jagger

10. Threats and Thrills

Eva and I found the next 3am girl a few weeks later. We decided on someone called Suzanne Kerins, who worked on the *Daily Telegraph*'s gossip column. Although Bryony had also worked on the *Telegraph*, we didn't let her brief tenure on 3am put us off Suzanne. She was blonde, pretty, had an air of deviousness about her and a good track record at covering parties and hunting out gossip.

Piers had given us permission to let the 3am team grow, so we also hired two young and keen reporters. They were Susie Harding, a small, quiet and cute brunette in her early twenties, and Dean Piper, a tall, muscular, blond and vivacious 21-year-old. He was the first man to work for 3am. They would help cover parties and hang out at clubs like Chinawhite and Funky Buddha. They would not have their photos on our two daily pages, but provided essential back-up on busy nights.

There were now five of us on the team, which meant we matched the size of the gossip columns on our rival papers.

Within weeks of our new team forming, our showbiz news reporter James landed the hottest scoop of the year. Through a top secret array of sources, he had discovered that Sven-Göran Eriksson, the England manager, was having an affair with Ulrika Jonsson. Sven's iceman demeanour had melted thanks to his regular bonkathons with the saucy telly star at her Berkshire home.

When James told me at work about the story he was working on, I, along with everyone else, didn't believe it at first. What on earth did beer-swilling Ulrika see in the bespectacled, dour, balding millionaire? While Ulrika was single, her fellow Swede was shacked up with fiery Italian other half Nancy Dell'Olio. Clearly these ladies knew something the rest of us didn't.

Everyone in the showbusiness department knew about James's

story, but we were, of course, all sworn to secrecy. We couldn't risk other papers getting their hands on it. Still, when a story of that magnitude started to leak within a newspaper, the bosses at work would have no choice but to bang it into the next day's paper as soon as they had enough evidence. It was all very tense and exciting, watching James, Kevin and Richard popping in and out of Piers's office all the time.

Piers rang up Ulrika's agent, Melanie Cantor, to inform her he was going to run the story the following day. Whatever she said must have convinced him that Ulrika was not going to deny the story or try to sue the paper.

Unfortunately for James, Piers had launched his war on celebrity several months earlier, and he was sticking to the promise he had made after September 11 to keep tittle-tattle off the front pages and stick to serious news stories instead. So when the time came to print James's red-hot scoop, Piers decided he didn't want to devote the entire front page of the next day's paper to the scandalous story. It was to be relegated to 3am. Not only that, but James's name wouldn't appear anywhere near the article.

A shell-shocked James emerged from Piers's office and sat in a glowering silence at his desk. Eva and I were then told what was to happen. We understood why James was so furious at not getting his byline on the story and seeing it splashed across our column.

'This is going to blow up in our faces,' I whispered to Eva.

There was an uneasy atmosphere in our department. I didn't blame James for being so pissed off. It was the biggest scoop of the year, and he couldn't take any of the glory for it. Eva and I were banned from telling anyone it wasn't our story, but there was no way we were going to stick to that. We'd look like the biggest byline bandits in the world, and when it emerged that it was James's story, Eva and I would be the laughing stock of Fleet Street. I just hoped Piers didn't expect us to go on GMTV and talk about the story, as *Mirror* reporters often did when they'd landed an exclusive.

The next day the paper ran the story across our column with a blurb on the front page referring to the unlikeliest love story of the year. Our predictions were right. James's friends on the other newspapers immediately attacked Eva and I, even though we'd had no choice in the matter. It soon became clear that every showbusiness journalist had an opinion, and it was that Eva and I were callous, cold-hearted cows who didn't have any decent stories of our own so had nicked James's sensational scoop.

We were gutted. I knew 3am had plenty of enemies at other papers and that we were always going to be bitched about, but I felt that the Sven and Ulrika saga had spiralled out of control. I didn't want to have anything to do with someone else's story.

When Patsy Kensit had called Piers the previous year to tip him off that she was having an affair with Ally McCoist, and that if he sent a photographer to her hotel that night the couple could be snapped, Piers ran the story on a news page under our names on 3am. At the time I found it odd that we had to go along with the pretence that it was our scoop. But this was very different. I rang my dad about it, as I thought he could advise me on what to do if anyone asked about the story.

'For God's sake, girl, have I taught you nothing? Take all the glory and spread all the blame!' he boomed down the phone at me.

I realized that that wasn't what I wanted to hear. In fact, Eva and I disobeyed the powers that be and told anyone who cared to listen that it was James's scoop. Piers must have been feeling bad about it too.

He sent an email around the entire office telling everyone that the Sven and Ulrika story had been James's and what a great reporter he was. He also rewarded James by packing him and his girlfriend off on a two-week freebie holiday to the Maldives. Still, it came as no surprise to anyone when James resigned from the *Daily Mirror* shortly afterwards to become the deputy news editor of the *Sunday People*.

The first big event the new 3am team covered together was the TV BAFTAs later that month at the Grosvenor House Hotel in Park Lane. Unlike the Film BAFTAs, at which the great and the good of the movie world behaved impeccably (with the exception of Russell Crowe, who'd duffed up a TV executive after he had edited out his painfully turgid acceptance speech), telly actors tended to be unable to control themselves around free booze. There was therefore usually A Scene.

I could never understand why the TV stars who unleashed themselves the most were always so outraged when their misbehaviour made the newspapers. If they knocked back enough warm wine to sink a booze cruise and subsequently performed outrageously in a room full of journalists, what did they expect?

The *EastEnders* actors always seemed to be the naughtiest. That was the case at pretty much every do. At the National TV Awards one year June Brown, aka Dot Cotton, had been photographed as she was helped out of the after-show party at the RCA and steered into a taxi. After we ran the picture in the column with a story about how the squiffy star had had trouble leaving the booze-fuelled bash unaided, one of the PRs for *EastEnders* rang in a furious state to inform us that June hadn't been pissed, she'd merely been pretending to be drunk for the photographers. Well, in that case, what an actress she truly was.

Jessie Wallace was always a surefire bet too. She played Kat Slater to great acclaim on the small screen, but off the *EastEnders* set the bubbly actress was just as feisty as her character. She would get into all kinds of trouble because of her aggressive behaviour, and not only at the BAFTAs: she once threatened to bash a stranger over the head with a snooker cue during a heated game in a Los Angeles bar, for example. You could always be sure she'd bad-mouth some of her co-stars (she was not the biggest fan of Barbara Windsor or Steve McFadden).

Eva, Suzanne, Susie, Dean and I were all looking forward to the party. With tanked-up soap stars in the house, we knew we were guaranteed some sort of bad behaviour.

We arrived at the party, which was taking place in one of the hotel's function rooms. It had attracted the usual gaggle of soap stars, many of whom tended to end up in the worst-dressed lists in newspapers and magazines. The *Coronation Street* youngsters were the worst culprits. Even the boys. How could you go so wrong with a smart suit? Easily, if you spent every day filming in the Rovers Return, it seemed. As for the girls, I'd never seen so much flesh on display. Forget about the rule about only showing a tasteful hint of cleavage if your legs are on show. Most of these young actresses preferred to get it all out, and the more ruffles the better.

As predicted, there were plenty of drunk stars from *The Bill*, *Corrie*, *Hollyoaks* and *EastEnders* hurling themselves around the dance floor. It wasn't long before two of the stars began to play up.

'Lucy Benjamin is losing it because of Steve McFadden,' whispered Suzanne to me.

'Brilliant! They're very temperamental. See if you can eavesdrop on them,' I said to her.

Suzanne nodded and took Susie and Dean with her. As Suzanne was new and Susie and Dean didn't have their pictures on the column, it meant they could venture out incognito. I'd certainly been feeling lately that my job had become much harder, as more and more celebs now recognized me. Knowing that a gossip columnist was hovering in the same room certainly put stars on their guard. It was easier with American celebrities who didn't know who we were.

Lucy, who played Lisa Fowler, and Steve, who played Phil Mitchell, had met on the set of *EastEnders*, where they played on-screen lovers. They were as highly strung and hot-headed in real life as they were in the soap. They were also in an off-screen relationship. They argued frequently and their bust-ups were regularly charted in the newspapers and magazines.

That night they had both clearly enjoyed a few drinks, and Lucy – who was wearing a huge sparkler on her engagement finger – was not happy with her boyfriend. But instead of discussing her displeasure with the female friend who had accompanied her, Lucy appeared to be acting out a scene from *EastEnders*.

Dean, Susie and Suzanne didn't find it hard to eavesdrop on the rapidly unravelling star. Anyone within a hundred-foot radius couldn't have helped but overhear Lucy's hysterics. Sobbing into her glass of champagne, the small blonde was wailing, 'Steve doesn't love me. He doesn't love me because he won't marry me. He always tells me he's not the marrying kind. But I so wish he would ask me. If he doesn't want to marry me, he should let me go. It's been two and a half years!'

The star then tottered over to a group of young blokes and tried to dance suggestively in front of them. We all stared at her. There must have been eighty people in the corner of the room, and Lucy didn't seem to care that everyone was watching her tragic performance. When her solo dirty dancing act didn't get her any attention from the men, she staggered back to her mate and burst into tears again.

'I love him. I love him. I so love Steve. Why doesn't he love me?' she cried.

She reminded me of how Jordan behaved whenever Dwight was in the vicinity.

Brave Susie took this as her cue to congratulate Lucy on getting engaged. The star had been flashing the diamond ring around all night and had waved it at photographers when she arrived at the ceremony. Maybe she was getting married after all?

'It's not a fucking engagement ring! It's a fucking present, all right?' she screamed at Susie, who quickly retreated.

Steve, meanwhile, stayed well away from the unfolding drama. Eva and I watched the actor as he walked straight past Lucy, rolled his eyes and blanked her when she tried to talk to him. Eventually, Lucy's mates helped her out of the party and into a cab outside. Steve just looked embarrassed.

We stayed until the party ended at 2am, just in case Lucy returned to have it out with Steve, who seemed to enjoy laughing and drinking with pals, including a curly-haired blonde who'd caught his eye.

The next day we typed up the Lucy and Steve story as the lead item in 3am with the headline 'Unlucy in Love', and detailed every bit of Lucy's sorry behaviour, describing the actress as an increasingly tragic figure. The story ran in the column the following day.

By lunchtime, when we were all busy working on the next column, the main 3am phone line rang.

'Hello?' said Eva. Holding the phone to her ear, Eva leant around her computer screen and started waving at me.

'What? Who is it?' I asked.

Eva mouthed something indecipherable at me and starting rummaging around in her desk drawer. 'Oh, hello. Yes, it's Eva here. How are you?' she said into the phone. She pulled out her small tape recorder and put the earpiece into her right ear. She clamped the phone to the same ear and turned the tape recorder on. We used these for interviews and when we were fronting up agents and publicists with stories about their clients that we were planning to run. Our lawyers always insisted that we had everything on tape. I got up from my chair and joined her.

She looked like she was about to explode into hysterics as she scribbled down the name 'Steve McFadden' on the notepad next to her phone. I sat down on her desk and listened in. I could hear Steve McFadden's voice berating her down the phone.

'I'm very well, thanks – apart from obviously being annoyed and upset about how you've been treating Lucy. I've got three things to say. You've been picking on Lucy since she's been in the show and I'm sick of it,' he barked, stopping at point number one.

'Steve, we don't pick on Lucy,' Eva replied in a measured tone.

'Yes, you do. You pick on her, and you know why? Because you're bullies,' he continued.

'We're not bullies,' said Eva.

'And I tell you something. I don't like bullies. Do you know what I do to bullies? I bully them back. That's what I used to do at school. And when I see any of you three . . .'

'We're not in school now, Steve,' Eva interrupted.

I put my hand over my mouth to stop myself from laughing out loud.

By now Suzanne, Susie and Dean had also gathered around Eva's desk and were listening intently. Eva meanwhile was on flying form and kept the enraged actor talking. In fact, there was no shutting him up.

'No, we ain't in school, we're in the big wide world called showbusiness, right? When I see you three out I'm gonna throw lager on you. And tell you to fuck off,' he shouted.

'Oh, really,' Eva replied.

'Yeah, really! You fucking watch me,' he growled, like his on-screen character.

'Oh, you're so hard, Steve,' Eva said, sighing.

'You fucking watch me, you fucking horrible bunch of c★★★s,' he shouted, getting into his stride.

'And what's the second thing you wanted to say?' she asked.

'I'm going to chuck fucking lager all over you until you can't do your fucking job any more, you c★★★s. Print what the fuck you want 'cos I fucking hate you.'

I had to jump off Eva's desk at this point, as I didn't want him to hear me howling with laughter in the background. Suzanne, Dean and Susie stared at each other disbelievingly. What a charmer.

'What's your problem?' Eva asked.

'What's my fucking problem, you c★★★? You fucking messed with my bird, picking on my bird.'

'We don't pick on your "bird". Is that how you refer to your fiancée?' she continued.

'You're a bunch of fucking bullies and I'm going to fucking bully you back, you fucking watch me, right,' he repeated.

'Why don't you just grow up,' Eva said, sighing again.

This was clearly too much for the 43-year-old actor, who then hung up on her.

'What a dick!' laughed Eva.

'Oh my God! He's a proper nutter!' I replied.

'You know how we normally don't believe anyone who claims they're a celeb when they ring us up? Well, I just knew it was him. There's no mistaking that gruff voice. I swear he thinks he really is Phil Mitchell,' she said. 'And I've got him on tape coming out with all those classic threats. I can't believe he was sad enough to slam the phone down though. How pathetic.'

Just then the phone rang again.

'I'll get it!' shouted Eva, as she put her earpiece back into her right ear and turned her Dictaphone back on.

'Hi, Steve,' she chirped brightly into the phone.

'Right, the third thing which I forgot to say is that Lucy's very emotional at the moment. She's had an operation on her cervix. She had an intrusive operation on her cervix. She's very emotional and so am I, and what I just said to you, I meant every word of it,' he shouted before hanging up on Eva again.

'Nice guy!' exclaimed Eva. 'I bet Lucy will be over the moon to hear that her bullying bugger of a boyfriend has called a gossip column to talk about her gynaecological problems.'

Eva rewound the tape on her Dictaphone and we listened to the whole conversation. Kevin joined us. We listened to it over and over and over again, each time laughing even more.

'He is going to get the biggest kicking from the *EastEnders* bosses,' I said, returning to my desk. 'They treat all the stars on that show like schoolkids and are so strict with them. They're going to go ballistic when they find out he's been calling up newspapers and threatening journalists. If he cares about Lucy so much, why didn't he console her at the party and take her home?'

'Fucking brilliant. Eva, write up every word of the conversation for tomorrow's column. Oh, Steve, you're so going to regret that,' sniggered Kevin.

We ran the full transcript of Eva and Steve's heart to heart in the next day's column with the headline 'EastEnder goes ballistic over our BAFTA bash revelations'. The article started:

Another day, another fan. This time it's the turn of *EastEnders* 'hardman' Steve McFadden, who was thrilled with 3am's exclusive coverage of his girlfriend Lucy Benjamin's extraordinary performance at the BAFTAs after-show party.

She had spent the bash sobbing into her champagne while wailing: 'Steve doesn't love me. He doesn't love me because he won't marry me.'

McFadden, who plays Albert Square's really dangerous Phil Mitchell, called Eva to discuss the nuances surrounding that fateful night.

Steve didn't ring us back to go over his views on our article. But we did hear that the *EastEnders* press office went nuclear on him, and it was explained to him very slowly and in no uncertain terms that he was never to call up a newspaper ever again.

Childishly, we couldn't resist running the entire phone conversation in the column again that Christmas. We had decided to run a series of favourite 3am stories from the year, and Steve McFadden's conversation with Eva was on top of our list.

Two weeks later, in May, Suzanne and I were dispatched to the Laureus World Sports Awards in Monte Carlo and then on to the Cannes Film Festival. Sadly, Jordan wasn't expected to attend the ceremony in Monaco that year. But Lady Victoria Hervey would be there, we were told.

She had long been a figure of fun in the column for throwing strops at parties and coming out with the immortal line 'Don't you know who I am?' when it was pointed out on various occasions that she had not been invited to a party she was trying to crash. We described her as 'Lady Vicky Horse Face' and we never hesitated to point out her headache-inducing bad dress sense and her rather chunky ankles.

Unfortunately, it was also pointed out several times a month, invariably by builders for some reason, that I looked just like her.

''Ere, love, are you that posh bird, Victoria Hervey?' asked a workman at Canary Wharf Tube station on the Monday morning before Suzanne and I were due to leave for Monte Carlo.

'No, I'm bloody not,' I hissed. I shuffled along with the rest of the commuters to get on to the escalators.

'All right, love, calm down. You 'er sister?' he continued, warming to his theme.

I had a total sense of humour failure, tutted loudly and stomped up the escalator.

My colleagues, led by Kevin, thought it was the best insult they had heard all year when I told them what had happened.

'You do a bit!' chortled Kevin.

'But we all slag her off for looking horsy and always write in the column, "Why the long face?" Great! What a bloody honour,' I snorted.

Suzanne and I had packed enough clothes to dress a small army of wannabe Girls Aloud members to get us through the black tie events of the next fortnight.

'Make sure you two scrub up well in the photos, please,' instructed Richard just before we set off for Luton to catch our flight to Nice.

We were booked into the Grand Hotel in Monte Carlo, where I had stayed the previous year, and I told Suzanne about the no-suntan rule.

'There's a gorgeous pool on the roof, but the office are expecting us to run around like blue-arsed flies so we can't really kick back up there,' I said to her while we walked to the pre-ceremony dinner.

Instead of throwing the lavish drinks party at the Monte Carlo Beach Hotel like the year before, the organizers had instead set up a sumptuous dinner at the Monte Carlo Sporting Club for all the celebs and the press.

There was a champagne party in the garden in front of the venue beforehand, where Suzanne and I posed with the likes of John McEnroe and Ian Botham. They were not exactly the sort of celebs we wrote about in the column, but we leapt on anyone vaguely famous in the hope that they'd misbehave later and that we'd already have a photo of us with them in the bag.

'This is boring as hell,' I whispered to Suzanne.

'Yeah. I hope it gets a bit livelier later on. No hope of an offer of a threesome here, is there?' she giggled, reminding me of my Jordan experience the year before.

We walked into the Sporting Club, where place settings for more than 400 people had been prepared for the night. Needless to say, the press were made to sit well away from the stars.

Everyone had adhered to the black tie dress code. All eyes were on Catherine Zeta-Jones, who slinked into the party in a black low-cut dress slashed to the thigh. Husband Michael Douglas was attached to her right arm. His hair had unfortunately turned an unusual hue of patchy chestnut, and he looked a good deal older than when I'd last seen him the previous year. German über-model Heidi Klum made her entrance wearing a floor-length, mermaid-style, white, peach and mint-coloured frock with matching headband.

Vinnie Jones and his wife, Tanya, then swept in. In keeping with his on-screen gangster image, Vinnie was wearing black trousers, a white shirt, no tie or bow tie and a pinstripe waistcoat buttoned up to the top. He could wear what he liked. Let's face it, who was going to dare tell Vinnie he wasn't allowed in without a dicky bow on?

We had spoken to Vinnie earlier on in the day at the celebrity golf challenge. He'd forgotten about our previous meeting when we'd interviewed Guy Ritchie at the *Snatch* premiere, and still had the air of someone who was about to lose his temper any second.

'So, Vinnie, what are you up to at the moment?' I had asked, hoping he wouldn't reply, 'About to bash your 'ed in, treacle.'

Luckily he regaled Suzanne and I with news of his new venture: recording an album of duets for Telstar with celebs such as Denise Van Outen and Billie Piper. Keeping a straight face was not even an option; it was a necessity in front of the soccer hardman turned Cliff Richard.

'Oh wow, that's amazing!' I trilled, trying to sound as impressed and enthusiastic as possible.

'I'm still waiting to hear back from Robbie Williams. I'd love to persuade Madonna, but I don't think she'll go for it,' he growled at us.

'Why ever not? Is she mad?' I replied, a bit too earnestly.

Suzanne nudged me to shut up while Vinnie eyed me suspiciously, trying to work out if I was being sarcastic or not.

After the dinner, Suzanne and I muscled our way into Jimmy'z nightclub, where I had hung out with Jordan and Dwight Yorke the previous year. Inside the packed club we ran into Jason Fraser, a celebrity photographer. He was single, in his mid-thirties, enigmatic, charming, good-looking and a millionaire. He was rumoured to have contacts in all sorts of fields and was on very good terms with the celebs he happened to stumble upon on holiday, such as Posh and Becks. He would take photos of famous people tanning themselves on the beach and looking stunning – unlike the rest of us mere mortals, who are usually sweaty, covered in sand and suntan lotion, and with greasy hair sticking up at odd angles.

I had met Jason twice before and was slightly intimidated by him. He was a big name in the media world. He had made a bundle with the first photos of Princess Diana and Dodi Fayed on holiday in the Med together in 1997.

Jason sold his pictures to the *Mirror* and they often ended up on 3am, but I never really dealt with him. He preferred to talk money and to check how big his pictures would appear on the page with Kevin or Piers, rather than with mere reporters such as myself.

The *Daily Mirror* paid less than the *Sun* and the *News of the World* for stories, so showbiz insiders who had tales to sell would usually bypass us and go straight for our opposition. But when I saw Jason at Jimmy'z that night, I was determined to persuade him to sell us his information instead. He looked like he'd enjoy a good flirt, and as he dealt with male journalists at the *Sun* and the *News of the World*, being a girl was in my favour.

He clearly liked to think he could charm the ladies. He was wearing a black Gucci suit and a fitted white shirt unbuttoned to nipple level. He had a gold chain around his neck with a crucifix hanging off it. He smelt strongly of aftershave. He looked like he was off to a James Bond fancy dress party. In fact, he didn't look like a snapper at all. Interestingly, he didn't have a camera to hand. I was to learn later that he preferred to walk around with a palm-sized digital one discreetly placed in his pocket. Jason didn't want people to take one look at him and instantly think he was a photographer. He preferred not to work at events. Although both were rich and famous, Jason was very different to Youngy in their field.

By and large, there were three main schools of photographers. The first group was invited to pretty much every party as they were discreet, charming and largely well behaved. They included Youngy, Dave Bennett and Dave Hogan. They had been covering events for more than thirty years and were generally more famous (and considerably richer) than the stars they photographed. I had enjoyed many a hilarious evening watching them at work and at play: they frequently argued among themselves like bickering middle-aged married couples. This brigade was all deep tans, flash watches, cashmere jumpers, leather jackets and expensive cars. They went on exotic holidays, made a fortune, oozed charm and were friends with celebrities.

The second class of photographers was your mid-range paparazzi who worked for agencies such as Big Pictures and Rex Features. They could be found penned in behind barriers outside the cinema at film premieres, award ceremonies and parties, screaming celebrities' names out at them and snapping away. They covered launch parties, photographed celebs on holiday and always seemed to be in the right place at the right time when topless soap stars were diving off yachts in Spain and the South of France.

And then there was the crème de la scum. These were men who were more like stalkers than trained photographers. They turned up at every celebrity party, were shabbily dressed and often reeked of BO. These men chased stars from clubs, bars and parties and had one mission in mind: they wanted to shove their cameras up the skirts of female celebrities. Their tactics involved either flinging themselves on to the pavement when the star in question got into a taxi, thus being in the perfect position to reel off shots of her panties, or they would run in front, alongside or behind the celeb, holding their cameras at skirt level and clicking away. Even though having a conversation with them on the phone was torturous ('I don't understand a word you're saying. Slow down. What? Who was wearing no knickers? No, I certainly can't use a picture like that in 3am. We're not a lesbian porn column'), I did buy pictures off them from time to time and paid them for stories.

He may have been nicknamed 'King of the Paps', but Jason didn't fit into any of these categories.

We were chatting and getting on well at the club when he suddenly whispered in my ear, 'I've got someone I want you to meet.'

'Who?' I asked.

'She's a very good friend of mine. I think it's time you two kissed and made up.' He grinned and walked off towards a gaggle of girls in sparkly dresses.

I was about to follow him – well, he was being obviously flirtatious now and I was intrigued to see who he was about to introduce me to – when I stopped in my high heels. There was Jason chatting away in the ear of Lady Victoria Hervey.

'Oh God, no!' I yelled at Suzanne.

Jason beckoned me over. I turned my back and pretended I hadn't seen him. 'Oh, no chance, mate. This is not happening,' I said to Suzanne, who couldn't stop laughing.

'He doesn't look very happy with you. Go on. Go and speak to her. You never know, you and Vic could become best friends!' Suzanne said, sniggering.

I sighed. 'I'm really not happy about this.' But I knew I had to behave. I stomped over like a sulky teenager towards a smiling Jason and a grim-faced Victoria Hervey. I didn't know what Jason was up to. Kissing and making up with Lady V wasn't exactly on my agenda that night, and I didn't appreciate being forced to make peace with her.

'Victoria, this is Jessica. Jessica, this is Victoria,' said Jason, as Victoria and I reluctantly shook hands and said hello.

It was too loud in the club to attempt to talk to her even if I had wanted to. And anyway, even when she was trying to be nice she still looked like she was chewing a wasp. But Jason was determined to make Victoria and I bosom buddies. He had a word in her ear, no doubt telling her about the benefits of being nice to me. She looked as reluctant as I was and glanced over his shoulder.

'Look, nice to meet you. See you around,' she drawled in my general direction.

'Yes, you too,' I replied.

'You see? I've sorted you two out. You can thank me for that. I told her to make an effort with you as you'll stop being bitchy about her in your column if she does. I'm sure she has lots of good stories if you get her on side,' he explained.

I grimaced. I didn't want to stop being nasty to her just like that. Besides, Kevin had a near-obsession with her and wouldn't like it if I decreed we had to start writing glowing articles about the stuck-up socialite.

The rest of the night, Jason oozed charm out of every moisturized pore. He bought Suzanne and I glass after glass of vodka and tonics, was unbelievably attentive and constantly cracked jokes. He was obviously very interested in me. He was talking to me so intently that I was practically leaning backwards over the chair behind. I was flattered, but also very happy Suzanne was there; he seemed quite manic and I didn't really know what he wanted with me.

I left the party with Suzanne feeling a little confused. Jason was much kinder and funnier than I'd given him credit for. Over the next two days, he and I spent a lot of time together talking about our jobs and how we'd got to where we were. The more I got to know him, the more I thought he wasn't the flashy playboy I had at first suspected he was.

'I've fancied you for so long. There's something about your eyes. They are so expressive. When I look at your photo on top of the column I am always drawn to them,' he said to me before he left Monte Carlo.

This guy clearly didn't believe in taking things slowly.

After three days in Monte Carlo Suzanne and I made our way to Cannes, which was about an hour away by car.

I had reported from the Cannes Film Festival for two years running when I was at the *Daily Telegraph*. As a journalist working for a serious broadsheet newspaper, I had enjoyed decent access to the stars; now that I worked for a tabloid the celebs were suspicious of, I could see that they used to have far more respect for me – although I did manage to accidentally knock a full glass of water all over Mel Gibson's lap during an interview one year.

Suzanne and I were staying at a rented studio apartment off the Croisette, over the road from Cannes beach. I would be out there for a week, while Suzanne was going to stay for the full ten days.

Most of the big parties took place during the first weekend and the main stars would leave towards the end of the second week, so there was no point in both of us staying. Eva, Dean and Susie weren't envious that Suzanne and I were in the South of France. They knew we had to deliver entire columns from there. And if we thought getting hold of party tickets in London was difficult at times, it was nothing compared to the lack of access the British press had at Cannes.

Every year the Cannes Film Festival took place over ten days and culminated on the Sunday night with the closing awards ceremony, the Palme d'Or. The handing out of the gongs was always the least memorable part of the annual event. It was all about the schmoozing, the parties, the private bashes on yachts and the celebs getting trashed at the Hotel du Cap.

Unfortunately, we also had to attend the daily press conferences with the stars of the films. These were held in the Palais des Festivals, a large building on the seafront.

More than 500 journalists squeezed themselves into the auditorium each time to ask a couple of movie stars largely banal questions. Not any old journalist could get in. You had to apply for accreditation and a pass six months or so before the festival. Not only did you have to get various bosses at your newspaper to fill out long forms to verify that you were who you said you were, you had to send photos as well as press cuttings from the festival the year before. That way the organizers could see if a journalist had written anything unflattering about the painfully bureaucratic event.

Once you were given the nod, you were handed over a press pass when you arrived in Cannes. The press passes were colour-coded depending on your level of importance, as decreed by the organizers. The top tier were allowed into the press conferences first, and they had white passes. Next were the pink passes with a yellow dot. Then there was the pink pass. At the bottom rung were the blue passes, followed by the yellow ones. The journalists with these last two types of passes around their necks were only allowed to sit in the press conferences if there were any spaces left after everyone else had taken their seats. The organizers seemed to handpick which journalists were allowed to ask questions anyway. The stars would sit along a table on a stage, with their names printed on a card in front of them. Oh, the indignity of being Leonardo DiCaprio and still having to wear a name badge. The press perched on the sort of desk and chair combos you'd find in university lecture halls, and stared up at them.

Despite this system, reporters still stamped on each other's feet and pushed each other out of the way to sit in on what was usually an agonizing hour of some stuck-up, pretentious actress droning on about her art.

The overseas journalists really came into their own and would ask the most long-winded questions, usually in their native tongue. By the time the panel of actors had been handed headphones so that they could hear the tedious question, which was usually to do with politics, in translation, everyone had forgotten what had been asked.

The worst bit of the press conference was at the end, when the foreign hacks rushed up to the stage, waving bits of paper for the actors to autograph. The British journalists, who mainly all sat together, would grimace in disgust at such unprofessional behaviour.

After filing over any interesting news lines that emerged from the press conference, it was usually time to start the daily stalking of the film companies' PRs.

Each movie company and movie company PR would set up shop in one of the seafront hotels lining the Croisette, the main thoroughfare in Cannes. The Croisette was usually packed with pickpockets, police, tourists hoping to catch a glimpse of the Hollywood stars in town, hundreds of journalists, film company executives, wannabe producers, directors and actors. In short, it often felt like battling your way up Oxford Street during the sales, albeit in the Mediterranean sun.

The film company PRs were there to garner publicity for their companies' films, and you would have thought that the best way to go about this would be to invite the press to their clients' after-show parties. Oh no. That would have made life far too easy for everyone. Trying to gain access to events became a daily form of torture for us. We would turn up every day to find out which parties the PRs were inviting press to, ask if we could have tickets, enquire why we couldn't have tickets, change tack and ask nicely, then scream and shout and swear and demand to know how they expected to get any publicity for their movies if they didn't invite any newspapers along. Apparently, it was often because the American actors hated the British tabloids and didn't want them there.

Usually they would cave in and we would get access, although most of the time, as with the spectacular party for *Shrek 2*, which took place in a castle, there were VIP areas strictly for the cast. It was always a bit of a kerfuffle. One year at the party for the All Saint's flop movie *Honest*, a local French gang tried to blag their way in and a gun went off outside the party during the fracas. No one was hurt. But what was truly startling was that no one was really surprised that the fight to get access into a Cannes party had resulted in gunfire. That's how messy the film festival was.

That May 2002, the main event was the *Vanity Fair* Cannes Film Festival party at the Eden Roc restaurant.

'Oh, God. We haven't got a chance,' I moaned to Suzanne when we found out the magazine was throwing an A-list party.

It was the same night as the annual MTV party at the Pierre Cardin villa, which was miles out of town and never really attracted the big stars. The party for the Brit film *24 Hour Party People* was taking place at the Hotel Martinez, too.

'Look, why don't you try to get into the *Vanity Fair* party and I'll cover the other two,' suggested Suzanne as we sat in the rented apartment we were sharing. It was a depressingly dark and dirty flat, so dusty that we had both become allergic to the place and couldn't stop sneezing.

I shook my head despondently. 'If I couldn't get into their Oscar party, then I doubt I'll make it into this one. It's at the Eden Roc, which is next to the Hotel du Cap, way out of town. I can't see them buying my excuse that I'm staying at the hotel and happened to stumble in by accident. You can just imagine the security they'll have,' I said.

I realized as I was talking to Suzanne that I wasn't getting into the spirit of things at all. I knew the reality of Cannes was that it wasn't glamorous. It was hard, hard work. Suzanne on the other hand was wildly excited to be there for the first time. But the real reason I was being all doom and gloom was because Jason had been ringing me constantly from London, and I couldn't wait to get back and meet up with him again. He was really laying it on thick, and I hated the fact that I was stuck in Cannes instead of going on dates with him.

To make matters worse Richard Wallace had called me the night before to break some big news. 'Your Uncle Dicky's off to the Big Apple,' he boomed down the phone.

'What? Are you leaving the *Mirror*?' I gasped.

'Noooo, Callan, you lady boy. I am off to New York to be the paper's new US correspondent. You're all going to have to survive without me,' he slurred, clearly having had a few celebratory drinks.

Even after moving on from being our showbiz editor, Richard had kept an eye out for Eva and me. He knew how to get the best out of us and we could go to him with anything. When tensions rose between us and Kevin, which they sometimes did due to a clashing of egos and temperaments, Richard stepped in to sort things out. We also went to him with our big stories, since he was head of news. But now he would be across the Atlantic. Yet again there was to be more turmoil in the office.

I was gutted. It had been bad enough when he'd left our department to move halfway down the office, but now that he was off to America I felt even lower than before.

But I was in Cannes and had to get on with things. I had to remind myself that I was there to work and the office would soon be checking up on us to see what stories we had. So far we had nothing.

Suzanne left the apartment for the *24 Hour Party People* bash at 9pm.

'Steve Coogan will be there and Johnny Vegas is meant to be too, so who knows what will happen. I'd better get down there early,' she said as she left.

I was going to try and blag it into the *Vanity Fair* party on my own. I knew Youngy was going to be there taking photos for the magazine, but there was no way I could ask him to smuggle me in. It was more than his job was worth, and it would have been unfair of me to ask him to jeopardize his relationship with the magazine. I'd already tried that earlier on in the year in LA.

I put on a green top from Press & Bastyan, a black Top Shop skirt and Zara high heels. I giggled to myself as I took a final look in the mirror. I certainly wasn't going to end up in the embarrassing situation of wearing the same outfit as somebody else. Not for a minute did I expect to see any of the Hollywood stars wearing high street fashion.

An hour later I left the dank, mothball-reeking apartment and hailed a taxi out on the Croisette.

The Eden Roc was intimidatingly swanky. The taxi rumbled down the long driveway, which was lit with torches. Tuxedo-clad Secret Service lookalikes growled into walkie-talkies as they prowled the manicured lawns.

'Oh, fuck,' I said out loud. 'How am I going to get in there?'

The taxi driver pulled up outside the entrance to the restaurant. A line of chauffeur-driven Mercedes, Daimlers and a Ferrari were parked outside, ready to whisk the guests inside back to their villas and hotel suites. I had turned up in a taxi. It was not looking great.

I paid the driver and tried to look confident as I clambered out of the back and made my way to the restaurant entrance.

Guarding the door was a pair of surly, black-clad skinny American women armed with clipboards. There was no turning back. I'd have to hold my head up high and act as if I had been invited and my mates were inside waiting for me. That trick may have worked in the past, but I wasn't so sure I would pass muster with this hatchet-faced duo.

'Oh, hell-air,' I said to them in my poshest accent and putting on my best Botoxed expression. At the very least I needed to look as if I'd had surgery just for the party.

'Good evening. May I have your name?' asked one of the women.

Were they this miserable to the real guests or only to the glaringly obvious gatecrashers, I wondered. But hang on. They wanted my name. What should I say? I said the first name that entered my head.

'Donna Air,' I replied.

God knows why her name sprung to mind. Thankfully the American hadn't heard of the Geordie ex-*Byker Grove* actress. I looked at the doorway with what I hoped was a nonchalant manner.

She scanned her list with a pen, but unsurprisingly couldn't find Donna's name.

'Did you RSVP?' she asked, peering at me suspiciously.

'I didn't personally. My PA should have. She's frightfully forgetful, you know. She's new, but I think I'm going to have to give her the boot. Are you telling me she forgot to RSVP? What an absolute disgrace,' I thundered, getting into my new persona.

'Well, your name doesn't appear to be here,' she said, eyeing me up and down.

And then, for no reason I can think of apart from maybe thinking I'd bray on for hours about my ghastly PA and bore her rigid, she let me in.

'Go in. It's fine,' she said, and moved aside so I could walk into the party.

'Thank you,' I replied and headed inside.

I couldn't believe my luck. Gatecrashing this event had been much easier than tricking my way into many far less glamorous ones. But I didn't allow myself the smallest smile of relief, as I was convinced I'd be rumbled. Instead, I went straight to the loo, spotting Youngy talking to Sting on the way.

I locked myself in a toilet cubicle, put the lid down and took a seat. I was scared rigid that the woman on the door may have come to her senses, had a change of heart, and would try to kick me out. Or maybe Donna Air herself had shown up?

I was getting paranoid now. I was in. And at least Youngy was there, so I wouldn't look like a total Norma no-mates. I opened the loo door, walked over to the sinks and re-applied my lip gloss.

'Hey, do you have any face powder? I'm so shiny!' drawled an American accent.

I turned around. It was the sultry raven-haired American actress Gina Gershon.

'Sure. Go for it,' I replied and handed her my Body Shop powder compact.

'Thanks,' she said and patted some of my make-up on.

I followed her out of the ladies' and headed back into the restaurant. The tables had been moved to one side so that people could start dancing. Sting and his wife Trudie Styler were dirty dancing together to Kylie Minogue's 'Can't Get You Out of My Head'. It was slightly gruesome. They looked like a pair of randy sixth-formers. I prayed they weren't about to start snogging each other.

I joined Youngy.

'Hey, have you seen who's outside?' he asked.

'Who?' I replied.

'Go out to the garden,' he said.

I wandered outside. There were a few tables of people including Mick Jagger, Rosanna Arquette, Matthew Modine and British actors Jason Flemyng and David Thewlis. Excellent, I thought to myself. Mick Jagger was always good value. Whenever I saw him at an event he usually moaned, 'Oh no, not you again,' and then good-naturedly agreed to do a photo with me. The last time I'd seen him was at a party in London at St Martin's Lane Hotel.

'I want to be in your surveillance section,' he'd said, referring to the section of 3am where we reveal where stars had been spotted and what they were doing. He spent the next ten minutes coming up with places he had been to that I could write about. Finally he settled on one. 'Can you write in 3am that I was spotted on the rue St Honoré shopping for a Magimix?' he asked.

I agreed, and two days later we ran Sir Mick's made-up story. But right then the Rolling Stones singer was being led by Gina Gershon on to the dance floor. I watched them from the garden. She had an extremely low-cut dress on. He joined her for a boogie and the pair were soon giggling away together. Somehow

I managed to corner Mick for a shot straight after. We talked about the films we'd seen and what parties we'd been to.

'There's that big MTV party on tonight, but I can't face going,' he told me. 'I went a few years ago and it was really crowded. I'm going home early.' And so he did, and without a woman in tow.

'So did you talk to him?' asked Youngy when I stepped back into the restaurant area.

'Who?' I replied.

'Leonardo DiCaprio. He's outside. I told you to go and look in the garden,' he said, laughing.

'Oh, blimey,' I gulped and dashed outside.

The actor was outside all right, surrounded by bodyguards. The first thing I noticed was that he was much taller in real life than I had ever imagined. He was well over six foot. But what was odd was that he had this baby face. It just didn't belong with his tall, strapping frame.

I couldn't work out why he had a group of security men surrounding him. The *Vanity Fair* party was strictly invite only (apart from me, and I'd lied to get in) and there were no more than fifty guests there. Plenty of them were A-list stars or important film makers anyway, so quite why DiCaprio felt the need to have bodyguards protect him I didn't know. But he was clearly bored by the sedate bash and after staring into space for ten minutes he decided to leave with his all-male entourage following him. I hadn't managed to get a photo with him.

It was now midnight and the party was thinning out. The guests had either left for their hotels or to carry on partying elsewhere. I looked around. The only celeb left in the room was the English actor David Thewlis. I knew he was going out with the actress Anna Friel, but apart from that I didn't know much about him. He noticed me staring at him.

'Hello. I know who you are,' he said to me.

'Oh, yes?' I replied, hoping he wasn't about to ask security to take me away.

'So, tell me about 3am. How does it work? What do you have to do at parties?' he asked.

And so David Thewlis and I sat down at a table and started to knock back a succession of Bellinis while I talked him through the ins and outs of working on a gossip column. He seemed obsessed with what really went on behind the scenes and we ended up getting legless together.

An hour later, while he was still drilling me on whether we made up our stories or if they were actually true, we realized we were the only people left in the restaurant.

'Shit. I'd better be going. I've got to meet my colleague at the *24 Hour Party People* party,' I said. I had told Suzanne I would meet her there at midnight, and it was now 1am.

'Come on, then. I'm staying up at the Hotel du Cap. I'll walk you up there and get them to call you a taxi,' he said.

We walked out of the restaurant and spotted a golf buggy which whisked lazy guests from the Eden Roc restaurant back up to the hotel, a short stroll away.

'Come on. Hop on!' he said, laughing, and jumped into the driver's seat.

I was not going to let the opportunity to go joyriding in a golf buggy around the grounds of the South of France's grandest hotel with a highly acclaimed British actor pass me by. So I got in next to him and screamed with laughter as he zigzagged drunkenly across the manicured lawns.

I had been expecting packs of rabid dogs to chase after us, with searchlights shining on us and sirens blaring. But there was nothing. It was eerily quiet. We'd managed to get away with it.

We giggled as we made our way up the steep stone steps of the hotel, and David asked the concierge to call me a taxi to take me back to Cannes. While I waited, I peered into the bar in the lobby of the hotel. The last time I had been there, George Clooney was racing around with a bottle of vodka. This time, though, the bar was completely empty. It was Saturday night and there were plenty of parties going on, so the actors and actresses would no doubt be whooping it up in the bar later on.

'Right, there's a taxi on its way. Good to meet you. That was a really interesting chat we had,' said David.

'No problem. Bye,' I replied.

He waved and made his way to his hotel room.

What a strange encounter, I thought to myself. But it had been very pleasant, and so nice to talk to a grounded British celebrity. I was feeling much happier altogether about being in Cannes.

Hugh Grant, me and Sandra Bullock

11. Turning Point

Very quickly Jason and I had something serious going. We saw each other pretty much every night. He was charming, funny, great fun to be with and full of advice on working at 3am. I was totally smitten. It was wonderful to be able to come home and nestle into someone's arms once more.

I found it strange, though, that people at work were not exactly over the moon for me that we were dating. I could see what the problem was. If things ended badly between Jason and I then he might well decide to punish the *Daily Mirror* as a result and refuse to sell the paper any more of his paparazzi pictures. It was now the beginning of the summer and the celebs would soon be jetting off on their holidays. Jason's stomping ground was the South of France at this time of year. I could just imagine the bollocking I would get at work if he and I split up over the summer and he blackballed the *Daily Mirror*. I didn't relish the double-whammy of being dumped and pissing off Piers.

Jason had started to take me on trips abroad when he was papping celebs. We'd be chasing after stars, remaining undercover at all times so he could snap them unawares. I found it a strange new experience not to speak to them.

The first job I accompanied him on was to St Tropez in June. I was already out there on holiday with some friends when he rang me up to tell me he had flown in. He'd had a tip-off that Natalie Appleton was getting hitched to her boyfriend, Liam Howlett from the Prodigy, in a village nearby.

'Meet me at my hotel and I'll take you with me if you fancy it,' he said.

I joined him and one of the French photographers he represented – Jason was also an agent to a team of snappers in France and sold their pictures all over the world. We drove to the village where Natalie and Liam were getting hitched that afternoon.

'Right,' he told me. 'One of my guys has talked a woman who lives on the road to the registry office into letting him take pictures from her sitting room window. We're going to the storage room belonging to the man who runs the café across the road from the registry office. Another of my guys has managed to persuade him to let us shoot from there. There's a big freezer in the room, but that's about it. It's on the first floor, and the view from up there is perfect. The window looks right out on to the registry office, so when they come out and do their own photos I'll have the perfect angle to do mine. You'll have to do what I say and stand way back from the window. We can't have anyone seeing us up there. Don't say a word either.'

I nodded. I knew how to operate at a party or an awards ceremony full of celebrities, but I had never seen stars being silently ambushed by the paparazzi without them realizing. It felt like a military operation and I didn't want to bugger things up for Jason. I had already been witness to the hairdryer treatment he doled out to pretty much anyone he felt had wronged him.

We let ourselves into the tiny room. Jason talked in rapid French to the other photographer. I couldn't understand a word (my GCSE conversational French module didn't cover what paparazzi said to each other mid-assault), so instead watched in fascination how they operated.

'Crouch by the freezer,' Jason whispered to me as he hid to the left of the window behind the curtain. 'When I say when, you can stand up but really slowly so you can see the people arriving,' he said.

Ten minutes later cars began to pull up. Jason was muttering in French to the photographer who was lying flat below the window, ready to pop up when Jason signalled it was time. They both had Hubble Telescope-sized lenses on their cameras and didn't utter a word to each other while bride and groom and their wedding guests entered the registry office.

'We'll wait for them to come out,' he quietly explained to me.

Jason rang up the photographer who was taking pictures from

the woman's front room down the road, and he confirmed he had snaps of Natalie being driven in a vintage car up to the registry office. He had checked the pictures and they were good shots. She hadn't suspected a thing.

Time ticked by and the three of us remained silent. Jason kept popping his head around the curtain so he could catch the happy couple when they emerged. I could see he was incredibly tense. This set of pictures could easily earn him £50,000 and upwards when he flogged them to various newspapers and magazines.

It was starting to get unbearably sticky in the room. The window was wide open so the two men could snap away, but there was no breeze outside and the sun was blisteringly hot.

Suddenly Jason motioned for me to stand up and take a look. I didn't dare move from the freezer in case I made a noise. He motioned at me again to take a peek. I got up slowly, stood on my tiptoes and saw Liam Gallagher standing just below with his girlfriend Nicole Appleton and their son Gene. Then I saw the bride and groom walking out of the registry office to the applause of their friends.

Jason poked his camera lens through the window and started snapping for a few seconds. The French photographer joined him. Then he suddenly stopped, and hid behind the curtain. He mumbled something to the other photographer, who did the same.

'Fuck! Fuck, fuck, fuck!' he said angrily through gritted teeth. 'Liam Gallagher keeps looking up here at the window.'

No one spoke. I was sitting on the carpet and leaning against the freezer and was now having awful visions of Liam Gallagher running into the café, racing up the stairs, smashing the door down and kung-fu-kicking everyone in the room. Liam didn't like photographers at the best of times, and he never hesitated in letting them know it.

'OK, he's looking away now. Fuck. That guy must have some sort of sixth sense or something,' Jason muttered, and he and the photographer carried on their ducking and diving and snapping act.

Five minutes later it was all over. Everyone had left the registry office, got into their cars and headed out of the village.

'Right, let's go. I've got to edit these pictures down and start selling them,' Jason barked at me, unlocking the door and pegging it out of the room.

I tried to keep up behind. We got into the French guy's car and he dropped us off at Jason's hotel.

It'd been exhausting just watching Jason work, but also so exciting. It was clearly a huge buzz doing this job, snapping away at stars without them realizing.

He had told me about the celebs who had agreed to have their photos taken by him on beaches, as long as it looked like they didn't know it was happening. You could tell who these people were because they looked so immaculate while sunbathing, with their perfect make-up, stomachs pulled in and not a hair out of place. Jason usually approached these celebs while they were on holiday. He had a range of contacts who would tell him when famous people would be going on holiday and where they were headed, and he would always fly business class so that he could come across them on the plane, charm them and talk them into agreeing to be photographed.

It was an offer most celebrities wouldn't say no to. He was going to take their photo whether they liked it or not, and if they agreed to play along then he would ensure they'd look simply gorgeous in the pictures and only sell the most flattering ones to the papers and magazines. As he was so well dressed, so immaculately turned out, so utterly charming, so discreet and engaging, celebs loved him.

Of course there were also those famous people whom he did not approach as he knew they would never agree to make deals; these included Kate Moss, Liz Hurley, Jude Law and Kate Winslet.

I was with him a few months later in Venice as he hunted down Kate Winslet and her husband Sam Mendes in the stunning Italian city's confusing labyrinth of backstreets. I had never been to Venice before and had certainly never expected to see it this way, the empty, narrow and cobbled roads a blur as we chased after the couple. Kate and Sam were constantly getting lost, and Jason, his Italian colleague and I would have to hide in doorways and shops every time they took a wrong turning and walked back in the direction they'd just come from.

After half an hour of chasing and hiding, Jason finally got the pair where he wanted them. They were giggling together as they ambled hand-in-hand through a busy square filled with tourists and pigeons.

'Quick! Scratch your head!' Jason shouted at me.

'What?' I replied.

'Just put your bloody hand on top of your head. Now stand still!'

I did as he said. I felt utterly clueless. But he knew what he was doing. Hedging his bets that Winslet and Mendes wouldn't notice two photographers taking shots of them in a square crammed full of sightseers, Jason swung his camera round off his shoulder and poked the lens through the gap between my hand and my head. He was using me as a prop. Mission accomplished.

Being on the front line of this sort of reportage was a whole new ball game to me. It felt so much more serious than chronicling the actions of Jade Goody, Jordan and Robbie Williams. Yet I couldn't help but feel that it was much more intrusive than my job. It was one thing if a celebrity collaborated with Jason on pictures, but when they were being captured going about their business, well, it just felt a bit like stalking.

It didn't occur to me that when I eavesdropped on stars having private chats in loos at parties I was being just as intrusive. Or when I spied famous couples fighting at awards ceremonies and sent photographers to try and catch out celebs who were having affairs with people they shouldn't. But that was exactly what my day-to-day job entailed.

Within a month of seeing Jason, we were already squabbling over my job. Jason did a fair amount of schmoozing himself, but he was not comfortable with the idea that I had to get all glammed up and charm celebs virtually every night, especially as those celebs were, on the whole, male. He was also teetotal and took a dim view of my boozy lifestyle.

'I think you're a binge drinker. You'd be able to do your job a lot better if you were sober. Why don't you try it for a while and see how it goes?' he suggested one day.

After I'd had a late night at the Dance Music Awards and ended up at the Elysium nightclub on one occasion, we had a big argument. I was extremely hungover and lost my temper with him. He issued me the edict that either I stopped drinking or it was over between us.

'Of course I don't want us to break up. I'll give up the booze,' I sobbed down the phone to him that day.

I told my best friend from school, Caz, a psychologist, what had happened.

'Jess! Just listen to yourself. You don't need to give up drinking. Christ, if you stop boozing, then we all have to,' she scolded me.

'I know. You're right. But maybe it'll do me good to give it a rest for a while,' I argued back.

'Well, make sure you're doing it for the right reasons. Are you happy with him? You haven't been together long and you're already having tearful bust-ups.'

She was right. We had already broken up once a few weeks after we had met. He was exciting, emotional and fiery, which could be fun but also very hard-going.

'Trust me on this one,' continued Caz. 'I've been there before. Yes, it's a rollercoaster of emotions and he's exciting and totally different from anyone else you've been with. But believe me, with the highs come the lows. You've barely been with him five minutes and you've already had a few fights, broken up and he's persuaded you that you're an alcoholic. This isn't you. Listen to what you're saying to me. Please, Jess.'

As I thanked her for her advice, my gut instinct told me to trust her. I had been friends with Caz since we met at secondary school aged eleven. We had been through our teenage years together. We had experimented with cider, Cinzano and Martini Bianco concoctions at fourteen, we'd compared love bites after snogging boys at the Gatecrasher Balls at the Hammersmith Palais, and we giggled and then felt guilty for years after we told lies to a nun at school. She knew me better than anyone. Of course Caz was right, I thought to myself.

Even so, I gave up drinking. I fought off Jason's suggestions that maybe I should try an Alcoholics Anonymous meeting, as I felt that was taking things too far. When I got upset or stressed, or had a fight with him, he assured me it was because I was 'no longer hiding behind the booze'. I didn't know what to think any more. Was he right? Had I been a hopeless alcoholic all along but just hadn't realized it? I never drank in the mornings, I sometimes drank at lunchtimes if I was out with a contact and I certainly had a few cocktails when I was at parties. But I never drank on my own.

'That doesn't mean you don't have a problem,' Jason said to me tersely when I tried to convince him I wasn't a washed-up boozer.

I was feeling very confused, but trusted Jason when he pointed out that I had not been alcohol-free since I was fourteen, so no wonder I was all over the place.

And then a few weeks later, Eva dropped a bombshell. She was leaving 3am to join the *Sun* as their Los Angeles correspondent. My first reaction was a purely selfish one. I didn't want my best friend at work to leave me.

'Oh, mate!' was all I could say before I burst into tears and hugged her.

She didn't say anything as I sobbed on to her T-shirt, leaving a wet patch from my tears. We were standing in the kitchen by the ladies' loo, where we had gossiped many times about work, colleagues and men.

'That's an amazing job. But I'm going to miss you so much. You can't leave me with this lot!' I blubbed.

'You'll be fine. Just think, we can finally go on holiday together! You can come out and visit me in LA,' she said, remaining stoic and unmoved by my sniffling, in true Eva style.

'Yes, I'd love to. But it's not going to be the same here. It will never be as much fun. It's going to be so serious. None of the others get me like you do. And there's no way I can gossip to them like I can with you,' I moaned.

'Well, you've got Jason now. At least you're not going on dodgy dates. He can look out for you. And give you stories!' she said, laughing.

We slowly walked back to our desks and I rubbed my blotchy face. It looked obvious that I had been crying, but I didn't care. Soon everyone would know that Eva was leaving and all eyes would be on me. I was the last original 3am girl still standing.

Eva interrupted Piers in the middle of his sunshine break to tell him the bad news. He was less than impressed and told her she was going to have to work out most of her notice period. And then he announced even more changes. Kevin was to be moved off 3am to concentrate on running the showbiz news desk, and I would now be in charge of the column.

Eva's departure meant the end of an era for 3am. I knew I would miss her terribly. She was someone I felt I could trust and depend on in an industry that had its fair share of two-faced back-stabbers. But now she was leaving, I was being given the opportunity to step up from being a 3am girl: I was now head girl of the column.

'We need to take our time with finding Eva's replacement. There's no point rushing it,' Piers told me soon after he had announced my new role.

Suzanne was working out very well, but we had to make sure we'd both get along with the new girl. To complicate matters, Piers decided he wanted someone from an ethnic background to replace Eva.

After sifting through countless CVs, letters and emails I narrowed it down to several girls, and after meeting them myself I asked Piers to interview them. We both agreed on a girl called Dominique Hines, who was from Jamaica. She didn't have much experience in newspapers and none in the showbusiness world, but we felt she had something about her. Unfortunately, by the time Eva had left for LA, things were already not working out with Dominique. She worked with us for a month and then left in October.

After a few weeks in my new role I began to realize just how difficult it was to oversee a gossip column, especially one with four girls and one bloke. As well as sniffing the scoops out, I had to go into Piers's editorial conference along with the other heads of department in his office at 11am every day and announce to the room what our main story was to be for the next day. If a story wasn't up to scratch then Piers would let you know in no uncertain terms. He once sent an email in response to a story that had run in 3am on a day he hadn't been in the office. It read:

I have three things to say about your lead story today:
a) Who
b) The Fuck
c) Cares.

The hunt was on to find another 3am girl.

'I'm beginning to think the third position on the column is cursed,' I said one day.

No one laughed. Everyone was beginning to think the same thing.

There was one natural candidate who I had long thought would be a fantastic 3am girl: Niki Waldegrave. Talking to her at Robbie Williams' ghastly premiere had reminded me of how approachable she was. She had been on the *Daily Star* in 2001 when they set up an imitation 3am column with the unfortunate title of The Bitches (this soon got switched to The Goss). She had also worked with Polly on the *Sunday Mirror* and was now on the *Sunday People*.

A small, pretty, slim blonde (or brunette, depending on whether she'd been at the hair dye that week) with a cheeky grin, a saucy glint in her eye, a tendency to be the last person to leave any party and an ability to get celebs to say the filthiest things to her, Niki was the perfect choice. Standing at 5 foot 1 inch in her stockinged feet – not that she would have been caught dead in anything other than sparkly stilettos or kinky boots – she was small but deadly. She was also from Yorkshire, which in Piers's eyes was the equivalent to being ethnic.

We offered her the job, which she accepted, and with her northern banter and the dirtiest sense of humour I had ever come across, Niki soon shook the department up.

'All right, *Coronation Street* barmaid?' Piers said to Niki one day soon after she started.

'For fook's sake, I'm not a *Corrie* barmaid. I'm from the land of *Emmerdale*. Get it right,' she boomed back at him.

We had never had someone so loud working for 3am, or someone who threw herself so heartily into the regime. For a start her ability to tackle hangovers put us all to shame.

'I feel fooking awful,' she groaned one particular morning. 'I don't remember getting home last night. Got a date tonight. Not sure if I can face it though. Mind you, I hear he's got a tongue like a lizard. If that's true, you'll never see me run so fast into a bedroom. That Linford Christie'll have nowt on me.' She grinned lasciviously and winked at me. Suzanne, Dean and Susie turned back to their computers with queasy expressions on their faces. 'Oh, Christ. I think I'm going to be sick,' she announced, for the benefit of the entire office. The female fashion writers nearby looked like they were about to pass out when Niki started retching at her desk. 'Bleurrrrggghhhhh,' she croaked at her computer.

'Oh, Niki! Go to the toilet. Please don't make that noise. You're making everyone feel ill,' I pleaded.

'Bleurghhhhhh. I can't help it. Oh God, I'm going to vom,' she shouted, and continued to make the most nauseating noise I had ever had the misfortune of hearing.

'Niki! Please go and sort yourself out in the loo,' I begged, covering my ears with my hands so I didn't have to hear her burping, groaning and making spewing sounds. But instead of choking in the privacy of the ladies' loo, she simply turned around in her chair to the bin next to her desk and vomited into it.

'Oh, that's better. I'm starving now. Does anyone want anything getting from the canteen? I could murder a spaghetti bolognese,' she said brightly, clapping her hands.

The Christmas party season soon got underway and I was still struggling with sobriety. In short, not drinking wasn't much fun at all. And it didn't make covering parties easy. With everyone else sloshed around me, I soon noticed how I must have seemed when I had been knocking back the bubbly. I hadn't realized that drunken people had a tendency to repeat themselves over and over again. I attended fewer and fewer parties as I couldn't face having to stay awake until the early hours of the morning without being on the same level as everyone else. I found it difficult to try and chat to celebs, who ranged from the slightly pissed to the roaring drunk. And that made me feel even worse about myself. I started to worry that I was unable to do my job sober.

I went to the What The Papers Say award ceremony, where 3am won the Showbiz Reporters of the Year award. I didn't have a drop of the champagne Suzanne, Niki and Piers were downing. And I attended the office Christmas parties completely sober. At the *Daily Mirror*'s executive's dinner at the Grill Room at the Café Royal, Piers finally snapped.

'You have become incredibly boring. Why aren't you drinking? I find people who don't drink are really dull,' he said to me loudly in front of everyone else who was sharing our table at dinner.

'I know, I know. It's not for much longer. I'm going to start up again,' I replied, deciding there and then to give up this sobriety lark. When your boss spells out your worst fears and labels you a bore, then you know it's time to do something about it.

Piers looked at me pityingly. I desperately wanted to tell him that I wasn't on the wagon for my own benefit. I was still doing this for Jason's sake, because in his eyes I had a problem.

Over Christmas, away from Jason and in the peaceful environment of my parents' house, I mulled things over. I was starting to understand that the problem wasn't with me, it was with me and Jason. After six months of sobriety I realized I didn't have a drinking problem. I had given it up just like that, but I had given it up for the wrong reason. It had all been to appease Jason, and I didn't like being controlled like that. It might have taken me half a year, but I now realized I didn't like how I had allowed myself to be changed by him.

I didn't want to alter my lifestyle for a man over whom my close friends and family had a number of question marks. They were all concerned about me. Caz's advice earlier in the year came back to me. We'd been having some terrible rows, and now I wanted things to change. I felt that at last I had reached that point.

In January I decided to start drinking again. It didn't take me long to get back into the swing of things.

At the after-show party for *Two Weeks Notice*, showbiz reporters were allowed to have a ten-minute chat with the stars of the film, Hugh Grant and Sandra Bullock. Grant was not a big fan of the British press, so we knew how torturous this meet-and-greet session at the Asia De Cuba restaurant at St Martin's Lane Hotel was going to be for him.

I had gleefully helped myself to the cocktails on offer at the do. I asked the PR if I could do a photo with Grant and Bullock.

'You can ask,' he grimaced, clearly not fancying my chances.

Hugh was in no mood to make small talk with who he considered the most loathsome sort of people. His attitude, combined with the many drinks I'd helped myself to, made me want to bound up to him even more.

'Hello, Hughie, Sandra, do you mind if I do a photo with you?' I asked.

'Sure,' replied Sandra Bullock.

Hugh put a fake smile on his face and nodded at me impatiently. I stood between them while Youngy started to snap away.

'Have you met Hugh before?' Sandra asked me.

Before I had a chance to say that I had pursued the reticent actor around many a party trying to cajole him into talking to me, he butted in. 'Yes. I know who she is.' And I don't think he meant it in a good way.

'Gee, I never know how to pose for photos with people,' laughed Sandra, attempting to lighten the mood.

'It's easy,' said Hugh, brightening up all of a sudden. 'Just pinch her,' he added, and then grabbed my bum before goosing me. And with that, he walked off.

Jason was furious when I regaled him on the phone the next day with the tale of having my arse grabbed by Hugh Grant. He wasn't best pleased either that I had started drinking again, and we had yet another explosive row.

'You will not be taken seriously if you drink. You need to step away from that whole showbiz reporter crowd and do your own thing. If someone makes a pass at you at a party and you're pissed then what's going to happen? You won't be in full control,' he screamed down the phone before hanging up.

I was beginning to despair. Where could we go from here? We had been dating for eight months and the arguments were getting worse. I tried to find solace at the *Daily Mirror*.

It was all change again at work. Dean and Susie quit 3am and Eva was not enjoying life in LA for the *Sun*. Suzanne moved across to the *Sunday Mirror* to work with Polly on her column, and Piers asked Eva to rejoin 3am. To my utter delight, she accepted. The new 3am line-up would be Eva, Niki and me. Piers described it as the dream team, and I finally felt that it absolutely was the best 3am line-up we'd ever had.

That April in 2003 Niki, Eva and I attended the Shaftas. In the 1980s, two reporters had decided to start up an alternative awards ceremony for showbiz writers to honour and celebrate the most outrageous fabricated stories that made it into the papers. The highlight of the evening was always the Princess Margaret award, in honour of two writers at the *Daily Star* (Pat Codd and Geoff Baker; Baker later became Paul McCartney's PR) who ran a story that Princess Margaret was to appear in *Crossroads*. It was complete bollocks. Soon after the story ran, the show was axed but the reporters then ran a follow-up story claiming the Queen's sister was utterly devastated that she would not be able to enjoy her walk-on part. Of course the whole thing was cobblers.

TV and radio host Johnny Vaughan usually hosted the awards, and each tabloid newspaper had their own table. The organizer, ex-*Sunday People* showbiz editor Sean O'Brien, even managed to secure sponsorship over the years. I'd never understood quite why Vodafone and UKTV G2 would want to be associated with a ceremony where showbiz reporters got annihilated, shouted abuse at each other and slapped each other on the back for their made-up stories.

The ceremony was usually attended by about eighty people, and consisted of showbiz reporters past and present and several friendly and fun PRs who were allowed to witness the event. Piers was always there. The editor of the *Sun*, the editor of the *Sunday People* and the editor of the *News of the World* were also guests on a few occasions. Of course not all the editors looked quite so pleased with their staff when they saw the amount of awards piling up on their table. The mantra everyone stuck to when they collected their plastic awards from Johnny was usually: 'It was true at the time.'

That year I was awarded Manager of the Year because of the rapid turnaround of staff. As he called me up to the stage, Vaughan announced, 'The moment Jessica took over the manager's job at 3am, she understood that story-getting was only half her job. The rest of her time would be spent pulling off a dazzling run of walkouts and sackings.'

I took the Manager of the Year award in good humour. Well, you had to really.

At least I hadn't picked up the most embarrassing award of the night. The Worst Showbiz Pundit went to Ben Todd at the *Daily Star* for telling Radio 5 Live on air that he didn't have any insight into why Kate Winslet had just split from first husband Jim Threapleton. 'I don't know. It was my day off and it was my son's birthday party,' was Ben's incisive contribution.

A few weeks later, in the middle of May, I took Niki with me to the Cannes Film Festival. She was dying to go and see the carnival of chaos for herself. Eva promised she'd go the following year.

We had rented studio rooms, similar to those you found in university halls of residence, next to the Carlton Hotel. This time it was a different block from the pit of horror Suzanne and I had stayed in the year before. The Resideal had a big garden and an outdoor pool. Not that we ever had the chance to test it out. It seemed popular with the pigeons, though.

Our rooms were next to each other. We each had a single bed, a kitchenette with a small fridge, a hob, a frying pan and a kettle, a TV and a small bathroom with a shower and a bath. Our rooms overlooked the garden and we each had a small balcony with a plastic table and chair. It was the perfect base for the festival as well as being in a fantastic location, just off the Croisette, where all the action was.

That weekend Jason rang me in a state of high excitement. 'I've just found out that Posh and Becks are having lunch at the Colombe d'Or Hotel with Liz Hurley and some other people. Right now. Get yourself up there immediately!' he announced down the phone.

Niki and I were walking out of the Majestic Hotel, where we'd been to see DDA film publicists to pick up invites to a Steve Coogan press conference for his movie *Around the World in 80 Days*.

'Right, Niki, we've got to get a taxi. We're going to find David Beckham!'

'You're bloody kidding me!' she shrieked.

I looked at her, one eyebrow raised.

'You don't understand,' she cried. 'I am so in love with him. I've got a life-size poster of him on me wall back in London. Apparently he's waxed all over! Oh, yes!' And with that she flew into the middle of the road to flag a cab down. We jumped in the back and told the driver to take us to the picturesque hillside village of St Paul de Vence. It was a twenty-minute journey, enough time for Niki to have stopped hyperventilating and calmed down.

'He's just been in the papers for having that new hairstyle of his. I prefer him with a shaved head personally, but the cornrow plaits are pretty kinky, I have to say,' she said, sighing, as she gazed out of the window at St Paul de Vence.

We pulled up outside the small hotel. It was easy to miss the entrance, which was just a doorway with a simple sign hanging above it. It may have looked understated from the outside, but this stone building with only twenty-six bedrooms was five star and ultra-discreet. Hanging from the walls of the hotel were paintings by Matisse, Picasso and countless others who once bartered for their bed and board with their art when they were impoverished young unknowns. The restaurant was in the garden, and guests sat at long tables under fig trees, ploughing through course after course.

We weren't the only ones who had heard the Beckhams were tucking into a gourmet lunch. There was a crowd of thirty excited tourists gathered by the two chauffeur-driven Mercedes which were parked outside the hotel.

'Oh, that's subtle, isn't it?' I commented to Niki. 'We're never going to get their attention with that rabble around the cars. They're going to have bodyguards keeping everyone back.'

'Look, Posh and Becks like 3am, so I reckon if they see us and we ask them a couple of questions, they'll speak to us,' said Niki.

'Yeah. But we don't want to get trapped among the rubber-neckers over there and find ourselves swatted away by the body-guards. Let's sit up on this wall. That way we're higher than the fans, and when Posh and Becks come out we can at least wave and pray they see us,' I suggested as I walked away from the hotel and towards a high wall.

'Do you reckon they will spy us up here?' Niki asked as I helped her up. She was still sore from a very eventful party at the villa that private club Soho House had rented for the Cannes Festival a few nights before, where she had been chased by security guards and Dobermanns and had hidden up a tree and then scurried over walls in her haste to escape. Although she had been banned from the celeb party at the villa, Niki was always up for a challenge.

'We'll just have to hope they do.'

Half an hour later the chauffeurs got out of their driving seats and stood by the passenger doors nearest the hotel.

'Right, that's our sign. They must be coming out any second now,' I said.

Five seconds later the excited crowd started to cheer as the Beckhams, along with their lunch companions Liz Hurley and David Furnish, emerged from the hotel and walked to their cars. David helped Victoria into one of the Mercedes and got in beside her. Liz and David stepped into the other one.

Niki and I stood up on the wall and waved madly. Neither Victoria nor David looked in our direction.

'Oh, bugger. We're so close! Those annoying tourists are in the way,' I shouted.

The chauffeurs closed all the passenger doors and got into their seats. But neither car moved. Eventually, one of the drivers' doors opened and a bald-headed chauffeur got out.

'Is Jessica still here?' he shouted to the crowd.

I frantically waved my arms at the chauffeur.

'Will you come over here?' he said.

Niki and I hopped down from the wall and pushed our way through the crowd, who were staring at us curiously.

The chauffeur was standing in front of the right passenger door of one of the cars. All the windows were blacked out. Niki and I stood there, looking at the chauffeur expectantly. Suddenly, the electric window lowered. There in the back seat was a smiling Posh Spice. Becks, with his hair tightly pulled back in cornrows, was sitting next to her, holding her hand and grinning at us.

'I thought it was you! How are you?' said Victoria. 'What are you doing here?'

'It's the Cannes Film Festival, so Niki and I are out here working. We thought we'd have a wander around the town here, but we noticed these cars and wanted to see who was at the hotel. Are you staying nearby?' I asked her.

'Yeah, we're at Elton's in Nice,' she replied.

'I like the new hairstyle!' I said to David, who still had a Jack Nicholson-style huge grin plastered across his tanned face.

Before he could answer, Victoria grabbed his head playfully and stroked his cornrows. 'He's burnt the top of his scalp sunbathing. Haven't you, babe?' she said, while he nodded and laughed. 'Nice to see you two. Enjoy yourselves!' she continued.

And with that, Victoria pushed the button for the window to close, the chauffeur stepped back into his seat and the convoy of cars drove off.

'Holy fuck. Did you see Beckham smiling at me?' gasped Niki. 'I think I'm in there.'

August was, as usual, a dead month, and the highlight of the autumn was when Eva, Niki and I were included in *FHM*'s Top 100 Sexiest Women poll. We had a photo shoot with one of the magazines's top photographers, decked out in sexy clobber. We soon came bumping back down to earth when we had the honour of coming thirty-first in Channel 4's 100 Worst Britons television poll. We beat the likes of Naomi Campbell, Cherie Blair, Vanessa Feltz and Simon Cowell.

Piers thought both results were fantastic. 'At least you're being talked about,' he pointed out to us.

I understood why we had been chosen as some of the country's most disliked people. I just couldn't get why *FHM* had thought we were sexy. That was until Eva announced, 'It's easy to work out. *FHM* tell us we've been voted in their top 100 sexiest women contest, we run a story about it in the paper blowing our own trumpets and give them free publicity!'

'Oh my God, you're right! Damn. I thought someone had said something flattering about us. The tabloid terrors have been manipulated for a change!' I said.

The Christmas party season was upon us again before we knew it. We held our showbiz department party in the private room at the Covent Garden Hotel. Piers dutifully turned up to join in with the drunken banter. After our three-course Christmas meal, he turned to me and said, 'Callan, can you ring Peter Stringfellow and tell him we're coming over to his club?'

I hesitated. Was it really a good idea to go to Stringfellow's with your boss? I shrugged and dialled the mobile of Peter's PA.

'Hi, Pat, it's Jessica from the *Daily Mirror*. I'm with Piers and some people from our department. Is it OK if we pop round? We're only up the road.'

'Course you can. I'll tell the doormen and let Peter know. He'll be happy to see you all,' she said.

Peter Stringfellow was one of those characters all gossip columnists had to get to know. It was a rite of passage. The reason? He was the source of stories and pictures of what celebs got up to inside his lap-dancing clubs. He was an absolute legend and, greying mullet, leopard-skin furniture and thongs on the beach aside, he wasn't sleazy at all.

Before 3am was born, most of the showbiz journalists were

men, so were more than happy to spend nights at Stringfellow's, where they got to sit at Peter's top table in the VIP section and enjoy free lap dances, food and champagne. But it was slightly different for me. A pole-dancing busty girl wasn't quite my thing. And even when the club launched their male strippers night, I ran out when a pumped-up perma-tanned Village People lookalike strode over to give me the treatment.

Visiting Peter at the club was a necessary evil, as I had to keep in with the lovable old rogue to stop him from giving stories to my rivals. He would call me when a famous face had been at the club and would send me pictures he'd taken of them in his Covent Garden strippers' emporium. He'd furnish me with details of which girls they had taken a shine to and how much they had splashed out on lap dances, and provide quotes for our articles. It was all done in a positive and celebratory way.

A few months before, in August 2003, Peter told me about how Colin Farrell had broken the no-touch rule with the girls by sticking his tongue down the throat of a brunette dancer and practically inhaling her lungs. The photograph spoke for itself really.

But a few days later that summer I had a call from Peter with a tale of a visit from a VIP guest which threw me into a bit of a dilemma.

'You'll never guess who I had in the club last night. The girls absolutely adored him,' he said to me.

'Who's that then, Peter?' I replied, thinking it would be one of the regulars, Simon Cowell, Chris Evans or Calum Best.

'Professor Stephen Hawking,' he replied.

'What?' I gasped.

'Marvellous man. I think he should be knighted, you know. He turned up with a few nurses and Tiger danced for him. He had a great time. The girls all love him, you know. And they've all read his books. I've got photos of him with some of the dancers, so I'll email them over to you. I'll give you a quote too,' he continued.

'Thanks, Peter. That's great.'

I didn't know what to do. Would our readers think we were

taking the piss out of him if we ran the photos and story? On the other hand, why shouldn't the wheelchair-bound author of *A Brief History of Time* enjoy a night out at Stringfellow's?

The best thing to do was to tell Piers and ask him if we should run it, I figured. I looked down the other end of the office and saw Piers sitting at his desk on the back bench, the area where the editor, deputy editor, executive editor and night editor sit at their computer terminals throughout the day and night and put the paper together. I got up and walked over to him.

'Piers, I've just had Stringy on the phone. He said Stephen Hawking was in the club last night. A girl called Tiger danced for him – she even put her foot up on his computer voice synchronizer keyboard thing. Apparently he loved it. Stringy's sending the photos over,' I said.

'What? Stephen Hawking was at Stringfellow's? Are you serious?' He was even more incredulous than I had been.

'That's what I said to Stringy. What do we do?' I replied.

'Let me know as soon as you get the photos. This I have to see,' he told me.

I walked back to my desk and checked my email inbox. Sure enough, there was an email from Peter waiting for me with an attachment of several photos of Hawking's night out. There was a picture of Hawking with five of the Cabaret of Angels dancers all gathered around him. I couldn't work out whether the *Daily Mirror* would get slated for running the pictures or not.

I emailed them to Piers. It wasn't exactly a classic 3am story, but I figured it would be something our readers would be interested in. Five minutes later Piers appeared at my desk.

'Great pictures. Love it. Run it,' he said, and strode off back to planning the rest of the paper.

In the next day's column we saluted Hawking for his night out. The article's headline was 'The Smutty Professor':

The 61-year-old Lucasian Professor of Mathematics at Cambridge University spent five hours in the club with his assistant Mark and two nurses.

Motor-neurone sufferer Stephen took a shine to 19-year-old Baby Spice lookalike Tiger, who was asked to dance for him repeatedly.

'She's one of the most gorgeous girls in the club,' reveals Peter. 'No wonder Stephen was having a great time. He wasn't the only one living it up though – his nurses were getting plenty of lap dances from the male dancers we have downstairs. It was a delight to have Stephen in the club. I was in awe – he's my all-time hero.'

We didn't get one single phone call, email or letter about the entire incident, which was totally unheard of as *Mirror* readers were never ones to keep their opinions to themselves. I had been expecting the worst, and that we'd get told we were making fun of him. We weren't, though. We were celebrating the fact that such a disabled eminent scientist was just like any other bloke who enjoyed a night out at a lap-dancing emporium. I felt our readers' failure to inundate us with berating calls marked their approval of our story. And I learnt never to underestimate the calibre of punter at the club. Anyone, it would seem, was up for a lap dance.

We had left our Christmas dinner and a group of ten of us walked into the club and were ushered up to the VIP area on the ground floor.

'You know, Callan, Stringy is one of the very few people in the showbusiness industry who would still welcome me with open arms if I left the newspaper business,' Piers said to me.

'How come?' I asked.

'He's a very genuine man. And he's so misunderstood. He's a great, great person,' Piers rhapsodized. 'I've known him for years and he's always been nothing other than a perfect host and, as you know, a great source of stories. Keep in with him.'

I sat down with Niki at a table. We giggled at some of our drunken male colleagues as their eyes remained glued to the lithe dancers' pert backsides.

Stringy made his entrance and sat down on his leopard-print throne at the main table in the VIP area. 'Hi, girls, how are you?' he greeted Niki and me.

'Really well. Thanks for letting us in with so many people,' I said, giving him a peck on the cheek.

'Oh, no problem. You know I am always happy to have you guys here. Go and have fun! I'll send some champagne over.'

Niki and I sat back down and surveyed the strange scene that was unfolding in front of us. Some of the blokes who worked with us on the paper were now sitting back in their chairs, looking like cartoon characters with their tongues hanging out of their mouths while girls writhed around between their legs and performed extraordinary feats of agility.

'This is gross. I really don't want to entertain the notion that Alun and John have got a little bit too excited by the dancers. I feel a bit sick,' I said to Niki. I winced as an athletic brunette thrust her peachy behind into *Mirror* photographer John's face right next to me.

'Oh, I don't know. I think it's great. 'Ere, d'you reckon I could audition for Stringfellow at the pole up there? It looks dead easy, don't it?' Niki asked me, pointing to a mounted area in front of us where two naked girls were hanging upside down from poles.

'No, Niki. Please try to resist. It's not one of your greatest ideas,' I said.

'Yeah, you're right. I'll come back and audition properly on one of the audition nights,' she replied.

Just then someone spoke into my ear. 'Excuse me, Peter sent me over to dance for you.'

It was a blonde lap dancer. She couldn't have been more than twenty-two and was wearing a short blue dress. I had paid plenty of visits to the club since joining 3am, but in those three and a half years I'd never had the urge to have a girl lap-dance for me. It just wasn't my cup of tea.

'No, thanks. That's very sweet of him but it's a bit wasted on me. I'm sure one of my male colleagues would appreciate your dancing skills much more than I would,' I said to her.

'Peter insisted I dance for you, though,' she replied.

I looked over at Peter's table. He waved cheerily at me and gave me a thumbs-up sign.

'Go on, Jess! I'll 'ave her if you don't! Don't be so mean to the poor girl,' Niki slurred as she knocked back a glass of champagne.

'No, seriously. I'm just not into it. I'm sorry. Please don't take it as an insult,' I said to the girl.

'I actually prefer dancing for women,' she said, smiling.

'Oh, for fook's sake, Jess. It's only a sodding dance. Don't be so borrrring,' Niki hollered in my face.

Not wanting to be seen as a dullard, I caved in. My male colleagues didn't notice the slinky blonde dance in front of me. Luckily they were far too preoccupied with their own limber minxes who were busy twisting their bodies around the boys' trembling thighs.

I was totally flustered by this girl bending over and touching her toes in front of me. Niki was loving it, but I felt utterly embarrassed. I didn't want to laugh as the girl may have thought I was laughing at her. Was I meant to be excited by her? Or was this for my male colleagues' benefit? I cringed at the thought.

At least it wasn't as bad as a male stripper parading around in his overstuffed thong. It still wasn't my thing, though. I was also jealous that I wasn't as flexible as her.

She whipped round to face me, slipped her arms out of her dress and rolled the clingy, short frock down to her waist to reveal her bare breasts, which she then thrust into my face. A camera flash went off. I gasped. She smiled and continued to wriggle around between my legs.

'That's a cracking shot! Glad you're enjoying yourself, Jessica,' laughed Stringfellow.

I sank even further into my chair. I was completely crimson with horror.

'Oh, you're fucked now!' sniggered Niki.

Thankfully the dancer finished her routine soon after. I decided that I had to leave before I found myself embroiled in any more disturbing encounters. I left Niki gazing up in wonderment at one of the dancers whirling around a pole, and tried to slink out of the VIP area unnoticed.

'Jessica! Where you going, love? Come and join us on my table!' shouted Stringfellow. So much for my sly disappearing act. Peter pulled out a chair beside him and patted it. 'Come on. I'll get my favourite dancer over. You'll love her,' he said to me as I sat down. He was determined to get the girls to work their magic on me. I cringed as a brunette strutted over to us.

'Come and sit on my lap,' instructed Peter. This was getting worse by the second.

'I would rather snog a tramp' was what I wanted to say. But I didn't. I didn't want to offend such a good friend of Piers's in case I got a ticking off. So I perched on Peter's knees, avoiding sitting on his actual lap.

'Isn't she great?' Peter shouted as the dancer shimmied up and down my legs.

'Mmm. Isn't she just?' I replied, trying to look like I was thoroughly enjoying myself. I glanced over to our table to see what was going on. Piers was sitting three seats away from us. He was appreciating the gymnastic abilities of one of the more dexterous dancers while one of the busty club masseuses was giving him a very vigorous head rub. Meanwhile, Niki was chatting away to a dancer about her hours and how much she earned in a night.

It was a defining moment, a real turning point, as I asked myself, had it really come to this? I began to think of my friends who didn't have jobs in the media. Did they ever find themselves in situations like this, all in the name of work?

Just as I was mulling over the horror of seeing my boss with his eyes glazed with pleasure, I noticed a bouncer rushing over to the VIP area. Niki had chosen not to take my advice, and was now being prised off one of the poles.

'Thought I'd give it a go!' she said, laughing, as she was escorted back to our table.

'Did you enjoy that, Jess? Give us a kiss!' chuckled Peter.

He gave me a peck on the cheek and I hopped off his knees.

'Callan! I can't look at you in the same way any more!' chortled Piers while the masseuse was pummelling his head.

'Thanks, Piers. Same to you,' I replied. He laughed and turned his attention back to the naked girl shaking her boobs in his booze-flushed face.

How had the showbiz department's Christmas party taken such a wrong turn? It really was time to make a move now.

'I'm just going to the loo,' I said to Niki, and rushed out of the VIP area and headed for the exit, pulling my coat on. Not daring to look behind me in case one of my colleagues saw me, I said goodbye to the doormen and ran out on to St Martin's Lane.

It had been a bit too seedy for me. There was always a big element of being one of the lads in this job, but this was taking things a bit too far. Niki had seemed to love every minute of the night, but by the end I had found it all a bit disturbing. Even more worrying was that I didn't want anyone to think any less of me at work for not getting into the whole spirit of a night out at Stringfellow's. And I knew that they would. It was all meant to be a bit of harmless entertainment, but it hadn't really been my idea of fun.

Stringy sent the incriminating photo of myself with the blonde lap dancer shaking her assets in my face to Piers the next day. Needless to say, it was forwarded around the office in no time. Jason took a very dim view of the evening and didn't find it funny at all.

I liked harmless drunken behaviour at office Christmas parties as much as the next person. But in my mind, no matter how much female newspaper journalists tried to convince themselves otherwise, it was still a man's world. I was never one to want to miss out on the fun. I just didn't want to be in the centre of it all.

Duncan James and me

12. A Deadline of One's Own

''Ere, Jess. You heard of that bloke John Hurt?'

It was the beginning of February 2004 and Niki and I were in the office putting together the column for the next day.

'Yeah. He was in *Alien* and *The Elephant Man*, and he's in *The Alan Clark Diaries* on TV at the moment. Why?' I grimaced. 'Niki! What is that? It stinks!'

Niki was on one of her health kicks – 'I think I'm going to have to eat nothing but dust this month, I feel so bloody fat,' she moaned most mornings – and was tucking into a tin of something smelly. 'Pilchards! They're lush. D'you want one? I've got some sardines in here somewhere too,' she said as she pulled out one of her metal desk drawers and rooted around.

'Yuck. No chance. Anyway, so what about John Hurt?' I was holding my cardigan over my nose to mask the smell of her tinned fish.

'Well, he was in Spearmint Rhino lap-dancing club on Tottenham Court Road last night and got chucked out for being too drunk and for trying to feel up the dancers! The dirty old bugger. He was rude to the staff too, so they got rid of him,' Niki said as she doused her pilchards with Sarson's vinegar. She kept a bottle in her desk drawer and liked to add it to everything she ate. As usual, the girls from the fashion department sitting next to us looked disgusted. 'This is lovely fodder. Even better with Sarson's on it. You sure you don't want to try it?' She grinned as she slurped a spoonful of fish.

'Niki, please stop. You're stinking the place out.'

'Oh, stop your moaning. It's healthy. Right, so what d'you reckon of the John Hurt tale?' she asked.

'It's a corker. Have you stood it up yet?' I replied.

'No. I'm going to ring the club in a few hours. There'll be no one there yet. But it's bang on. My contact was there and saw the whole thing happen. I reckon the club will confirm it on the record as they were so pissed off with him. He's not exactly our typical 3am celebrity though, is he?' she asked.

'No, but he is a legendary boozer and hellraiser. And the fact that he's in his sixties and has decided to start living it up again and get turfed out of a lap-dancing club is just up our street,' I said.

I decided to hold back from telling Piers as I knew he'd love the story, and although Niki was 100 per cent behind her trusted source, we still needed someone from the club to officially confirm it. The last thing we wanted was to get Piers all excited about a story before we'd had it officially confirmed by a PR or agent, only to have to tell him we were unable to run it. That would send him off into an irritable mood and no one needed that.

'Bingo! I got 'im,' crowed Niki as she put her phone down a couple of hours later. 'A spokesman for the club has just given me a statement. He said, "We can confirm John Hurt was escorted out of the premises. He had obviously had too much to drink so we stopped serving him because he was intoxicated." I told him everything we were running and he was fine with it. The funniest bit was when Hurt tried to sign his name on his credit card slip, ballsed it up and, when he was told to do it again, barked, "Do you know who I am?" What a star!'

Niki typed up the story for the next day's edition of 3am and went into great detail about how he tried to touch up the gyrating girls, made one waitress cry after he shouted at her and pointed his finger in her face, and was eventually marched out of the club by angry security men. He wasn't a pop singer, a soap star or a socialite, but we liked the fact that such a distinguished actor had behaved as badly as the young party people we usually wrote about. No one was off-limits now, especially those who got kicked out of lap-dancing clubs for allowing their hands to wander.

At 6pm Niki and I asked our new 3am boy, Dan Carrier, to man the phones, and left the office together to go to *Empire* magazine's annual Film Awards at the Dorchester hotel. Jude Law's new girlfriend, Sienna Miller, was on the guest list as well as the stars of the previous year's box-office success *Love, Actually*, who were expected to sweep the board. The party was taking place at the hotel after the ceremony, and always attracted a good crowd.

'Oh my God! You'll never guess who's here tonight!' I exclaimed.

Niki and I were examining the seating plan outside the function room at the hotel. We always scanned the plans so we could work out which stars were sitting where and how close we'd be to them.

'Who?' she asked as she pointed to Sienna Miller's table.

'John Hurt! He's presenting the Career Achievement award to Sigourney Weaver. This is going to be interesting. Did his people ever ring you back after you put the story to them?' I asked her.

'I tried. But you know what it's like. Agents refuse to comment on their clients' private lives and hate dealing with the tabloids. I tried to speak to the agent but they were unavailable, so I left a message with my name and number saying that we were running a story on Hurt in tomorrow's paper. We've given him the right to reply, but no one rang back. The statement from the spokesman for Spearmint Rhino is good enough.'

'Great. So he doesn't know the story is going to appear in tomorrow's paper then? OK. Well, when we see him let's get his version of events,' I said.

Niki and I joined the other guests at the round tables to watch the ceremony. After the awards, instead of stalking Sienna Miller like every other showbiz reporter there, Niki and I headed straight for Hurt.

He was knocking back wine from a huge glass, and by the looks of it he had been at it throughout the evening. I suddenly felt sorry for him. He was standing on his own and wasn't in a great state. Was it such a good idea to ask him about his evening in Spearmint Rhino? He looked like he could keel over at any moment. But before I could tell Niki that I had an attack of the guilts about taking advantage of a pissed-up luvvie, she'd already started talking to him. And he didn't look threatened by Niki at all. On the contrary, he looked quite happy peering down her top.

'Oh, hello you. I'd love to be a woman. You have beautiful

clothes. All soft blouses and pretty skirts. I like dressing up. Every man wants to be a woman. And ones who deny it are lying,' he slurred.

'Oh, really?' she asked.

'Er, Niki, what's going on?' I asked as the plastered star wobbled in front of us.

'He's out of his mind! I love 'im!' she replied.

'You're a naughty one. What are we going to do with you? I bet you've got really big nipples. Show me,' he demanded.

'I'll show you mine if you show me yours,' she replied.

How had this got out of hand so quickly, I thought to myself. Still, I didn't attempt to intervene as Niki was getting on famously with the old goat. She was helping him unbutton his shirt so she could examine his man boobs.

'They're not that big,' she concluded. Thankfully she didn't take Hurt up on his offer to flash her nipples at him.

He was just getting into his stride now. He started singing incoherently at us. We were standing either side of him while he warbled in our ears when he suddenly gripped the back of our necks tightly and lunged for both of us. It was like being trapped by a randy office perv at a Christmas work's do. Luckily we were faster, younger and much more sober than Hurt, so we managed to duck away from his slobbery kisses just in time.

The lecherous actor then shut his eyes, looking like he was going to have to take an impromptu nap on the floor. It was time to round things off double-quick.

'We hear you went to Spearmint Rhino last night, you naughty thing!' I said.

He pulled a face. 'What a peculiar place. Horrible, awful place. These girls, they look so young and all they're interested in is money. It's all "money, money, money". You can see it in their eyes. Is that how you all are? You girls, all you want is money?' The pie-eyed old rogue wasn't quite so amusing now. He was getting a bit angry and had planted a trembling hand on each of our bums. 'Do you girls offer yourselves? Do you? Do you?' he slobbered in our ears.

'Right. Well, how utterly charming to meet you, Mr Hurt. Have fun!' I said loudly, grabbing Niki's hand.

He staggered over towards a chair next to a blonde publicist. Within ten seconds she was ducking his furry tongue too.

The hellraising antics I had witnessed of some stars were not a patch on John Hurt's extraordinary performance. Just went to show – the old ones really were the best.

A month later Niki handed in her resignation. It didn't come as a complete shock to me. She had been missing life back up north in Yorkshire for months, and finally decided after Christmas 2003 that she was going to return to the house she and her brother Jon shared there.

'I'm so sorry, Jess, but I really miss it up there. London's doing me 'ead in. Me and our kid have got a lot to sort out in the house since Dad died and I just want to be up there. I've had a cracking time on 3am though. Never a dull moment!' she grinned, with tears in her eyes.

She left with an appropriate bang in a spectacular outfit at the office Christmas party. The theme that year was royalty. Most of the men at work tried to outdo each other by hiring the most lavish period costumes they could, and there were several Henry VIIIs and a Charles II (someone had actually managed to borrow the heavy outfit Rufus Sewell had worn in the BBC drama about the English king). Piers came as Louis XIV, the Sun King, and there were lots of Williams and Harrys. I went as a Jewish princess to the cries of, 'But you're wearing your regular clothes!'

However, Niki's ensemble horrified everyone, even Piers. She decided to turn up to the bar we had hired in Canary Wharf as dead Princess Diana, complete with a steering wheel around her neck. Strangely she didn't win the costume contest that night. The column was certainly going to be a much duller place without her.

As I waved goodbye to yet another 3am girl and welcomed in her replacement, a tall, slim and sly brunette called Caroline Hedley, I began to ask myself why so many people had come and gone on 3am while I had remained. It was coming up to my fourth year on the column, and one of Piers's first pieces of advice came to mind: 'Five years is long enough on a gossip column.'

Piers had spent five years running a gossip column, and my predecessor at the *Daily Mirror*, Matthew Wright, had also bowed out after half a decade. If I listened to Piers, I had another year and a half left.

But I wasn't ready to go yet. I was still enjoying aspects of my job. I still loved the feeling of sitting down at my computer terminal in the morning, excitedly writing up my gossipy tales from the night before and choosing which paparazzi pictures of celebrities looking ropey to put into the next day's column. The buzz of knowing that every day was different, and that anything could happen at the parties, clubs, bars and awards ceremonies I was going to attend that night, was still very much there.

But I couldn't deny that things had changed for me in the office. As head of the column I had whole new worries and stresses to deal with. I had struggled with staff issues and was finding that pounding the beat at parties at night while trying to cope with my fiery relationship with Jason was really exhausting.

With all this preying on my mind, I returned to Los Angeles. Eva and I were at the Oscars again, and we checked into the Beverly Hilton once more.

This was the third time I was going to be attending Elton John's Oscar party in LA. I couldn't help but notice that I was not anywhere near as excited as I had been that first year. We were now on the guest list and had been told that we'd get a picture with Elton and David Furnish. I had a nagging feeling that it had been so much more satisfying when we'd had to fight to get into parties. Not that I was complaining about being a guest at the A-list bash, far from it. But why was I now feeling a bit blasé about the whole thing? Was it because I knew the drill and what to expect? Still, it was a hell of a lot better than sitting in the office back in London, I said to myself. I sincerely hoped that I wasn't beginning to think of going to the Oscars as the tiniest bit tiresome.

Eva and I had managed to wangle tickets to the Miramax pre-Oscar party, which was taking place the day before the Academy

Awards. Thanks to that *Vanity Fair* article, head honcho and Hollywood movie supremo Harvey Weinstein had allowed Eva and I to attend his BAFTA party at the Sanderson Hotel that year, so we'd asked his London PR if, as long as we were on 'best behaviour' (his words, not ours) we could come along to the movie company's bash at the St Regis Hotel.

We were given the go-ahead and were soon posing for pictures with Quentin Tarantino, who spoke at a billion miles an hour about how he was in the middle of editing *Kill Bill: Vol. II*, and with Scarlett Johansson, who was girly and sweet.

But after an hour at the party, which was filled with high-fiving, short, not very attractive movie producer types, one of the PRs sheepishly walked over to Eva and I. 'I just thought you girls should know that Jude Law has complained about you,' he said.

I was dumbstruck and absolutely furious. 'But we haven't gone anywhere near him! We saw him here with Sienna, but they're so dreary we stayed away. We haven't even looked in his general direction. He'd only make a scene if we did. How can he complain about us, we haven't done anything!' I said crossly, almost breathless with exasperation at Jude's diva-like performance.

'I know that, and I really appreciate it. But he's complained about the mere fact that you're even here at the party,' he explained.

'What does Jude think we're going to do? Trip him over, stuff canapés up his nose and shout, "You've got a lollipop head and a receding hairline!" into his face? Can we honestly not be trusted?' I was getting very angry. What was wrong with him? Did he really feel so threatened by us?

'Come on, Eva. Let's go and wind him up and say hello to him. He'd probably try to get the British Embassy to extradite us back to Britain.'

The PR went pale. 'This is exactly why I didn't want to tell you about Jude's complaint! Please don't play up,' he implored. 'Look, all I wanted to say is that Jude isn't happy about you being here, but he's been informed you are guests of Harvey Weinstein's and you're not going anywhere. So please just be good.'

'You are having a laugh!' I exclaimed. 'Oh my God, I'd love to have seen the look on Jude's face. Did he pull that constipated expression? My night has just got a whole lot better.'

Eva wasn't pleased either. 'Doesn't he have better things to worry about? Like whether he's going to win the Best Actor Oscar tomorrow night? If that was me I'd be far more concerned about my chances of going home with a gong than whether two gossip columnists are at the same party as me.'

In the end it just wasn't Jude's weekend. He lost out to Sean Penn the next night and within ten minutes of arriving at an after-show party with Sienna Miller, it got raided by police and shut down.

It wasn't Martine McCutcheon's weekend either. The ex-*EastEnder* had jetted out to do an endless round of meetings with Hollywood movie bosses. Like many British actresses before her and since, Martine found the LA merry-go-round far tougher than she'd imagined. For starters, there was the lesson in etiquette at Hollywood parties which she had failed to pick up.

We witnessed this the next evening at Elton John's Oscar night party at trendy restaurant Pearl. Martine was there, hitting the free booze with great gusto.

'Eva! Quick! Look who it is!' I whispered.

We had just arrived at the bash, and Joss Stone was performing onstage. We'd located the VIP area, which was simply a small cordoned-off section of the restaurant, and had spotted Sharon Osbourne in there, as well as Prince, who was skulking in a corner, surrounded by friends. Simon Cowell and his girlfriend Terri Seymour were bickering by the Portakabin loos outside, when Martine staggered past us. She was wearing a long, floaty frock, which trailed behind her.

'Oi! Get off me flamin' dress!' she suddenly screeched at a shocked guest who had accidentally trodden on the train of her designer dress.

So much for the demure persona she had been touting around Hollywood. Martine had recently given an interview in which she had claimed studio bosses were so keen on her, 'they said I'm England's answer to J-Lo.' She had a very vivid imagination, it would seem.

After drunkenly muttering to herself, she then attempted to talk her way into the VIP area. The security men clearly hadn't been informed about this Cockney Jennifer Lopez. After a few more – failed – attempts, Martine turned her attention to the entertainment and drunkenly danced to Joss Stone's set before calling it a night and staggering out of the party.

We flew back to London the next day. We were delighted when Virgin Atlantic upgraded us to upper class. This was a total godsend, and we planned to flop into the beds and catch up on some much-needed sleep.

As we settled into our huge seats and waited for take-off when we could change into the giant romper-suit pyjamas they had provided us with, Jude, Sienna, his mother and three pals arrived.

I tried to suppress my giggles, but they came out as a snort. Jude spotted us immediately. His pretty-boy face scrunched up into a tight ball of fury. Ever the gent, he swapped seats with his mother so that she was near Eva for the entirety of the flight, rather than him. He must have come close to bursting a blood vessel as he glared at his mother in horror when she merrily made small talk with Eva. Poor old Jude.

Our trip to LA had definitely not been as exciting as on previous occasions. I couldn't shake off this feeling that I'd been there and done that. I was also feeling in turmoil because my relationship with Jason was by now in its final stages.

I had been with him for nearly two tumultuous years, but, as with Tom, my work for 3am came before the relationship. Evenings and weekends with Jason were now spent mainly arguing. The fighting soon spilled over into the office, and barely a day went by when I wasn't battling with him on the phone at work.

Finally, after a huge shouting match one weekend in May over something trivial, something clicked in my head, and having listened to months and months of advice from my friends to walk away from him I finally decided I could take no more.

I had been seeing a therapist since January at Jason's insistence. He'd been so furious with me when I had decided to take up drinking again that when he advised me to see a therapist for my alcohol problem I had accepted. I realized it would probably be a good thing for me to see a professional and offload all my feelings about my relationship anyway. I didn't want to ring up my friends all the time and cry about the latest insult he had hurled at me.

The weekly therapy sessions lasted four months and I learnt how to walk away from him. In the end I had to let him feel like he had decided to let me go. I wished I had gone to the therapist months before; it felt like I'd wasted so much time locked in such a mismatched relationship. I'd never thought I'd allow a smooth talker to sweep me off my feet. I'd always assumed I could see through all of that.

But I hadn't. Despite my initial thoughts, my intuition telling me that this man wasn't for me, I fell for everything he said. If any of my friends had told me they'd met a guy who had declared his undying love on the first night they'd kissed, I would have cracked up laughing. But I didn't when it happened to me. It took me two years to realize I should have trusted my feelings.

I didn't answer his phone calls or texts and was relieved a week later when Eva and I were sent to the Cannes Film Festival.

By the time Eva and I got to Cannes, I was so drained from the aftermath of so much fighting with Jason, I didn't have the strength to tell her we had finally broken up. It was a strange feeling. I had told Eva so much about my private life during the four years we had worked together, but now I just wanted to keep it to myself. It wasn't that I didn't want her to know my business, I just felt so worn down by Jason I had lost some of my spark. I didn't even feel like crying. I simply didn't want to talk about it.

I had allowed myself to get into this mess, so I was going to have to sort my head out on my own and without sharing it with anyone. Who wanted to hear yet another tale about Jason, I thought to myself.

Soon an altogether bigger matter dominated our conversations in Cannes. There had been rumours back in the office that Piers was going to have his knuckles seriously rapped over photos that the *Daily Mirror* had splashed on its front page of a British soldier allegedly abusing Iraqi prisoners. As a result, wherever Eva and I went, British journalists kept asking us about the whispers that Piers was about to get the sack.

'How are we meant to know? We're here in Cannes, aren't we? You're hearing the same rumours as we are,' I told one of them.

It was the truth. Eva and I were no wiser than the others. As far as we were concerned, it was business as usual back at the office. We were informed that we had to concentrate on bringing in 'sleazier' stories from Cannes. But then one morning I got a hysterical phone call from Caroline.

'Piers has just been marched out of the office! He wasn't even allowed to get his coat. Everyone is just sitting around in total shock. The photos are rumoured to be hoaxes, but Piers wouldn't back down and apologize,' she cried down the phone to me.

'Bloody hell. I can't believe it. Shit. I really don't want to be stuck out here in Cannes right now. Let me tell Eva. I'll call you back,' I said.

Eva and I had been sitting at the table in the tiny living room of our rented apartment, going through the list of press conferences for the next day. She looked up at me. 'He's gone, hasn't he?' she asked.

'They turfed him out without letting him go back to his office. I never thought it would come to this. I can't imagine the paper without him,' I replied.

We sat in silence, just staring at each other.

'Who do you think will be hired as the new editor?' I said.

It was the question on both of our minds.

'Who knows? Who knows what's going to happen now?' Eva said.

'I know what you mean. I feel so useless being out here. I'd much rather be back at Canary Wharf finding out what's going on. Who cares about Brad Pitt and Angelina Jolie? I never thought I'd ever say that!'

But we had to care, of course. Angelina was the talk of the town. Rumours were rife that Jolie and Pitt had been doing more than practising their lines together off the set of their movie, Mr and Mrs Smith. Brad and his wife Jennifer Aniston were out in Cannes, staying at the Hotel du Cap. Brad was publicizing *Troy* and Jennifer had come along for the trip, and no wonder: Angelina Jolie was also at Cannes promoting *Shark Tale*. She had brought her adopted son Maddox along with her, and they were also staying at the du Cap.

Earlier that day, Eva and I had attended the press conference for the animated movie. Angelina's co-star Will Smith had all the journalists giggling with his outrageous flirting. Both actors had provided voiceovers for the aquatic-themed cartoon, and Will could not keep his admiration for his co-star to himself. Angelina's fish – all pouting lips and batting eyelashes – was a total turn-on for the star.

'When I saw Angelina's fish, I started eating sushi!' Will whooped to the audience.

'Does that woman ever blush?' I whispered to Eva as we watched Angelina give the married actor an ever-so-slightly patronizing smile. 'Every man who stars alongside her just seems to turn into a gibbering wreck. She's got remarkable powers. What's her secret?'

We had just been told by a contact that morning that Angelina had turned down an invite to the after-show party for Brad's film *Troy* the night before. The lavish dinner had taken place at the Hotel du Cap, but the actress had decided to give it a miss. It was a strange thing to do for someone who professed to be friends with Brad and was staying in the same hotel where the bash was taking place. It wasn't as if she wasn't up for partying: she had already attended another Cannes party. Her absence gave even more weight to the Brangelina rumours. We were told she hadn't attended in order to spare Jennifer's blushes. Yeah, right. Whatever made her sleep better at night, I thought to myself.

At the same press conference, Angelina didn't react when a journalist asked her, 'You've worked with some of the sexiest guys in the world in the past few months. Did you at any time have a crush on any of your co-stars?'

Eva and I nudged each other. How was Angelina going to get out of this one, I wondered.

'I think you're fishing for something,' she purred.

'Let's ask the real question. Have you slept with any of your co-stars? Spit it out, lady!' Will interjected.

Well done, Will, I thought. He'd been cheeky enough to ask the question we all had been dying to ask, but which would get us chucked out of the press conference if we dared.

'I have not been naked with any of my co-stars,' she said, smiling enigmatically.

'That'll put Jennifer Aniston at ease, won't it? Not. Angelina really is something else,' Eva whispered to me.

A few hours later, as Eva and I sat in our apartment discussing Piers's sacking, the Brad-Angelina-Jennifer tale was put on the back-burner.

'I feel so out on a limb here. Do you reckon they'll bring us back to the office?' I asked her.

'Nah. It's probably best we are out here. It must be a nightmare in the office. Let's just keep our heads down and carry on,' she replied.

That night every British hack wanted to discuss only one topic, and it wasn't Brad and Angelina's supposed affair. If only the two celebrities knew that the talk of the tabloids was actually a man they'd never heard of called Piers Morgan.

Over the next few months, life changed even more on 3am. Richard was announced as the new editor of the *Mirror* to my utter joy. And Eva announced she was pregnant. She'd been seeing a guy who had nothing to do with the media for a while after meeting at a gig.

'Bloody hell! When you go all out to shock me, you really go for it, don't you! That's brilliant news. I can't believe it! The first pregnant 3am girl!' I said to her, hugging her in the loo.

'I've only told a few people as I'm under three months. But I had to tell you. Please keep it zipped,' she said, smiling.

'Of course I'll keep it quiet. I know it's impossible to keep anything secret here, but I promise I won't breathe a word,' I assured her.

My head was spinning with all of the changes. In my personal life I was now single again and resolutely so. Jason had stopped contacting me and all my friends and family told me how relieved they were that it was over between us. At work, Richard was now the editor and Eva was going to have a baby. It meant that she'd be off on maternity leave the following July, which would also be the five-year anniversary of 3am.

Piers's advice about spending no more than five years on the column kept coming back to me. The dates tallied and I began to feel that everything was now starting to point in that direction. But I didn't know what to do. Where would I go? I vowed to reassess everything in the New Year. It was December and the party season was about to kick off. I needed to concentrate on that.

I had moved into a new flat in west London and was mulling over whether to attend the post-premiere party for *Phantom of the Opera* on the night of the sixth of December.

'Oh, come on, don't be so dreary. The party's at Olympia; it's round the corner from you! Come and say hello and have a quick drink.' My PR friend Simon was determined to get me out of the house. It was a cold night, I was still surrounded by boxes from the move and all I wanted to do was stay in.

'Don't make me feel guilty. I just can't be arsed. I'm so tired. I'm getting too old for this job,' I moaned.

'Oh, shut up. You're twenty-nine. Stop being boring. I expect to see you there. We don't have to stay long. You don't *have* to get drunk, you know. I can come round to your flat afterwards to take a look,' he answered brightly.

'You're not a friend. A friend would listen to my woes and let me wallow in my own misery at home. Fine. I'll come. But it's only a Tuesday night. I'm not getting pissed. There are too many events in the next few weeks. I can't start December feeling really hungover,' I replied.

'What. Ever. See you there,' said Simon.

What was wrong with me? Usually I'd happily give up a rare night off at home in order to cover a glam party or hang out with a friend like Simon. But since moving into my own flat and living by myself, I had started to appreciate the joys of staying in. However, my job wasn't about staying in, it was about premieres, award ceremonies, celebrity parties. Since when did I turn down a big after-show bash to think about curtains, pots and pans, for goodness' sake, I thought to myself.

Two hours later I had changed into a skirt, knee-high black suede boots and a black top and jumped on to a number 28 bus. I had missed the film, but the party was about to start at the exhibition centre in Olympia. The stars of *Phantom of the Opera* would be there, and Simon was bringing one of his clients, Duncan James from the boy band Blue. Luckily the singer was single and would no doubt be looking to charm his way into some lucky lady's affections that night. I was confident that I'd definitely get a spicy story for the column the next day. It wouldn't be a waste of time going out after all.

'Let's have a glass of champagne. Don't look at me like that, Jessica. It's just the one.' Simon forced a glass into my hand and gave one to Duncan. 'Well, cheers everyone!' he said.

We all mumbled cheers and tasted the champagne. I looked around me. The party was now in full swing. There were at least 400 guests, all drinking and dancing and putting the canapés away. The stars of the film, Gerard Butler, Emmy Rossum, Minnie Driver and Jennifer Ellison, stayed in a roped-off VIP area.

Duncan was chatting to Andrew Lloyd Webber while Simon and I were surveying the scene.

'Are you still loving it at 3am?' Simon suddenly asked me. He was looking at me suspiciously.

'Of course! Why do you say that?' I replied a bit too quickly.

'Oh, nothing. You just don't seem your usual bouncy self. How long are you going to stay, do you think?'

'What on earth are you asking that for? I don't know. I haven't even thought about it,' I lied.

'Hmmm. Right, madam, we've got a lot to talk about when we're in Miami.'

Simon and I had booked a week's holiday in Miami in January.

We were going to meet up with our friend Dan, who was living in New York where he was number two at a weekly showbiz title.

'I don't know what you're talking about. Everything's fine!' I trilled.

Simon knew me too well and could see I was putting on an act. But it wasn't the right place to be probing me on my 3am crisis. 'Come on. Let's have another drink,' he replied.

Three hours later and Simon, Duncan and I were full of festive cheer. We were all hopelessly drunk. In fact, we were in a far worse state than anyone else at the party.

Simon had started chatting up a bloke who had caught his eye, but Duncan decided he didn't approve. 'He looks like a hobbit! You can do much better than that,' Duncan said, laughing.

'Oh, shut it. He's not a hobbit, he's lovely!' slurred Simon, who was giving the small and not very attractive chap admiring glances.

'No, he's not. I'm not having it,' replied Duncan.

'Don't tell me what to do, Duncan. I can talk to any man I want to.'

'But he's a hobbit!'

'He's not a hobbit. What's your problem?'

By now the man had moved away from the unfolding spectacle, but in their drunkenness Simon and Duncan hadn't noticed and were getting louder and louder.

'What on earth's wrong with you two? Calm down!' I interrupted.

But Duncan was on a roll. 'Simon! Will you listen to me? He's not good enough for you. He's a sodding hobbit!' he shouted. He suddenly smashed his champagne glass against a table we were standing next to and brandished the jagged stem in the air.

'Duncan! What the fuck are you doing?' screamed Simon.

Duncan stormed off and Simon ran after him. I followed. They headed into the men's loo and I stood outside, listening to the pair of them drunkenly screech at each other.

'I'm your PR! You can't tell me who I can and cannot fancy!' Simon shouted, as the bickering duo spilled out of the men's.

'But he's a hobbit!'

'Will you shut up about the hobbit?'

Everyone milling around the men's loo was now watching their hissy fit.

'Be quiet! I don't know why you're arguing about this guy anyway – he's legged it,' I said, interrupting them.

Duncan pushed past me and raced back into the main room, where the party was winding up.

'What's up with him? He's gone mad!' I asked Simon.

'He's pissed,' he replied.

We chased after Duncan and found him about to leave the party. He was swaying a little.

'So, where are we off to now?' he asked. He looked like he'd completely forgotten what had just happened.

'How about my flat? It's round the corner. You two can sort out your girlie problems away from the eyes and ears of everyone here,' I suggested.

We walked out of the party and the group of ten paparazzi guys who were waiting outside started to shout and snap at Duncan. Simon and I stood away from him so we could make sure we weren't in the background of any of the photos.

'Let's get a taxi,' I suggested, and stood by the kerb looking for one. I felt a pair of arms wrap themselves around my waist. It was Duncan. He pulled me close to him. 'What are you doing? Get off!' I said, laughing.

Just at that moment the photographers started to take pictures of us.

'Stop it! He's only messing about,' I said.

What was I thinking? Duncan was the last celebrity to leave the bash and the snappers were loving the fact that the drunken singer was grabbing a girl outside. Arguing back and trying to remind them I was a journalist and not his latest squeeze had no effect. They clicked away, and Duncan was by now fully basking in their flashlights.

'Quick, let's get into the taxi!' shouted Simon, who had flagged down a cab.

He opened the door and I got in. Duncan followed behind me,

but before Simon could get in, the pop star slammed the door shut in his face.

'Just start driving!' Duncan instructed the driver.

'What are you doing? What about Simon! We can't leave him there!' I laughed, covering my mouth in shock at the thought of Simon stranded on the pavement.

Just then more flashes went off outside. Some of the photographers had shoved their cameras against the taxi windows and were snapping away at us. I realized it looked deeply suspicious: Duncan and I were in the back seat, and I had hidden half my face with my hands. The taxi driver accelerated away, but the snappers weren't ready to let their prey go, and ran alongside taking picture after picture.

Duncan was utterly pissed and smiled broadly at them. I was feeling terrible for Simon. I pulled my mobile out of my handbag and rang him. He answered after one ring.

'Where are you? Are you all right?'

'I'm walking up to High Street Kensington. I can't believe you abandoned me!' he screamed in a high-pitched voice.

'I didn't! Duncan is the one who slammed the door in your face. Ask him. He's lost the plot. Stay where you are, I'll get the taxi to turn around and pick you up,' I said.

The cab made a U-turn in the road and we soon found Simon standing just past Olympia and looking distinctly unamused. I opened the door.

'Get in,' I ordered. 'We're going to mine.'

He sat next to Duncan and I shouted my address to the taxi driver as the pair kicked off again. Five minutes later, with the duo still ranting away, we pulled up outside my flat. As I opened the door and walked in, Duncan and Simon were still squabbling about the short guy at the party.

'Why are you two so obsessed by this man? Are you two secretly at it or what?' I said.

Duncan appeared not to have heard. He was looking around my flat. 'Have you got a garden?' he asked.

'Well, it's more of a walled patio to be honest. It's through the bedroom.' I led them through my small bedroom and opened the pair of glass doors which opened out on to the patio. I flicked the switch which lit up the coloured light bulbs strung along one of the walls. 'And this is my tiny garden,' I explained.

But as I gestured towards the mass of overgrown weeds and the mysterious triffid-like plants growing out of the paving stones, Duncan and Simon started hurling another round of abuse at one another.

'You are being so vile, Duncan!' shouted Simon as Duncan pushed past him and stormed back into my bedroom.

I followed Simon as he went after his client.

'Will you get out of there?' I heard Simon yell.

As I reached the door I could see Duncan was now lying in my bed, under the duvet.

'I'm tired. I just want a quick nap. Leave me alone for a bit,' said Duncan, who had now shut his eyes and was snuggling against my pillow.

'Get out of Jessica's bed! What are you doing? She's a journalist. You shouldn't even be at her flat for a start!'

'But she's your friend. She's not going to fuck me over. Don't you trust your mates, Simon?' replied Duncan.

'Oh, shut up. I know she's a friend, but haven't I taught you anything? You just don't go back to a journalist's house, regardless of whether they're a friend of mine or not. You just shouldn't do it.'

Duncan leapt up from under the duvet, grabbed me, pushed me against the wall opposite the bed and tried to kiss me. I ducked my head away from him, but he held me by the shoulders and tried to lunge at me again.

By now Simon was shrieking. 'Get off her! Duncan! Right, that's it! I'm taking you home. We are going to have some serious words tomorrow. I don't know if I can continue to represent you.'

I was still standing against the wall, and Duncan was now heading for my front door.

'I'm so sorry, Jessica. I'll call you later. Duncan, stop right there!' Simon ran past me and I heard the pair swap further insults as they stomped up the metal stairs from my basement flat to the street.

I'm so glad I went for just the one drink, I thought to myself as I got undressed. Why hadn't I stuck to my guns and spent the night studying sofa material swatches instead? Duncan had nearly glassed Simon at the party, they were presently waking up my entire street with their screams of abuse, and I was going to have four hours' sleep at the most and was definitely going to wake up with a cracking hangover.

'Hello?' I croaked into my mobile.

'You still asleep? Wake up, kiddo. Did you pull Duncan from Blue last night?'

It was Tom.

'What? What time is it?'

'It's 8am. I've just been told the picture desk at work has been sent photos of you and this pop star looking cosy in the back of a cab last night. Did you shag him? He's got a very silly haircut, you know.'

Tom had left the *Mirror* a few months before to join the *Sun* as their defence editor. He was now married to the girl he had started seeing a few months after we had broken up. We had become good friends, and he quizzed me relentlessly on my love life. He had heartily approved when I broke up with Jason.

'What picture? Oh, shit. I remember now. No, I didn't do anything with him. His PR is a very good mate of mine and we were all going back to mine but Simon wasn't in the cab then. I inadvertently covered my face up at the wrong moment. Oh, shit. I bet it looks really dodgy, doesn't it?'

'Oh, for goodness' sake, kiddo. You should know better! Hiding your head looks like you're trying not to be photographed. Of course it looks dodgy!'

'Bollocks. I didn't do anything, I promise.'

'Yes, whatever you say. You do realize those pictures have been sent around to every newspaper, don't you? Everyone's going to think you pulled him. Oh dear!' He laughed.

'Right. I'll call you later. I need to get to the office now,' I said and hung up on Tom, who was still chortling away.

The shock of Tom's phone call had distracted me from what I now realized was a thumping headache. A shower didn't help. I quickly got dressed, left the flat and half-walked, half-ran towards the Tube station.

Calm down, I said to myself, it's only a silly picture. It was entirely innocent and it wasn't as if anyone would actually run the photo. None of the gossip columnists wrote stories about each other. It was a sort of unspoken rule. Would our readers really be interested in the disastrous love life of a journalist from another paper? Well, only if it involved a celebrity, I thought with a pang of horror.

But then I was sure Simon would ring the other papers and explain what had really happened. It would be fine, I reassured myself.

By the time I arrived at Canary Wharf, flashed my pass at the security gate and made my way up to the twenty-second floor, my hungover panic had subsided. I didn't know what I had been worrying about. Tom loved to wind me up and still knew how to get a rise out of me. I got out at my floor and walked over to my desk.

'Oi, Callan! Nice new boyfriend you've got there!' shouted Richard. He was standing outside the frosted glass editor's office, which was now his.

'Er, what?'

'Yeah, yeah. For sure, for sure. Your boy-band lover! Nice guy!' He laughed.

I followed him to the picture desk, where Richard instructed the picture editor to show me what he had on his screen.

'There you go! Right – I want you to run that photo very large in tomorrow's column. And refer to yourself as a mystery girl until the end of the story and then reveal that it's you,' he barked at me.

'But it's not true! Nothing went on. Simon Jones was with us. I know it looks a bit suspect, but those are the facts.'

'Now, now, Callan. Don't lie to your Uncle Dicky. You're running the photo and that's final,' he replied, rubbing his hands together. He sat at his desk on the back bench and started to whistle annoyingly.

'But, Richard, I'm going to look like such a dick. Everyone's going to think I did pull him and that I want to run photos of us in the taxi. Oh, please don't make me,' I begged.

'Well, that's what happens when you get into taxis with pop stars,' he replied, then winked and carried on whistling loudly.

I walked to my desk and the other end of the office where Eva and Caroline were now giggling over the photos of me on their screens.

'OOH! How's lover boy this morning?' asked Eva.

'Shall I go and buy my wedding hat now?' said Caroline.

'Oh, please don't. Nothing went on! Simon dragged him off me before anything happened. Not that I would have done anything anyway!' I replied as I sunk into my chair.

'Ha, ha! Yeah, right!' laughed Eva.

'Oh, please! Richard says we've got to run the photo in the column tomorrow. It's going to look like I'm a Duncan fanatic!' I whined.

So this is what people go through when they've been snapped in a compromising picture, I thought to myself. I now knew exactly what it felt like to be on the other side of the fence. The photo spoke for itself. I hated to admit it, but some of those people who had denied anything improper had gone on when they'd been snapped with someone may have been speaking the truth.

'OH MY GOD! Those photos have gone round to every paper and magazine, you realize?' Simon asked me when he rang half an hour later. 'I've been doing your PR and denying it all. I don't know what happened last night! Duncan and I found a taxi after we left yours, carried on arguing and then he suddenly screamed, "Stop the cab!" and got out. I was so livid I didn't beg him to stay or go back and get him. He's just rung and apologized for being so pissed and losing the plot. He's mortified about the paparazzi pictures though.'

'Gee, Simon, thanks so much for convincing me to come out for just the one drink last night,' I said, laughing.

After spending the morning batting off calls from journalists at other papers and denying that Duncan and I had been playing tonsil tennis with each other, my mobile rang. I couldn't bear the thought of going through the whole saga again. But it wasn't who I'd expected.

'Hi, Jessica. It's Duncan here. I'm just so sorry about last night. I don't know what came over me. Simon gave me your number as I told him I really wanted to apologize to you. I'm sorry if I've put you in an awkward situation,' he said sheepishly.

'Oh, don't worry. That's very sweet of you to ring. You know you've got a very good publicist there. You don't want to lose him. I wouldn't tell him that the boys he fancies look like hobbits, though,' I advised him. 'He gets a bit oversensitive, especially after he's had a magnum of champagne. I don't think it's worth glassing him over.'

After the parties were all over, I went home for the Christmas break. Throughout the holiday, I had never felt so tired and despondent. I knew it was time to make a decision about my future as a 3am girl. Eva would be off to have her baby in the summer, and we'd have to go on yet another hunt for a replacement. Could I face it yet again? We had endlessly joked that the third position on the column was cursed, and it really did feel like that now. Three definitely wasn't the magic number.

My nagging worry was that I was getting a bit bored of rushing around parties almost every night, hardly ever seeing my friends and being older than most of the celebs I wrote about. I was about to turn thirty, and my five-year anniversary on 3am was months away.

I asked my father for his advice as we polished a bottle of wine off together on Christmas Day.

'Five years is long enough, my girl. You don't want to be pigeonholed for ever. I didn't stay on gossip columns for more than that,' he said. 'You know it's time to go when people you meet tell you that you look twenty years older in person than you do on your picture byline.'

'But no one's said that to me yet!'

'"Yet" is the keyword there. There's nothing worse than some old bird trolloping about from one party to another, bloated from booze and long lunches, all wrinkly and old and tired. No one wants to talk to that. And no man will want you then,' he continued, warming to his theme of doom and gloom.

'Oh, how marvellous. Anything else I can look forward to?' I asked.

'Yes. I've seen enough gossip columnists go mad from far too many years of drink and bitterness. It's time to move on, Jess. Don't end up in the Priory, please.'

I knew he was right. If my dad was advising me that the end of my 3am career was in sight, then it was time to make a plan. He had been in journalism long enough – forty years to be exact – to dole out insider knowledge. He may not have known who most of the celebs I wrote about were, but he knew when the time was right to leave a gossip column on a high note, as he himself had done more than thirty years before.

I was horrified at the idea of turning into an embittered, fat, alcoholic gossip columnist and still doing the job in twenty years' time. While male gossip columnists seemed to be able to get away with doing the job well into their sixties, not one woman was doing the same. A middle-aged man could still put on the charm at parties, but it seemed that a woman of a similar age was expected to leave the hunt for celebrity scandal to the younger, prettier, slimmer girls out there. Which male celebs would want to flirt and spill the beans to a matronly middle-aged mum? The sad truth of the matter was that no one would. I would have to leave while I was still on top of my game and had my dignity intact.

It wasn't just the age issue that was putting me off the job. In the *Vanity Fair* article there had been a quote from Peter Mckay, a legendary journalist on the *Daily Mail*. He'd described us as 'victims', which had left me feeling confused and a little troubled. Was I really a victim and not a pioneering, go-getting gossip columnist? I was fully aware that Piers wanted to capitalize on the ladette and *Sex and the City* culture that everyone was obsessing about. But was I not in control as much as I had assumed, and did that mean my gossip columnist techniques were actually little more than feminine wiles and an ability to hide myself in loos in order to escape from bodyguards and eavesdrop on celebrities' conversations?

All these questions were going round and round my head. To top it all I had also started to feel increasingly guilty about some of the stories we wanted to run.

Along with the other tabloids, we had found out that a certain female celeb was pregnant. A freelancer was touting the story about from paper to paper. The star was under three months and it soon became apparent that she was keen for the papers not to run the story as she was planning on having an abortion. She had just broken up with her cheating boyfriend. We were all set to run the story when her lawyer sent out letters to the press spelling out in no uncertain terms that if we ran anything on her pregnancy it would contravene the terms of the Press Complaints Commission's Code of Conduct. As she tearfully went for an abortion a few weeks later, she was trailed by paparazzi. No one ran the pictures or touched the story.

The sad truth of the matter was that I would have run her abortion story in the column if her lawyer hadn't threatened us. Initially I hadn't thought for a minute that it would be wrong to run this story. I was blinded by the fact that this Brit was a big-name star and courted the press when it suited her. All I could think now, however, was what if it had been one of my friends who had been hounded by the media in such a manner when she was making the heartbreaking decision to have a termination?

I was also increasingly stunned by the way supposed friends and flatmates of celebrities would dish the dirt on them for a few thousand pounds. One TV personality rang up a friend of hers who happened to work on the *Mirror* to find out who had been making money out of her misery following a story I'd run when she'd been dumped by yet another boyfriend. It all left a very nasty taste in my mouth. The truth was one of her closest pals – her flatmate, in fact – was doing the dirty on her.

I was starting to feel guilty. I had paid her flatmate and in so doing encouraged him to spill the beans on her private life. I made myself feel better at the time by thinking that if I hadn't bought the story then he'd only have sold the tales to another paper. But by paying him £3,000 in cash, I was simply whetting his appetite and making an already unstable and insecure celeb even more unstable and insecure.

A lot of the stories I ran were with the collaboration of celebs and their PRs. Most music publicists spun lies about their clients in order to get them in the papers. This happened regularly with 3am. Unfortunately, the PRs wouldn't always get round to telling the pop stars that they'd told fibs about them to the press, so outraged singers would often blame the newspapers for making up stories about their love lives. The *Daily Mirror* lawyers would never have allowed us to print any stories without proof to back up our claims, which is why we always taped every conversation with a PR. Even when we agreed with the publicist not to quote them by name in the article but described them as 'a friend' or a 'source close to the star', we had them on tape confirming the story.

I always felt sorry for girl-band members who would read in 3am that they had split up with their long-term boyfriends. Their love lives were used as bartering goods with us. Basically every aspect of a celebrity's life was up for grabs when they had something to promote, whether they wanted it to appear in 3am or not. It was simply the nature of the game, and everyone in the showbiz industry played a part in it.

Sometimes some very mysterious sources of information would pop into my inbox. One of them kept their identity hidden and emailed me out of the blue about the British actress Kate Beckinsale. She had just broken up from her long-term boyfriend, actor Michael Sheen, and put out the usual statement that no one else was involved. But I was assured otherwise. The mystery person informed me that Kate was now going out with Len Wiseman, who had just directed the acting couple in vampire horror film *Underworld*.

'Just another request, please could you avoid implying in the article that the information supplied had anything to do with Michael. I wouldn't want Kate to get funny with him, especially as she could make things difficult regarding his access to their daughter, Lily,' read one of the emails I received out of the blue.

I rang Kate's publicist in LA, thoroughly expecting either an outright denial or, as was usually the case with American PRs, no answer at all. But I was taken aback when the publicist rang me back and confirmed that Kate was now with Len.

The unknown source – who used a hotmail email account with Kate's name in it – didn't want cash for their tip-off. But he or she did ask for me to donate the sum I would have paid for the story to a charity of my choice, which I did. Was this someone acting on behalf of Michael? I never found out.

Usually the sources I used were clearly not very honourable. One such source was an actor who starred in *EastEnders*. I got to know him at the National TV Awards one year, and we exchanged mobile phone numbers.

'I'll tip you off when any scandal happens with the rest of the cast and in exchange will you hold back any negative stories you get on me? And write positive things about me?' he asked.

I agreed. He had a partner and kids, but this star had recently been snapped at a hotel late at night with a girl who was most definitely not his other half. I didn't think about the part I played in helping him cover up his infidelities. All I was concerned about was getting stories off him about his *EastEnders* colleagues.

This actor was as good as his word and rang me up one day from his dressing room to tip me off that one of the show's stars had just been given his marching orders. He whispered it down the phone to me and begged me never to reveal he had blabbed on someone who was meant to be one of his close friends.

I assuaged my feelings of guilt about helping this guy's quest for fame by convincing myself that if I didn't enter this agreement one of my rivals would. It was my job to uncover these sorts of stories, and I was expected to go to any lengths to do so.

On occasion techniques would backfire. Sometimes reporters made what was known as blagging phone calls. This was when they rang a doctor/hospital/credit card company/estate agent/hotel to obtain information by pretending to be a celeb or an aide or family member of the star. Either a reporter would do it themselves or they'd pay a private detective who was used to this line of work to do it.

A freelancer had been touting a story around that a famous British celeb was pregnant. He had pulled her medical records and found out that she'd been visiting a Harley Street gynaecologist.

The star's PR issued her denial to every journalist who rang with the story. This didn't automatically mean the pregnancy was untrue, though. But Piers and Richard always refused to run stories on stars expecting babies unless the star had confirmed it themselves. Who wanted to publish an exclusive about a famous person being pregnant if they were under the twelve-week danger period and ran the risk of having a miscarriage? Or even worse, an abortion. We had run two stories when we first started 3am about two female celebs who were pregnant. Both were under twelve weeks, and neither of them gave birth. That was a lesson learnt.

In fact, on this occasion the star was not pregnant. It emerged that her mother-in-law (who had the same surname) was going through the menopause and was being treated by the same doctor. It was a close call.

There were occasions when we got what we deserved. One time a big-name celeb fled abroad to have her baby. The media was on an intense mission to track down the A-list actress and be the first to reveal the details of the birth. One reporter hit upon the ingenious idea of pretending she was suffering from food poisoning to get admitted to the hospital we thought the celeb would be giving birth at, so she could then happily sneak about while dressed up in a gown with a drip in her arm.

As impressed as we were by her idea, this poor girl became a laughing stock when it emerged that – after she had been taken in as a patient – she'd got the wrong hospital. The actress went on to give birth to her daughter away from the prying eyes of the press.

I was outraged that the celeb got away with it. It didn't even occur to me at the time that I was the one in the wrong.

By the start of 2005, I realized I'd had an absolute blast on 3am but in the words of many who criticized my job on a tabloid, I'd turned into the sort of person who would sell their grandmother for a juicy scoop. We used to joke in the mornings at work about whose life we were going to ruin that day. And increasingly that was exactly how it was feeling to me.

Caroline, Jean-Christophe Novelli and me

13. Behaving Badly and Bowing Out

It was amazing what we could blag once we put our minds to it. In January 2005 we persuaded a major London store to lend us clothes. Piers was right after all. There were plenty of freebies out there if we only had the cheek to ask.

I had assumed the store would just let us wear clothes they lent out for photo shoots. But they actually let us loose on the shop floor to peruse the latest designer collections and to borrow clothes which then would be sold. The security and price tags would be removed from the outfits we chose, and the press office would bike them over. We just had to make sure we didn't get any spillages or cigarette holes on the glitzy frocks.

After wearing a £500 dress to the Brit Awards that February, I woke up the next day to discover the pink slinky number reeked of stale fags. We had promised the PR that we'd return our outfits that day. There was only one thing for it. While I showered, blow-dryed my hair and got ready for work, I gave the dress a good airing by hanging it up in the garden.

By the time I got into the office it smelled a lot fresher. I checked it for any drink or deodorant marks, wrapped it up with Caroline's and Eva's borrowed dresses and biked them back to the store, where they were promptly displayed on the women's floor again, to be sold to unsuspecting shoppers.

'Almost as good as new, eh?' I said to Eva.

'I know. It's a vile thought, isn't it? Luckily we haven't stained any of them. Yet,' she replied.

In April, Caroline and I were sent tickets to the Tio Pepe Restaurant Awards at the Grosvenor House Hotel in Park Lane. Looking at the guest list, it wasn't exactly brimming over with celebrities, but we knew French chef Jean-Christophe Novelli would be there and were keen to get him on side. He had just been announced as the new host of *Hell's Kitchen* on ITV1, and we knew the fiery lothario would be good value.

Caroline and I had dressed up in borrowed frocks for the restaurant awards, even though it wasn't a seriously glitzy event, mainly because we liked the idea of using the store as a giant dressing-up box.

As soon as we arrived at the hotel, we saw Novelli.

'Right, let's get him. If we tell him we'll big him up in the column and back the programme, he should give us spicy stories in return. I'm sure loads of kiss-and-tell girls will come crawling out of the woodwork once *Hell's Kitchen* airs,' I said to Caroline.

We made our way over to him just before dinner was about to begin.

'Hi, I'm Jessica. This is Caroline. We work at the *Daily Mirror*. We wanted to wish you luck for *Hell's Kitchen*,' I said to him.

Novelli was taller in person than I had expected. But his black hair was every inch as greasy as I'd envisaged. He slowly eyed Caroline and I up and down. 'Why, sank you ladeeyz,' he purred. 'You two are like summer and winter.'

'I beg your pardon?' I replied.

He looked at Caroline and I, peering down our cleavages. 'Tell me – are you single?' he asked me.

'Er, yes,' I replied and then instantly regretted my honesty.

Was I now asking for it? Shit, he was a fast mover, I thought to myself. He had a reputation for pulling female journalists who interviewed him and were bowled over by his Gallic charm. Each to their own. To me he was slimy, had greasy hair and a big nose. I wondered what his famed seduction technique was.

'OK, zer are three reasons why you are single,' he continued loudly. 'One. You cannot cook. Two. You are psycho. Or three, you are sheet in bed.'

Caroline burst out laughing.

'Oh, you're a charmer all right, aren't you?' I asked him.

He shrugged at me, smiled, gave me a wink and walked off.

'Is that how he does it? Is that how he eases the knickers off all those women? How bizarre. What a strange man,' I said to

Caroline as we watched him waltz off to give the eye to some unlucky women at the dinner.

After the ceremony and meal, the guests moved to the Zeta Bar at the Hilton. Caroline and I bumped into Northern Irish actor James Nesbitt. The *Cold Feet* star was always fun to talk to at parties and awards bashes. He liked to make the most of the alcohol on offer and always chatted away in a friendly fashion to Eva, me and the other girls who had worked on 3am over the years. He could be outrageously flirtatious. At the National TV Awards one year, he had staggered over to me at the after-show party at the RCA and slurred in my ear, 'You look like the sort of girl who takes it up the arse,' before his mate, a BBC PR boss, dragged him away. He never tried anything on now, thank goodness, and we always had a laugh with him.

'Hi, Jimmy, how are you?' I asked.

His mischievous eyes twinkled away as usual and he gave me a wink. 'Oh, I'm grand. What are you doing here?' he asked.

'Oh, you know, thought we'd see who was here and what they're up to. I reckon that Jean-Christophe Novelli comes from the same charm school as you,' I said, laughing.

Other than James, there was just a *Footballers' Wives* actress and Ronnie Corbett, so Caroline and I decided to go to the Met Bar nearby to see if there were any other celebs knocking back cocktails. I told James where we were going and he told us he'd see us there.

Caroline and I walked the short distance to the Metropolitan Hotel and stepped into the bar. It was pretty much empty apart from a table with Novelli, who'd left the Tio Pepe party before us, and some of his friends. He saw us and waved.

'Hey, ladeeyz, come and join us!' he shouted.

'We may as well. Who knows what gems he might come out with?' Caroline whispered to me.

We sat at their booth and the chef immediately turned to me to regale me with tales of his prowess. Hadn't he heard of foreplay, I wondered.

'So, when did you last 'av sex?' he asked me.

'None of your bloody business,' I replied.

'I 'ad it five hours ago,' he said, laughing.

'How lovely for you,' I said, grimacing at the thought. I wasn't in the mood to even flirt with Novelli for the sake of getting some funny stories out of him. He seemed to think that every word he uttered would make me want to rip my knickers off. I was relieved to see Nesbitt appear.

'Oi, Nesbitt! Over here!' I yelled, waving my arms.

At least with his Irish charm he managed to get away with his cheesy mock chat-up lines. He joined our table and Novelli was sufficiently distracted for a bit to stop sharing with me any further tales of his acts of heroism and daring in the bedroom.

'I think I'm going to go. Are you going to stay much longer?' Caroline asked me.

'I'm going to stay for a bit. With these two lady killers in the room, you never know what could happen,' I replied.

Half an hour later after some intense cocktail downing, James leaned over and whispered to me, 'I've got a room at the Grosvenor. Do you want to come back for a bit? You look like you need rescuing from him.' He jerked his head towards Novelli.

'Sure. Why not? I'll come back for a bit,' I replied.

We said our goodbyes to Novelli and walked back to the hotel along Park Lane.

I didn't think Nesbitt meant anything dodgy by his offer. I had been privy to some very interesting stories about him in the past but I hadn't run any of them in 3am, mainly because I didn't have proof. In his eyes I hadn't done the dirty on him and was a trusted member of the press. In turn, I didn't expect him to be stupid enough to make a pass at me.

He was married to his drama school sweetheart and had two daughters, but Nesbitt had been busted plenty of times over the years for illicit romps. Almost every time the girls had sold their kiss-and-tell stories to the newspapers. And every time Nesbitt had been wracked with guilt, professed his love for his wife and family and begged for forgiveness, which he always got.

I asked him about all of this as we arrived at his suite.

'Why do you do it? And why do you always get caught?'

'I just fall in love easily' was his response.

'Is that it? Is that your excuse?'

'Oh, don't start. I can't help it. I've been an eejit, I know. Now, what do you want to drink?' he said, poking around in his minibar.

'You know, you've got to be careful or you're going to head for another fall,' I said to him. I suddenly felt protective of the balding actor. There was something helpless about him. 'You've had it pretty easy. Your wife has stood by you. But there's going to be another young kiss-and-tell professional around the corner waiting to catch you out. You've got to give these girls credit. They know exactly what they're doing and they target famous blokes who can't help themselves when they see a pretty face and a pair of giant tits. One journalist I know even leads a team of these lethal blondes out to parties and clubs and points out the celebs she wants them to try and pull. She's like a pimp, this girl.'

'Why? What does she do then?' asked James, handing me a gin and tonic.

'Well, her glamour model mates then home in on the drunk stars and practically every time the bloke will ask them back to his hotel room or wherever. What they don't realize is these girls have cameras in their fake designer bags so they can capture the whole sordid business. And this journalist gets a photographer to discreetly follow the couple back to wherever they end up, in order to snap them together.'

James shrugged. He obviously didn't think he had anything to worry about.

'It happens every time,' I insisted. 'You actors are so dim. If a gorgeous pouting model looks too good to be true, it's usually because she is. Just watch out, Jimmy. Steve Coogan's wife has just left him because two girls did a kiss and tell on him recently. He denied having full-blown sex with them, but that's not the point. You've got to watch out for yourself.'

James got himself a drink. 'Oh Jesus, that sounds awful. I've got filming tomorrow,' he said to me, waving a script for *Murphy's Law*.

'Well, you better not get too drunk then,' I replied.

He clearly didn't want to take any of my advice on board. Why was I trying to be his PR, I wondered to myself. It wasn't my job to rescue him from the clutches of the kiss-and-tell brigade. I was a gossip columnist. It was my job to uncover his misdemeanours and report them.

Three hours later we had finished off his minibar with gusto. He had shared all sorts of shocking stories involving the cast of *Cold Feet*, tales that I knew I could never write about as I had no proof he had told me. And I couldn't turn him over like that.

I felt sorry for Nesbitt. It was no wonder so many girls sold their stories about him. He was good fun, but after a few drinks he opened up about his life far too easily and blabbed all sorts of insider secrets. Even if I *could* stand any of the stories up, I just couldn't bring myself to run them. Watching him knock back yet another drink, I realized that he seemed so lonely. When he was away from his family in London filming on set, it was no wonder he ended up in trouble.

'You really shouldn't invite women back to your hotel room. You could give girls the wrong idea entirely,' I ticked him off.

'Don't be like that,' he said. 'Anyway, I can't believe you're in my hotel room and I haven't made a pass at you yet!'

'Don't even think about it!' I gasped.

'Oh, you know I'm only joking,' he said, laughing.

I got up to go to the bathroom and decided I would go home straight after. I was knackered and my head was swimming with all the stories he had shared and which I couldn't do anything with.

Suddenly there was a knock on the bathroom door. I jumped.

'What is it?' I shouted.

'What are you doing in there?' James asked.

'I'm on the loo!'

'Can I come in and watch?'

'Oh, bloody hell! Course you can't! Bugger off!'

So much for feeling sorry for him, I thought to myself. He was unbelievable. I was sure he was joking but I didn't want to hang around and see, especially after all that booze.

'Look, I've got to go now,' I said as I walked back into the room.

He was pouring a miniature bottle of gin into a glass and topping it up with Red Bull.

'You can't. I'm just sorting a drink out for you,' he slurred.

'No, I really have to go now. Just keep out of trouble. And don't ask girls if you can watch them pee,' I said, leaving the room.

And to think James had been the one to gallantly 'rescue' me from the slimy Novelli.

My disillusion with my job increased. At the beginning of May I flew to Nice for the Cannes Film Festival, and I was sure it would be my last one. I did still enjoy the absurdity of it all, though. A hilarious party had been thrown for Paris Hilton, who arrived an hour and a half late, having kept the 200 guests there waiting. She headed straight for the dance floor and danced for ten whole seconds (I timed her). She then turned to her friend and announced, 'I'm, like, so bored.' And then she left.

The hottest party in town that year was the *Star Wars Episode III: The Revenge of the Sith* bash. It was the long-awaited final part of the prequel trilogy, and organizers had spent hundreds of thousands of dollars on the event at Le Bâoli club. We had been welcomed with open arms to the press conference and photo call – they were happy for our publicity then – but we were informed in no uncertain terms that we were not welcome at the after-show soirée. We knew we had to get in, and were saved when Caroline and I spotted a girl carrying a pile of envelopes embossed with the *Star Wars* logo to the concierge at the film PR's hotel.

Caroline walked over to the concierge's desk and pretended to look up a phone number on her mobile while she eavesdropped on the girl, who was now talking to the man behind the desk while handing over the precious invites.

The girl walked back towards the hotel lifts and Caroline scurried over to Austin, a photographer on the *Mirror*, and me.

'Right. I've got the name of the man picking the invites up. Austin, you've got to pretend you're him,' she said urgently.

'Nice one. Right. What's his name?' he asked.

I was panic-stricken. When I first started at 3am I wouldn't have hesitated to pilfer party invites. But now I just felt bad about doing it. 'You can't do that. What if you're seen? That's stealing. Some poor bloke's going to get the sack. And what about when we get rumbled at the party? Our pictures are on the top of the column, so the PRs know who we are and that we're not meant to be at the party,' I said.

Caroline looked at me suspiciously. 'What's wrong with you? We've got to get into the party. We have no choice. Richard will kill us if we don't. It's not stealing. It's, um, well, it's not stealing.'

I knew she was right about getting into that party no matter what but I felt genuinely bad about nicking the invites. Surely there had to be another way in. Caroline and Austin were whispering and looking at the concierge desk. No one had arrived to claim the tickets yet.

'Jess, we've got to do this now before the man comes to pick up the invites,' Caroline said to me.

'Yes. You're right. Go for it. I'll be up the road,' I replied. I didn't want to be around to witness it. I walked out of the hotel lobby, past the doormen and out on to the packed street. I turned right up the side road where our apartment was located. I couldn't believe how I had wimped out. I felt like such a failure for being so scared. What had happened to me?

Just as I walked around the corner, I heard footsteps behind me, getting closer. I spun round. Caroline and Austin were racing towards me, laughing uproariously.

'Shit, what happened? Did you get caught?' I asked as they dragged me by the arms and pulled me towards the security gates of the Resideal. Caroline punched in the pin code and we piled into the garden.

'Will you tell me what happened? Are they looking for you? Did they see where you were going?' I was frantic with worry now.

Caroline opened her bag up and handed me the thick pack of envelopes. 'Austin surpassed himself,' she said. 'He pretended he was the guy who had been sent to pick up the invites and was asked to sign for them. He signed the name Darth Vader. The concierge didn't bat an eyelid.'

We now had ten invitations at our disposal. I was pleased we were going to the party but was still feeling ambivalent about the way we'd gone about it. Any smugness I might have felt was short-lived anyway as two hours later I received a call from the movie's PR to say that our earlier efforts at persuasion had paid off and the film company had caved in to the demands of the British tabloid reporters, granting us access to the bash.

To top it all, the party was dismally lacklustre. There were a few Stormtroopers on the red carpet, but that was as far as it went with the *Star Wars* theme. The stars of the film, Natalie Portman and Hayden Christensen, were locked into a VIP area and we ended up watching the likes of Lisa Snowdon wolfing down the greasy canapés.

It was on the flight on the way back to London that I thought about handing in my resignation. I really hadn't felt the usual buzz and excitement in Nice that I'd felt the previous years. I had definitely become too blasé. Part of me also felt like I'd seen it all. I'd witnessed too many celebrities behaving badly, and had heard almost too many true scandalous stories. Only earlier that month I'd turned down an offer from a famous socialite to piss on a pregnancy test stick in front of me to prove she was expecting. I'd also learnt about a British pop star who froze her own poo in ice-lolly containers and then wrapped them up in clingfilm, which she would use for kinky games in bed with her husband. Forget about how she had dreamt up such a peculiar hobby, what on earth did their sheets look like in the morning?

There was another story I'd been told recently. A PR friend of mine told me about a recent shoot with a client of his. He had stumbled across the famous pop star in her changing room naked and squatting over a plastic cup into which she was peeing, purely because she couldn't be bothered to go to the toilet.

'It was beyond vile,' he told me. 'She didn't even take it to the loo to empty it out. She just left the warm cup of urine on the floor for someone else to dispose of. What's worse is that she didn't even bat an eyelid at the whole situation, let alone at being caught pissing into a cup.'

Nothing could shock me any more.

I knew there were a couple of music gigs coming up that I would enjoy, so I decided to wait until they were over before resigning. It was an important decision, one that filled me with fear and dread but that also felt absolutely right.

For the moment, though, there was the Ivor Novello Awards. I was particularly looking forward to it because a very interesting celeb was meant to attend: Pete Doherty.

'There's something about him,' a friend who had met him told me. 'He's got this iconic quality and has an air of a Byronic crusader about him. He's got huge brown eyes and looks like a baby deer. He's fiercely intelligent, and all women want to mother him.'

The shambolic singer had been nominated for one of the awards. He had a reputation – among others – for pulling out of events, ceremonies, parties and his own gigs at the last minute so I wasn't holding my breath, but I was hoping he'd make it.

I was intrigued to meet him in person. He had only started dating Kate Moss in February 2005, but the couple had become instantly smitten and rarely a day went past without the love-struck duo being plastered all over the papers and magazines holding hands and smooching.

I was surprised at the furore over Kate's relationship with the junkie Babyshambles singer. Pete may have been in and out of court for class A drug possession and was a frequent visitor to various rehab units around England, but Kate was not exactly nun-like. She was a renowned party queen, and we had had an endless supply of stories about the supermodel's scandalous deeds behind closed doors over the years. She was also highly litigious and her lawyer didn't shirk from going after the newspapers.

It wasn't shocking to me that the blonde, scruffy fashion icon had fallen for a notorious bad-boy rocker. She simply liked cool, reckless free spirits. So I was keen to see if he really was this godlike, radical bohemian who oozed sex appeal in person. Kate

Moss was meant to have great taste; I just wondered if that extended to men.

At the awards ceremony I hung out with the rest of the TV, radio and print journalists inside as we all waited excitedly for Pete. The only topic of conversation was whether the rocker was going to make it or not, especially given the spreading rumour that he hadn't won the award.

Jamelia, Natasha Bedingfield, The Darkness and Lou Reed all trooped in and made their way down the media line-up, chatting to everyone. But we all had one eye on the entrance to see if Doherty would grace us with his presence.

'He's not coming, is he? The lunch is just about to start and everyone's sitting down,' I said to a rival from the *Mail*.

'He's a rocker. He'll make a big entrance,' he assured me.

Lunch came and went and there was still no sign of Pete. I hovered at one of the press tables on the balcony overlooking the room where the guests were tucking into their meals. Surely if Pete was going to turn up, he would just slip in through a side entrance, I thought to myself. Kate would have definitely trained him on how to arrive at these events in order to avoid the media. She herself never spoke to the press. Apart from posing for one or two photographers at the very few parties with a press presence she ever attended, Moss steered clear of courting the media. Her voice had been heard on only a few TV adverts, and apart from that she was one of the most ultra-secretive stars of our time. Which merely added to her mystique. Until she met Pete, that is.

'Quick, there he is!' A radio journalist nudged me, pointing to the door.

We rushed out of our seats and made our way towards the singer, who was standing at the entrance with a friend. He was much taller than I had imagined, at least 6 foot 2 inches, and not quite as skinny and underfed as he was usually portrayed. Still, his skin was sallow and he was covered in moles. His hair was greasy and he had an air of unkempt squalor about him. He was wearing a loose white T-shirt, a thin blue jacket, scruffy jeans, boots, and had a battered straw hat on. Oddly, he had felt-tip marks all over his hands and a zigzag scrawl on his right cheek.

'Hi, Pete. Good luck for the ceremony,' I said to him.

'Thanks. Thanks a lot,' he replied.

He sounded much better-spoken than I expected. He also smelt of BO and his hands and nails were filthy. I had no idea how Kate Moss could bear to let him put his tongue in her mouth and paw at her. I could see immediately what my friend had meant when she'd said women wanted to mother him. There was nothing sexual about him at all. I just wanted to steer him in the direction of the nearest bath and introduce him to the concept of soap and deodorant.

He happily posed for a picture with me and instead of rushing off to escape the press – there were about five of us now circling him like ravenous sharks – he hung around in the entrance hall, chatting to us.

'So, how was your holiday in the South of France with Kate and Lila last week?' I asked.

Pete, Kate and her daughter had been living it up at the Hotel du Cap and had just arrived back. I was fully expecting Pete to tell me to piss off. But it was worth a go. He had a dazed look in his eyes that indicated that he might not be thinking too quickly.

'Yeah, it was great. Lila is lovely. She is quite switched on for a two-and-a-half-year-old. She calls me "Potty Pete". Kate really spoiled me in Cannes. I'm skint, you see,' he explained. He spoke in a very quiet, gentle voice and seemed extremely at ease chatting to us. Usually anyone in Kate Moss's set steered clear of the media as it was deemed uncool to be seen seeking publicity, or even being polite to journalists. But Pete had no such concerns. It didn't take much to persuade him to open his heart up and talk more about Kate. It was the first time he had spoken so candidly about the British icon. 'Kate's been there for me. She's my rock. Not my rock of crack though!' he said, laughing.

For a spaced-out druggie, I was surprised at how quick-witted he was turning out to be. It was a bad joke, but all of a sudden that mucky, sordid, undesirable persona seemed just like a bit of an act.

Pete got into his stride and was soon explaining how Kate had helped keep him off heroin. Well, for that week anyway. 'Kate said to me, give up heroin or we can't be together and you can't meet Lila. I've had implants sewn into my stomach. Look,' he said. He lifted up his grotty T-shirt to show us his bruised, slightly rounded belly and the bulging scars where the implants had been stitched in. 'It's been three months now and my implants are biodegradable,' he continued.

A junkie with an eco-conscience, I thought to myself.

'It gets easier but the implants are only for heroin. It's not for all drugs,' he pointed out.

I didn't see the point of that at all. Unless he didn't want to kick the habit.

'How does it feel to know that Kate's mates have all warned her off you and said you're a bad influence on her?' I said to him.

'You must be joking! It's more like the other way round,' he said, laughing.

So it was true. According to Pete, she really was an even bigger party girl than anyone had imagined. Not that we were able to publish details of her legendary behaviour. No one ever had tangible proof. It was only several months later when the *Daily Mirror* captured her on film chopping up and snorting lines of white powder that we were able to write about her in that way. Her career was to only get better after she was nicknamed 'Cocaine Kate', even though she was routinely criticized for glamorizing drugs and the druggie lifestyle.

Pete would not stop talking about Kate. It had been twenty minutes and he was enjoying gabbling away. 'I've written a new song for her. I wrote it yesterday. One of the lyrics is "There is a lesson I have learnt. If you play with fire you will get burnt,"' he said, wide-eyed with awe at himself.

I didn't dare glance at the other journalists who I was standing with. I could sense everyone was trying not to laugh. The Babyshambles frontman was supposed to be this profoundly prodigious musical talent. But he simply reminded me of the sort of dog-eared eccentric boy who was in a school band. With lyrics like those, it was no wonder he didn't win an Ivor Novello Award for songwriting that afternoon.

But Pete was still not in the mood to sit down and join some of the biggest names in the music industry at the ceremony. He was now explaining to us what the scrawls were on his face and body. 'I've got these fans who turn up everywhere I go and they draw on me. Look. This lightning mark on my cheek is my lucky felt-tip flash,' he said.

'Are you playing Glastonbury next month?' someone asked.

'Yeah. Kate and I are taking a gypsy caravan. She doesn't like me talking about her though. I'll get a clip round the ear for saying all this.' He giggled and put a stained hand over his mouth.

Ten seconds later he'd forgotten all about the bollocking his missus would give him for talking so merrily away to tabloid reporters. He just wouldn't shut up.

'So, are you and Kate going to get married this year?' I asked.

Surely now he'd keep his trap shut?

'We're driving through Gretna Green next weekend so who knows? I might be able to persuade her!' the love-struck singer sniggered.

Finally his mate, who was thoroughly bored by now, nudged him. 'Pete, man, the ceremony's about to start, we've got to sit down,' he said.

And with that Pete and his pal said their goodbyes and sat down at their table.

He was not quite the wildman rock and roller everyone made him out to be. More like a smelly posh boy. So much for his huge sex appeal. What on earth did Moss see in him? I wondered if his singing was any better than his songwriting.

Two months later at the Live 8 concert in Hyde Park, the whole world found out what Pete Doherty was really like in front of a mic. His performance of the T-Rex classic '20th Century Boy' with Elton John was ear-shatteringly bad. He was off-key, mumbled the lyrics he had managed to remember and bumbled about the stage looking dazed and confused.

Pete had absolutely zero stage presence and no star quality. He was worse than a fifteen-year-old schoolboy who had smoked a banana skin and thought he was Jim Morrison. For some reason he had a lighter in his mouth for most of the car crash collaboration. It was a disastrous duet and Elton John looked as if he wanted to drop-kick Doherty into the booing crowds. Pete had a ludicrous explanation for ballsing it up.

'I wasn't lost for words and I wasn't out of it on drugs. Just before I went on stage Peaches Geldof squeezed my bum hard and whispered something rather suggestive to me. It left me in such shock I didn't know where I was,' he said soon after.

Just in some park in London with three billion people watching you, mate. How easy to forget.

My next encounters with rock and rollers was at a music festival in a forest in the middle of Sweden.

3am had decided to launch a campaign to get legendary Brit band Status Quo on to the stage at Live 8. The Quo had opened the original Live Aid concert in Wembley Stadium in 1985 with 'Rockin' All Over the World'.

This time around Sir Bob Geldof had offered them a slot onstage which they were unable to play as they were meant to be performing in Ireland that evening. They wanted to play an earlier slot, but Sir Bob wasn't budging.

As part of our campaign – it was called 'No Show Without Quo' – I appeared on GMTV to put the *Daily Mirror*'s case forward about why the ancient rockers should get the audience air-guitaring once more. They were legends, I argued, and unquestionably should be part of the historic line-up.

When I flew out to Ronneby to interview Francis Rossi (the dark-haired one) and Rick Parfitt (the blond one), the middle-aged stars had a further reason for wanting to appear on the Hyde Park stage. They could hardly remember a thing about the original Live Aid performance because they had been far too drunk and drugged up to their eyeballs.

'Apparently we were back onstage for the finale of "Feed the World". I only know because I've seen the film of it,' Francis told me. 'But I do remember falling off a table with David Bowie just before we went back on. Geldof got angry with me because I'd said there were lots of drugs around.'

Rick butted in at this point to correct his pony-tailed onstage partner: 'You were wrong. There weren't "lots of drugs". There were fucking shedloads.'

'Fifteen minutes after coming offstage, I was completely drunk,' continued Francis. 'I don't recall anything else. So it would be great if we can remember it this time.'

Watching Rossi and Parfitt playfully bicker with each other and strut around in their trademark drainpipe jeans, I couldn't help but be in total awe of them. I had assumed they'd be sad old battered grandads. They were anything but. I found out that during their forty-year career they had sold more than 112 million records, had had 61 hit singles (more than any other band in the UK) and had played to more than 25 million people over the years.

They were warm, funny and took the piss out of each other constantly like some sort of comedy double act. They didn't act like divas, had no outlandish demands and were incredibly down-to-earth multi-millionaires who clearly lived to perform onstage.

During the interview they invited me to join their entourage backstage at the Ronneby Rock Festival. The band were headlining at the concert later that day in front of 30,000 Swedish fans.

Daily Mirror photographer Austin was with me and we were given Access All Areas passes and told by their tour manager that we could stand at the side of the stage with the roadies and technicians during the Quo's performance. It was a blisteringly hot day and Austin and I giggled over pear cider about the fact that we were now honorary members of the Status Quo crew.

'They're like an old married couple. I never thought they'd be so funny,' I said to Austin as we sat near the stage, watching thousands of black-clad goth Swedes headbang to thrash metal.

'You've been won over by them, haven't you?' Austin asked me.

'Too right. They're just so honest about everything – drugs, drink, women. Rick said he couldn't even remember if he was re-married to his ex-wife whom he's now back with. They're total legends! Pete Doherty could learn a thing or two from them,' I said, laughing.

A few hours later we were directed up to the main stage. Austin and I stood to the left-hand side of the stage where the sound technicians were busy fiddling with knobs and dials. Rick and Francis ran onstage to a collective roar from the audience of tens of thousands of fans, who started to chant, 'Quo! Quo! Quo!' They were both wearing their drainpipe black jeans, box-fresh white trainers and shirts.

The drummer beckoned to Austin to stand behind him so he could get some great shots of the back of Rick and Francis, who by now were in the midst of 'Whatever You Want' and doing their synchronized back and forth guitar-waving.

I'd been to concerts by the Rolling Stones, Madonna, Oasis, The Prodigy, Elton John and Girls Aloud, but I'd never seen an audience lose it so much as they had at this one. From kids aged seven to grandparents in their sixties, everyone seemed to know the words to the Quo's tunes. The band were unbelievably energetic onstage and seemed decades younger than their fifty-five years. Watching Rick race around and toss his blond mullet about, it was hard to believe he'd had a quadruple heart bypass a few years before.

By the end of the concert I had been converted into a total Status Quo fan. The effect they had on their fans was amazing and I discovered I knew more of their songs than I had realized. I was dying to become one of their roadies and join them on their tour of European rock festivals that summer. It all looked like so much fun. They were like one big happy and lairy family.

'Why don't you and Austin join Francis, his PA and Andrew, the keyboardist, in their people carrier going back to the hotel?' suggested the tour manager at the end of the concert.

The band had given Austin and I two rooms free of charge at their hotel. We were booked under the names of two roadies who had been unable to join the band in Sweden. I was told that I'd be staying in the room of someone called Meat Dish.

We climbed into Francis's people carrier. Rick Parfitt was in another people carrier with the other band members.

'Are you guys like the Royal Family – you've got to travel separately so if you crash then at least some of the Status Quo members will survive?' I asked Francis.

He was sitting behind me and was fiddling with a plastic bag.

'What are you doing?' I asked him.

'I'm going to have a smoke. Do you want some?' he replied.

I had never thought of the Quo as epic drug-takers, but that's exactly what they were once like. Francis gave up booze and cocaine in the 1980s when his septum started to rot and some cartilage fell out in the shower one day. Parfitt had admitted in the past that at the height of his coke-taking days, he was splashing out £3,000 a week on the drug. Those times were now long gone for the duo.

I leant over the seat and peered closely. He was expertly rolling up a huge spliff. He lit it and the car instantly ponged of strong weed. I knew the band no longer did hard drugs and Francis made no secret of the fact that he smoked pot, but I didn't think he would actually offer me some.

'Thanks. That'd be great,' I replied.

I hadn't been much of a smoker since I had left university nine years before. But there was no chance I was going to pass up the opportunity to get stoned with a legendary rocker.

I had shared a spliff once with Gwen Stefani's rocker husband, Gavin Rossdale. When I'd written in the column a few days later that the joint had been very badly rolled, one of his aides rang to tell me that Gavin wanted me to know that it had been his friend who'd skinned up that spliff.

This joint was perfectly rolled, and I realized I had underestimated Francis Rossi. The star was some sort of superhuman toker. It was the strongest stuff I had ever smoked. I had two drags and passed it to Austin.

'It's a bit strong,' I said to him as I tapped him on the shoulder.

'It'll be fine,' he replied and slowly inhaled three huge lungfuls.

Francis watched Austin and I as we sat back in our car seats and stopped talking. 'That's shut you two up,' he commented.

'I'm just a bit tired, that's all. We were drinking pear cider all afternoon in the sun,' I replied.

Twenty minutes later we pulled up to the hotel. Austin and I were no longer slumped in stoned silence. We were now in totally embarrassing hysterics. Francis looked pityingly at us as we tried to get out of the people carrier but struggled to stand up straight.

'Look at the bloody state of you two!' he said, laughing.

I tried to reply but was unable to. We were giggling so uncontrollably, no sound was coming out of either of our aching mouths.

'Well, I'm going up to my room. I think the others are going to the hotel bar. Nice to meet you two. Bloody hell. Sort yourselves out,' he chuckled, as he shook his head at us and walked off perfectly sober. The spliff had failed to affect him at all.

Some of the other band members headed to the bar and I pointed towards them to let Austin know that we should join them. Austin nodded but neither of us moved. We were now howling out loud and had lost the power of our legs.

We stood in the hotel lobby for the next ten minutes trying to straighten ourselves out. It didn't help that one denim-clad fat goth after another trooped into the hotel at that point to head for the bar. We were finding everything we looked at ludicrously amusing.

Finally, the giggles subsided.

'Please stop it, Austin. I can't stop laughing. It's really painful now. Let's go to the bar. We've got to pretend everything's fine and that we're normal,' I pleaded with him, fighting more giggles and now desperately trying to avoid entering the realms of stoned paranoia.

I strode off purposefully down the long corridor which led to the hotel bar, with Austin bouncing off the walls behind me. But after what felt like twenty minutes we were still in the corridor.

'Austin, what's going on? Where's the bar? This corridor is endless. When's it going to end? It's like the bloody Channel Tunnel in here,' I gabbled.

I was now overwhelmed by paranoia and thought we'd have to sleep in the never-ending corridor. There really was no light at the end of the tunnel. But all Austin did was lean against the wall and crack up into more hysterical laughter. He had tears running down his creased face now, and his eyes had shrunk so much they had practically disappeared.

'Austin! Stop it! What are we going to do?' I shrieked.

'We've got to keep going!' he just about managed to articulate.

I marched down the corridor and kept looking back every second or so to make sure the giggling photographer was still upright and following me. Eventually the corridor came to an end, and we stumbled into the packed bar.

Exhausted with laughter (Austin) and paranoia (me), we slumped into two empty chairs at the table where the rest of Status Quo's band and roadies were enjoying a few beers.

'All right, you two?' asked the bassist, John.

'No, not really. We had one of Francis's spliffs on the way back to the hotel. I'm bollocksed,' I replied.

'Oh, dear. Yeah, I heard that he'd dosed you two up! Look at the pair of you,' he replied, looking distinctly unimpressed.

We stayed in the bar for the next hour. Austin thankfully had stopped sniggering and was now transfixed by a bottle of beer. I spent the rest of the evening jabbering away to John about Adidas trainers and how I couldn't find the exact colour I wanted.

We then wobbled out of the bar and lost it again, spending the next fifteen minutes doubled over in the endless corridor, cracking up with laughter.

It had been one of those unforgettable assignments. I had been well and truly buggered up by Status Quo, smoked under the table and shown how it was really done. They were true rock and roll legends. I was so glad I hadn't resigned before meeting them.

A week later I was on another flight, this time to Germany. Coldplay were performing at a huge outdoor stadium in Cologne and Chris Martin had agreed to an interview with me beforehand.

He had made no secret of his dislike of the press (he had lashed out at a few paparazzi since getting together with Gwyneth Paltrow) and usually ducked out of the whole media game. In 2003 he was arrested in Australia after a fight with a photographer who had snapped the singer while he was surfing. The charges were dropped, but Chris was still no great admirer of the fourth estate. However, the band had just kicked off their world tour and Chris had decided to finally let me meet him.

I was intrigued to find out what he was really like. I had seen him at a few events – the Q Magazine Music Awards, the NME Awards and the Nordoff-Robbins Awards – but he had resolutely refused to chat to reporters.

Coldplay's record company, EMI, had flown me over and put me up at the same hotel as the band. Their PR took me to a meeting room a few hours after I had landed, and shortly afterwards Chris and bassist Guy Berryman strolled in.

The three of us sat at a long table in high-backed chairs. I kept expecting Chris to hit a button under the table when I asked a question he didn't like so that I'd be ejected through the window. But Chris was nothing like the miserable 'knobhead student' Liam Gallagher had once described him as. He was very witty and flirty, and denied being the macrobiotic-food-munching teetotaller he had been labelled. Weirdly, he also liked to talk about stirrings in his jeans.

'Did you just see on the news today that Tom Cruise has proposed to Katie Holmes? He announced it at a press conference in Paris,' I said to him at the start of the interview to ease him in gently. What better than to gossip a bit about Tom Cruise's bizarre activities?

'Well, actually, I've got Tom to thank for teaching me the ways of the woman. The first sex scene I ever saw was between him and Kelly McGillis in *Top Gun*.' Chris grinned at me. 'I was thinking, "What the hell is going on in my trousers?" It was all in silhouette so it was very harmless. But when you watch it when you're thirteen it's like "wow".'

Not quite the answer I had been expecting, but I obviously welcomed his openness. He was also keen to explain why he didn't take drugs.

'I don't do anything like that because it means I can't do music. And I can't have sex. And if you can't do those things, then what's the point?'

He was on a roll now and was soon telling me about the time he went for a walk around Hyde Park in the middle of the night to clear his head when he'd been recording the band's last album. 'I jumped over a fence in the park and saw this other guy jumping over the fence too. And then I remembered they warn you not to go on your own because of soliciting in parks at night,' he explained. 'If I was gay I'd be happy to admit it. It would be great to have a service like that. I wish there was a park you could walk into and there were girls under every tree waiting for it.'

A wish surely not shared by his wife, Gwyneth?

He then revealed why he had agreed to a grilling from me. 'I know we are only in the 3am column because of Gwyneth. I used to be so down on the whole gossip thing, but now I think you need it.'

It was an eye-opening opinion from someone who had once so detested the press and the whole media-showbiz circus. He wasn't upset or riled by 3am any more, because he regarded the column as nothing but entertainment. He no longer took himself so seriously, and now that he saw the light side of the gossip column, he could see that I wasn't a two-headed terrifying beast.

To prove how he had grown to appreciate 3am, midway his concert that night Chris said into the microphone in front of 30,000 screaming fans, 'Is everyone having a good time tonight? Jess from the *Mirror* – are you having a good time?'

I think I screamed the loudest.

They had been three great stories to work on, and they had reminded me how much fun the job could be. Pete Doherty had been intriguing, Status Quo had been mad and Chris Martin was a funny and charming guy and had called my name out at a major concert.

But my mind was set. After months of discussions with two of my best friends who also wanted to have a grand adventure before it was too late, we decided to jack in our jobs and go travelling that October. We kept our plans top secret as we all had to give three months' notice period to our bosses. We wanted to save up as much money as possible before we resigned, and didn't want our offices to get a whiff of our plans before we were ready. Sarah was working as a media lawyer at a TV production company, and Sam was a director of a PR firm. We were all single and itching for a new challenge in life.

My mother didn't take the news so well when I announced my plans over Sunday lunch.

'Why would you do that? And a backpack? Get out of here. Only teenagers do that. Are you crazy? Your window of opportunity is shrinking by the day,' my mother informed me after I broke the news to her.

'What? What window? What are you talking about?' I asked, appalled by what I suspected she was referring to.

'You know what I mean. You're thirty. And you're going backpacking. Can't you find a nice banker here in London?' she replied.

My father was more encouraging.

'Ignore your mother. You have a great time. Just don't go bungee jumping or hurl yourself out of planes,' he said.

A few weeks later, at the end of June, I sent Richard an email at work asking if I could pop into his office for a quick word. By the time I walked from my desk to his bunker at the end of the room, I was shaking. I was about to finish my time at 3am. The ride was coming to an end.

'Don't tell me you're up the duff too?' he joked when I sat down in one of the chairs at his glass conference table.

'No. Nothing like that. If I was it would be the immaculate conception if my luck with men these days is anything to go by,' I replied.

'Oh, how lovely, Callan. Come on then, spit it out.'

'Well, um, I've come to see you because, well, I'm leaving 3am to go backpacking around the world,' I stuttered.

Richard paused. I had no idea what he was thinking.

'What? Fucking hell. Well, we're going to really miss you. But you know what? Bloody good for you. Go for it. I only wish I'd done that when I was your age,' he said, grinning at me.

I was relieved he was being so supportive. And slightly put out that he wasn't begging me to change my mind and stay. Not that I would have. I had already booked my ticket.

'I wanted to give you my three months' notice starting from today.'

'Fine. No problem. Put it in writing, will you? So where are you going then? I'm going to put a bet on that you'll be found dead of an overdose in a blood-splattered lady boy drug den in Bangkok on your first week!' He laughed, rubbing his hands together.

'Richard! I'm not even going to Thailand.'

I told Eva, who was about to go on her maternity leave, that I was leaving. 'I've had five fantastic years of celebrity mayhem. Now it's time to give it all up and see what happens,' I said to her.

'Yeah, but how are you going to cope without *Celebrity Big Brother*, *Heat* magazine and all those awards ceremonies?' she asked.

'Yes, well, you may have a point there. I'm just going to have to go cold turkey,' I said, laughing. 'Shit. Do you think they have *The X Factor* in India?'

Word whipped around the office in no time. It was too late to turn back. I knew I had made the right decision. It was the right time to go.

The last three months at 3am was a final round of parties and concerts. I went to *Glamour* magazine's Women of the Year Awards, *the* glitziest bash of the year, and posed with *Desperate Housewives* star Teri Hatcher, who'd jetted in to pick up the Editor's Special Award and was dazzling that night in a stunning glittery cocktail dress.

I attended the Live 8 concert, during which I got marched out of the VIP area by security after sneaking in via the kitchens. They noticed I was wearing the wrong wristband when I attracted attention to myself by laughing loudly at Channel 5 talk-show host Matthew Wright's jokes.

But the highlight of that time was definitely Eva giving birth to a baby boy she named Josh. I had never seen her looking so happy. It was clear that the only late nights she was going to have from now on would be spent rocking her son back to sleep. Things had changed so much for the two of us.

By the end of September it was time to go. I had attended more than 1,250 parties, premieres, awards ceremonies, concerts, product launches and after-show bashes. I must have knocked back at least 6,000 glasses of champagne, wine and cocktails. I had become an expert at stalking celebs and posing next to them for photos. I had been threatened and called a minger and a c★★★ by actors, singers and presenters. I'd been asked to have a threesome with Dwight Yorke and had zipped Jordan's naked body into a PVC catsuit after watching her pee. I had drunk mojitos with members of Coldplay until 6am, got helplessly stoned with Status Quo and watched shamefacedly as an England footballer hot-footed it out of my flat after I'd snogged him and admitted I was a journalist.

On Tuesday 27 September I left the twenty-second floor of One Canada Square for the final time. As I swiped my security pass at the door to the editorial floor, I knew I'd always be infatuated with the ever-so-grubby world of showbusiness journalism and the excitement of uncovering a great tabloid scoop. And I would always be a fan of the circus that is celebrity culture, too. What was not to love?

Once a 3am girl, always a 3am girl.

Acknowledgements

At the risk of making this sound like the worst sort of Oscar-style speech, I'd like to jump up and down and scream my thanks to my agent Lizzy Kremer at David Higham Associates for persuading me in one conversation to write the book and for steering me in the right direction throughout the entire process. And for enjoying a juicy gossip session. You so should have been a 3am girl.

A massive thanks to Katy Follain, my unflappable editor at Penguin, for making it all seem so effortless and for being so chilled. I'm still determined to get you and Lizzy out on the lash.

Thank you to Carly Cook, Clare Pollock, Sophie Brewer, Liz Smith, Nikki Dupin, Naomi Fidler and Ana-Maria Rivera at Penguin for all you've all done. And for loving a showbiz scandal. Wish I'd known you all when I was doing the column!

To Polly, Scottie, Kev, Meths, Sinead, Jo and everyone who worked at the *Daily Mirror* showbiz department – what a disgraceful five years. And to think I started out such a wide-eyed youngster.

A huge thanks to Eva, my partner in crime and the keeper of the secrets. Ssshhh!

Piers and Wallace – thanks for hiring me in the first place and for teaching me the ways of the showbiz beat. And then some!

To James Herring and Cath Taylor, thank you so much for all your indispensable advice. And disgraceful lunches. And dinners.

Tom deserves a hearty pat on the back for his fantastic cuttings research for me. Truly, thank you. What a star!

Scare, Walders, Kez, Mortner and Lash – the Slovakian Circus. Thank you for being the best travelling companions ever. What went on tour very much stays on tour. Always!

To Caz and Juli, your decades of piss-taking will stay with me always. And thank you, Caz, for counting the olives.

Simon, Sundraj and Dan – cheers, you thin and gorgeous

showbiz boys, for involving me in terrible escapades and for being such outrageous gossips. This is the kind of shit I live for.

To my parents and my brother Jamie – thanks for patiently listening while I've droned on and on over the years about my *Mirror* antics and laughing in all the right places.

What a superstar you are, Steff, for keeping practically every *Mirror* article I ever wrote. You are a Jewish mother and a half!

Daddy, thank you for being my journalistic inspiration. Big trouble!

And finally, thank you, Charlie, for all your loving encouragement. And being the gorgeous mensch you are.